On Kiddie Porn

On Kiddie Porn

SEXUAL REPRESENTATION, FREE SPEECH AND THE ROBIN SHARPE CASE

Stan Persky and John Dixon

NEW STAR BOOKS

VANCOUVER

2001

New Star Books Ltd.
107 - 3477 Commercial Street
Vancouver, BC   V5N 4E8
www.NewStarBooks.com
info@NewStarBooks.com

Cover by Steedman Design
Typesetting by New Star Books
Printed & bound in Canada by Transcontinental Printing
1 2 3 4 5   05 04 03 02 01

Publication of this work is made possible by grants from the Canada Council, the British Columbia Arts Council, and the Department of Canadian Heritage Book Publishing Industry Development Program.

NATIONAL LIBRARY OF CANADA CATALOGUING IN PUBLICATION DATA

Persky, Stan, 1941–
  On kiddie porn

  Includes bibliographical references and index.
  ISBN 0=921586-77-9

  1. Children in pornography — Law and legislation — Canada.
2. Obscenity (Law) — Canada. 3. Freedom of speech — Canada.
4. Privacy, Right of — Canada. 5. Sharpe, John Robin — Trials, litigation, etc. I. Dixon, John, 1943– II. Title.
KE9070.P47 2001   344.71′0547   C00-910981-1
KF9444.P47 2001

for our teacher
Bob Rowan

CONTENTS

ix   PREFACE

I   ONE   *The Making of a 'Pervert'*

28   TWO   *The Making of Canada's Kiddie Porn Law*

98   THREE   *Judge Shaw Decides*

128   FOUR   *An Appeal to Reason*

166   FIVE   *At the Supreme Court of Canada*

219   NOTES

237   INDEX

PREFACE

In *On Kiddie Porn* we study the making of Canada's 1993 child pornography law and analyze the court decisions arising from Robin Sharpe's constitutional challenge to that law. Such an examination inescapably raises a remarkable number of issues, from the nature of justice and democracy to popular attitudes towards children and young people.

Our use of the colloquial term for child pornography in our title is not meant to suggest either flippancy or a disregard for the serious issues raised by sexual crimes against children, but to signal that the debate about the law occurs in a wider context of politics and culture which must be taken into account in any effort to understand the law's meaning.

Indeed, the very notion of what constitutes child pornography is at issue, hence the use of the term "sexual representation" in our sub-title. You might think that the definition of child pornography would be self-evident. It's not. Though a phrase like "sexual representations of children" seems to encompass the concept of child porn, it turns out that most of the elements of such a definition, as they appear in the Canadian child pornography law, have been contested.

When we talk about child pornography, do we mean strictly photographic representations, or should we include drawings, paintings, computer-generated images, and even written material – products of the imagination involving no use of actual children? Should the representations covered by such a definition be limited to "explicit sex" or do we also intend nude photographs or written advocacy and fictional accounts of sexual relations with young people? Whom are we referring to when we use the word "children"? Eight-year-olds? Sixteen-year-olds? Twenty-year-olds? All of these questions are part of a debate that is further complicated by a political and social dimension in which various ideological views are in conflict.

As our examination of the issues makes clear, we view sexual assaults on children – as do practically all Canadians – as serious crimes for which there ought to be appropriate law enforcement and judicial penalties. We also take the position that there ought to be a child pornography law that prohibits the production, sale, distribution, and even the mere possession of any sexual representation of children and young people that requires the commission of a crime for its creation. Such representations should be regarded as an extension of the crime that made possible the representation and should be prohibited.

However, we're also concerned that a child pornography law not violate constitutional protections of such fundamental freedoms as thought, belief, and expression, values central to democratic life. In our account we make it clear what kind of law would protect children and simultaneously satisfy the requirements of the Canadian Constitution. Our view tends to reflect the position of civil liberties associations across Canada.

On Kiddie Porn begins with a narrative account of the arrest of Robin Sharpe and the charges of violating the child pornography law laid against him. In the ensuing discussion we establish the social and cultural context of the law.

We then turn to the story – untold till now – of the crafting of the child pornography law in the early 1990s, relying on internal documentation from the federal Department of Justice. In subsequent chapters we examine the controversial decisions of the B.C. Supreme Court and the B.C. Court of Appeal, both of which found a section of the child pornography law in violation of the constitution. Finally, we scrutinize the decision on the law made by the Supreme Court of Canada in January 2001.

Our aims are relatively modest. While we try to make sense of the issues and to show, in plain language, why the court decisions are both interesting and important, we do not attempt to develop a general philosophical account of sexual representations and public fascination with them, nor do we evaluate the hotly contested claims of social science about the degree of harm caused by child pornography. With respect to the latter, we confine ourselves to an examination of the weight given by judges to those claims. Our guiding concern has been to resist extraneous controversy and argumentative digression in the service of the reader who wants a fairly clear, comprehensive, and, we hope, useful narrative.

Given that both the judiciary and civil servants are prevented by custom and law from commenting on these issues outside their prescribed roles, we believe our interpretation of judicial decisions and political actions – in addition to explicating the issues – will be helpful to readers who want to understand how the courts and various administrative bodies work. Though we offer criticisms of government agencies and their decisions, we are basically sympathetic to a necessarily reticent judiciary and civil service. We think there is an underappreciation of the range of talents and intelligence that so many Canadian judges and civil servants bring to the "burdens of office," as one of our teachers, philosopher Joseph Tussman, succinctly phrased it. In that sense, our book is an affirmation of democratic institutions.

Several people have been kind enough to help us during the writing of this book and we wish to acknowledge their invaluable assistance. Robin Sharpe made available to us his manuscript about the case, Scott Vrecko gathered research materials for us with admirable efficiency, Tom Sandborn called our attention to information we would have otherwise missed, Darin Feist provided computer support services, and the B.C. Civil Liberties Association – especially policy director Murray Mollard and executive director John Westwood – supplied us with useful documentation. We have benefitted throughout from the expertise and advice of various experts, especially Phil Bryden, associate professor of law at the University of British Columbia, and lawyer Richard Peck, counsel for Robin Sharpe. We are also grateful to New Star publisher Rolf Maurer for initiating this project, as well as reading and editing the manuscript, and to our astute editor, Audrey McClellan, for making it more readable. Finally, our thanks to Lanny Beckman for keeping the home fires from burning down the house. Naturally, all remaining errors of fact and interpretation are the responsibility of the authors.

Stan Persky
John Dixon
Vancouver, B.C.
April 2001

On Kiddie Porn

ONE

The Making
of a 'Pervert'

On April 10, 1995, a sixty-one-year-old Canadian citizen, John Robin Sharpe (known as Robin Sharpe) was detained by U.S. Customs officials at SeaTac Airport in Washington state. Sharpe was en route to his home in Vancouver, B.C., returning from a holiday in Sri Lanka via Amsterdam and Seattle.

According to Sharpe, "there were minute but detectable traces of some fine Amsterdam marijuana in a pocket of a carry bag." When a U.S. Customs "sniffer" dog became "frisky" while examining his luggage, Sharpe was taken aside by Customs officers. They meticulously searched his baggage.

The American officials found a good deal more than traces of an illegal substance. In Sharpe's suitcases were several computer disk copies of a collection of pornographic stories he'd written, which he referred to as his "*Boyabuse* stories" (and which were subsequently described in court documents and the press as "a text entitled *Sam Paloc's Flogging, Fun and Fortitude – A Collection of Kiddiekink Classics*"). In addition, there were what Sharpe described as "about ten photos of two nude blond boys in their late teens, gay lovers at the time, hugging, kissing and hamming it up for the camera," which he had slipped into one of many folders of tourist photos that he'd taken in Sri Lanka. Finally, there were "various longhand notes on foolscap; journals, impressions and rudimentary essays and stories" on which Sharpe had worked. In retrospect, Sharpe would characterize himself as "incredibly stupid" for attempting to travel across international borders carrying such material rather than discarding it.[1]

Sharpe was detained for a couple of hours and then, to his surprise, everything was returned to him (except film taken from his cameras), and he was released to continue on his way to Vancouver. Despite being "profoundly fearful" during the time he'd been detained at the airport, once he was released, "even more stupidly I again did not discard the photos and disks . . ." Instead, he was so relieved to be free that he convinced himself the material he was carrying "was not of real interest to the authorities" and simply boarded a Greyhound bus bound for Vancouver. "If stupidity were a capital offense," Sharpe later remarked, "I should be dead."

Predictably, U.S. Customs promptly contacted its Canadian counterparts, alerting them to Sharpe's imminent arrival. When the bus pulled in at the Douglas, B.C., border crossing into Canada, Canada Customs officials immediately went through Sharpe's luggage and found precisely what they had been told to expect. Sharpe was detained and an RCMP officer, Constable MacDonald, took Sharpe to the nearby Surrey police station where he was processed, but not questioned, and held overnight. He was released early the next morning after promising to appear in Surrey court at a later date.

After his detention, Sharpe retained a lawyer, attended a couple of court appearances, and prepared himself for a further appearance, slated for mid-July 1995, at which he expected charges to be laid. However, the court appearance was set aside for unspecified reasons and the case appeared to go into limbo for several months. Unknown to Sharpe, the delay was caused by the police investigation being turned over to the jurisdiction of Detective Noreen Waters, a member of the Coordinated Law Enforcement Unit (CLEU) and the Vancouver Police officer responsible for child pornography cases. She began to gather evidentiary materials for a case.

From Sharpe's point of view, "very little happened for about a year and I assumed that maybe they weren't going to bother with me." He rationalized the possibility that the case might be dropped. "After all, the ten photos of the two blond boys did not depict any explicit sex or even arousal and they were arguably over eighteen at the time. Both were still friends and we joked about all the trouble their pictures had caused." As for the writings, Sharpe hoped that perhaps they might be seen as "too literary." In short, as Sharpe later admitted, "I became complacent."

Indeed, he became sufficiently inattentive to his legal situation that he took out of storage a suitcase containing nude photographs, mostly of young men from the Philippine Islands, that he had shot over the course of several years during holidays he had taken there and in other parts of Asia. Along with the suitcase, which was on top of the dresser in his bedroom, Sharpe also had a few bound copies of his stories, as well as other manuscripts, some of which he'd submitted for publication to gay magazines. Copies of such magazines and various books were stored on his bookshelves.

Sharpe's complacency was abruptly ended at 7:55 a.m. on May 13, 1996, by insistent knocking at the door of his modest suite in an apartment building located in the Kitsilano neighbourhood of Vancouver. Sharpe was asleep. When he got up, with only a T-shirt in hand to cover his nakedness, and opened the door a few inches, three police officers, led by Detective Waters, made their way through and into his living room. They were armed with a warrant to search Sharpe's apartment for kiddie porn. Waters, whom Sharpe had never met or heard of previously, told him that his writings were "the sickest stuff I've ever read."

Literary judgment rendered, Sharpe was arrested for a second time, handcuffed, and taken outside. A paddy wagon arrived and he was driven to the Vancouver police station at 222 Main Street, where he was booked, fingerprinted, and placed in a cell with a few others. He wasn't released until about 5 p.m., with a promise to appear later. When he returned to his apartment, the police were still going through his possessions and taking photographs. Sharpe wasn't allowed in and eventually spent the night at a friend's.

When he returned the next day, any illusions he'd had about the case being dropped were dispelled by the shambles of his bedroom. As he picked up the clothing strewn about his room, he noted that the police had seized his computer, monitor, and keyboard; culled his library of various books; and taken away several albums of photographs.

Sharpe would be charged with several counts of violating Canada's child pornography law (Section 163.1 of the Criminal Code, or as it's colloquially known, "the kiddie porn law"). The law was enacted in 1993 as an addition to the existing law against obscenity in the Canadian Criminal Code (see accompanying box).

The main point of the law, in plain English, is that it's a crime to make, distribute, or simply possess any visual representations of people under the age of eighteen engaged in sex, or to advocate, either through pictures or writing, sex with people under eighteen that would be a crime according to other sections of the Criminal Code.

The Child Pornography Law: Section 163.1[2]

(1) In this section, "child pornography" means
  (a) a photographic, film, video or other visual representation, whether or not it was made by electronic or mechanical means,
    (i) that shows a person who is or is depicted as being under the age of eighteen years and is engaged in or is depicted as engaged in explicit sexual activity, or
    (ii) the dominant characteristic of which is the depiction, for a sexual purpose, of a sexual organ or the anal region of a person under the age of eighteen years; or
  (b) any written material or visual representation that advocates or counsels sexual activity with a person under the age of eighteen years that would be an offence under this Act,

(2) Every person who makes, prints, publishes or possesses for the purpose of distribution or sale any child pornography is guilty of
  (a) an indictable offence and liable to imprisonment for a term not exceeding ten years; or
  (b) an offence punishable on summary conviction.

(3) Every person who imports, distributes, sells or possesses for the purpose of distribution or sale any child pornography is guilty of
  (a) an indictable offense and liable to imprisonment for a term not exceeding ten years; or
  (b) an offence punishable on summary conviction.

(4) Every person who possesses any child pornography is guilty of
  (a) an indictable offence and liable to imprisonment for a term not exceeding five years; or
  (b) an offence punishable on summary conviction.

(5) It is not a defence to a charge under subsection (2) in respect of a visual representation that the accused believed that a person shown in the representation that is alleged to constitute child pornography was or was depicted as being eighteen years of age or more unless the accused took all reasonable steps to ascertain the age of that person and took all reasonable steps to ensure that, where the person was eighteen years of age or more, the representation did not depict that person as being under the age of eighteen years.

(6) Where the accused is charged with an offence under subsection (2), (3), or (4), the court shall find the accused not guilty if the representation or written material that is alleged to constitute child pornography has artistic merit or an educational, scientific or medical purpose.

(7) Subsections 163(3) to (5) apply, with such modifications as the circumstances require, with respect to an offence under subsections (2), (3) or (4).

For example, if someone writes something "advocating" anal intercourse between adults and people under eighteen, that could be a crime in itself, because it's illegal in Canada for adults and people under eighteen to engage in anal sex.[3]

Since we will subsequently repeat parts of the text of Section 163.1 of the Canadian Criminal Code and analyze the law in considerable detail, we won't pause here to discuss the particular aspects of it that would give rise to a complex legal case eventually reaching the Supreme Court of Canada.

For now, we'll confine ourselves to pointing out a couple of ways in which the materials found in Sharpe's possession might provide law enforcement officials with evidence of a violation of the child pornography statute. While one might think that the violation of the law would be obvious in any given instance, it turns out that it isn't, and that the Crown is required – given the constitutional presumption of innocence in our system of law – to do considerable work to establish that a crime has been committed.[4]

In a "Report to Crown Counsel," dated May 7, 1996, concerning Sharpe's arrest more than a year earlier, and prepared by police detective Waters – a report Sharpe did not receive until after his second arrest – we see the kinds of evidentiary material being gathered to make the case against Sharpe. Among the report's documents are such items as an assessment, made by Dr. Jean Hlady of the Child Protection Service Unit of the B.C. Children's Hospital, of the ages of males represented in Sharpe's photographs, as well as extensive reviews of Sharpe's writing by Detective Waters, Marc Everitt of the B.C. Film Classification Branch, and Mary-Louise McCausland, director of the B.C. Film Classification.

The assessment by Dr. Hlady, for example, is intended to establish whether the youths represented in the photos are under the age of eighteen, the first step in determining if the representations are a violation of the law. Deciding whether those portrayed are "engaged in sex" or whether their sexual organs are being depicted for "a sexual purpose" would, of course, require further judgment.

A more direct example of an analysis of possible violation of the law concerns the prohibition against "advocating" illegal sexual acts with persons under eighteen. Thus, McCausland writes about Sharpe's fictional tales, "These stories convey, through a sense of the narrator's satisfaction, that the sexually violent acts being carried out both against the children and by the children are pleasurable, satisfying and beneficial for all involved. It is this theme, and the fact the abuse of children is presented . . . as being non-traumatic, that led me to determine that these works of fiction counsel adult sex with children and are therefore child pornography as defined by Section 163.1 of the Criminal Code." McCausland's determination, inferring that the sexual representations in Sharpe's fictional writing amount to "counselling" illegal acts with children, is the sort of judgment that would provide law enforcement officials with grounds for regarding the material as a violation of the law.

Although there was initially no coverage of Sharpe's case in the print media, television crews attempted to videotape Sharpe entering and leaving the courthouse at 222 Main Street, where he was required to make periodic appearances. Sharpe's lawyer was anxious to avoid publicity and the TV crews generally met with little success.[5]

However, one day shortly before a hearing where Sharpe expected formal charges to be filed, a woman knocked at the door of his apartment, introduced herself as Suzette Myers of UTV (now Global TV), and asked for an interview. Sharpe declined, explaining that he didn't yet know what charges he was facing, and suggested that she contact him after his next court appearance. Myers thanked him and left.

While the request for an interview might have been sincere, it also served as a ruse to surreptitiously videotape Sharpe. In mid-October 1996, Myers hosted a three-part special series about child pornography on the UTV evening news, which featured Sharpe in all three segments. Sharpe appeared, variously edited, in each of the programs. Sharpe's apartment building, a well-known Kitsilano landmark, was shown, along with footage of Myers walking down the corridor, followed by a close-up of the number on the apartment door and a brief clip of Sharpe himself at the door, apparently taken by a hidden camera in the sports bag Myers was carrying.

Myers warned her viewers that they might see material that was not suitable for children and which might be "extremely difficult" for most adults. On the first day of the special, the clips of Sharpe were juxtaposed with an extended segment on a particularly horrific child murder case in Belgium, which was then in the news.

Myers also reported that the Vancouver Police were allowing TV cameras in to film their collection of child pornography for the first time so that the public could learn "what child pornography really is." Detective Waters, described as an undercover officer and one of the principal local sources of information for the TV program, then showed Myers materials from the police collection. Oddly, although the genitals of those in the photos were covered by "post-it" notepaper, the faces of the people portrayed in the pictures, and hence their identities, were not similarly protected. While the materials shown had not been seized from Sharpe, it would have been easy for viewers to assume they were.

Almost predictably, the broadcast was followed by the first of several abusive, anonymous phone calls made to Sharpe's publicly listed number. The full brunt of the abuse would not occur for some time, however. By the time publicity about the case reached its apogee, Sharpe would be represented as the stereotypical dishevelled "dirty old man," whose face on the front page of the morning tabloid fulfills parents' worst nightmares about "perverts."

The term "pervert" was regularly used in the city's daily tabloid paper, the *Vancouver Province*. During 1993, for example, when the Canadian Press news service wrote stories about the federal government's new child pornography law – stories that didn't include the word "pervert" – *Province* headlines over those news items declared "Ottawa targets porno perverts" and "Grits rip stalker, pervert bills." The paper was clearly using the term as not merely informational, but to convey editorial moralizing and to sensationalize the story.[6]

Sharpe himself later became the focus of an anonymous poster campaign in his Kitsilano neighbourhood. The handmade posters, which featured a newspaper photo of Sharpe, warned residents of his presence in the vicinity and gave his address (the poster was prominently reproduced in a *Province* news story about the campaign, although the address was blacked out). In the building where Sharpe lived, newspaper clippings about the case were posted near the elevator, and someone wrote on them in magic marker: "This pervert lives in this building."[7]

Sharpe wasn't the only alleged pornographer in the news at the time. Journalists were preoccupied that autumn with a far more sensational front-page story of child pornography, one that would lead to a certain amount of journalistic controversy about the coverage of such issues.

Around the time of the UTV special, in September 1996, a Burnaby, B.C., elementary school principal, William Bennest, fifty-two, was charged with making and possessing child pornography, sexual touching and assault of a boy under fourteen, and procuring the sexual services of a male under eighteen. Bennest, to that point a respected member of the community, was also a semi-closeted homosexual man active in various gay athletic and cultural organizations.

The story of the charges against Bennest, who was immediately suspended from his job without pay, was page one news, and television cameramen didn't have to look far for dramatic footage as panicked parents rushed to the school to protect their children. Indeed, the panic was sufficiently intense that the police felt the need to step in and quickly assure parents that Bennest was not suspected of having had sexual relations with any of the students in his school.

Once the "public hysteria . . . settled," as the gay newspaper *XtraWest* later put it, the Crown examined the evidence that the police had collected, and "the most serious charges fell, one by one." In December 1996 the charges of sexual touching and assault were dropped, and in October 1997, at Bennest's trial, the charges of making child pornography and procuring from a minor were stayed. Bennest pleaded guilty to one count of possessing child pornography and was given a two-year suspended sentence by Judge William Kitchen, who justified the suspension of jail time by noting that, in significant ways, Bennest's "life has been destroyed."[8]

That, however, wasn't the end of it. Upon Bennest's sentencing, the police pronounced themselves "disappointed" that he would not serve time in jail, and Detective Waters, in a local CBC radio interview, called for the funding of a special police pornography squad. Waters offered the opinion that "adult porn can be disturbing as well," citing bondage, sadomasochism, and bestiality. Various citizens' groups called on the B.C. attorney general, Ujjal Dosanjh, to reopen the investigation of Bennest.[9]

Criticism of the judicial system was heavy enough that Vancouver regional Crown counsel Austin Cullen was assigned the task of reviewing the police and Crown handling of the case. In a report issued in February 1998, about a year and a half after Bennest's arrest, Cullen found that an initial report from one police investigator had blown the case "out of proportion." Further, Cullen criticized another police investigator for making "indiscreet and inaccurate comments" to the media, and concluded that the case relied too heavily on the evidence of a questionable source. Cullen's report was endorsed by former judge Josiah Wood, who was then advising the Delta police in an investigation, launched at the request of Vancouver's police chief, of the Vancouver police department's handling of the Bennest case. As a result of Cullen's report, the Crown dropped its pending appeal of Bennest's sentence.[10]

The editor of *Xtra West*, a newspaper that had a natural interest in the Bennest case given the frequent conflation of issues concerning child pornography with those of pedophilia, gay prostitution, and homosexuality itself, was sharply critical of both the police and the media. "It's far too easy," argued Gareth Kirkby, "to accept as unadulterated fact the media headlines and stories featuring reports from police . . . It's doubly important that journalists keep a clear, unemotional head when writing about alleged crimes."[11]

In pointing to the periodic "demonization" of people accused of child pornography crimes, we want to be quite clear about our point. It's not that there are no demons out there. The notorious case of B.C. serial murderer Clifford Olsen in the 1980s is still sufficiently alive in the memory of many Canadians to dispel any such illusions. Nor are we simply making a plea for the presumption of innocence of those accused of crimes, or offering a reminder that crimes come in different degrees and that it's important for a community to be able to distinguish between those that constitute a serious threat to the security of the polity and those that don't. Both of those points are significant, but subsidiary here.

Rather, the main danger of media (or police) sensationalism is that it poisons the well of public discussion. Lynch mobs are not ideal panelists for reasoned debate, and the analysis and argument that we'll be making subsequently require a climate in which dialogue and careful reasoning can be sustained.

It might be appropriate, at this point, to reiterate our view of child sexual assault (or "child abuse") and child pornography, so that readers can understand the direction of the argument we'll be making. As noted in our preface, we view such assaults as serious crimes for which there ought to be appropriate law enforcement and judicial penalties, and we take the stance that any sexual representation that requires the commission of a crime for its production should be regarded as an extension of the crime that created it, and thus prohibited. That is, we'll argue that the mere possession of certain child pornography ought to be regarded as a crime.

Although our position is unremarkable within the spectrum of available views, we should note that it is more conservative than that of philosophical libertarians (who argue, for example, that consensual sex with children and its representation should not be criminalized), those who argue for the elimination of age of consent (to be replaced by a concept of consent), and even some courts that have ruled that mere possession of child pornography ought to be protected by constitutional concepts of privacy and freedom of belief, speech, and expression. However, our view is also one that is more politically liberal or moderate than the existing child pornography law under which Sharpe was charged or than the views held by those who describe themselves as protectors of "family values" and want to see the law extended (for example, by raising the age of consent to eighteen).

Having established that we're not "soft" on the issue of child pornography, we observe that one of the things notable about such declarations is that there's a powerful, if unstated, social requirement to make them, given the dramatized state of discussion of the issue.

That is, since there's near-unanimous agreement on the seriousness of sexual crimes against children and on the need for some kind of law against child pornography, one might think that the assertion of agreement with the predominant perspective could go unspoken on the grounds of redundancy. But that's not the case.

Indeed, the absence of such a declaration is one of the grounds for suspicion that someone's opposition to child pornography is in fact "soft." The failure to accompany one's views on the subject with a visceral expression of disgust for child pornography and pornographers is taken as a failure rather than as an assumption about shared views.

What this indicates to us is that there's considerably more at stake here than a literal expression of a view, and it turns out that discourse about child pornography is embedded in a much wider political debate about sexual mores in our society. This is a point neatly captured in a column by Peter Wilson of the *Vancouver Sun*, written at the time of the 1993 legislative hearings on the proposed child pornography law.

Wilson cites the legislative testimony of Keith Kelly, then executive director of the Canadian Conference on the Arts (CCA), who was voicing concerns of artists about the proposed law. Wilson writes, "Defending free speech in the arts should be easy. You want people to be able to speak their minds, you want them to be able to express themselves, you want the exchange of ideas to flourish. What could be more tapioca-bland than that?

"Except that in Canada," Wilson continues, "you always have to defend yourself first. You have to say . . . No, I am not in favour of child pornography. No, I am not in favour of violence in our society. No, I am not advocating the moral destruction of our citizenry.

"Take, for example, a recent statement . . . by Keith Kelly: 'Canadian artists are not child pornographers, and there is a wide consensus regarding the need to protect children from exploitation and abuse. In this, the CCA has no objections to the legislation.'"

Wilson remarks, "Let's look at that first bit again. 'Canadian artists are not child pornographers.' Sad, isn't it, that it even has to be said . . . 'Canadian artists are not child pornographers.' It's more than a touch pathetic that it has to be said at all . . . Or, are you having doubts already?"[12]

Wilson's point is that even the relatively uncontroversial defense of free expression, when made in the context of child pornography, must be accompanied by assertions of adherence to the prevailing public mentality on the topic.

One of the useful things done by "social constructionist" thinkers – people who analyze the historical development of categories, concepts, and social institutions to demonstrate that they're not simply "natural facts" – is to show us the fluidity and ambiguity of ideas and definitions about sexuality, sexual representation, children, and "child abuse."[13]

It is relatively well-known that both historically and cross-culturally, people have held (and are holding) diverse views on how to define and see children, and there's a similarly broad array of attitudes and opinions about what constitutes appropriate sexual behaviour by, and in relation to, young people.[14] In many cultures, for example, girls are customarily betrothed and wed at early pubescence to fully adult men. In Canadian law, the establishment of fourteen years as the age of consent goes back more than a century — perhaps reflecting the circumstances of a largely agricultural society at the end of the nineteenth century — and was derived from even older British common law that set the age of consent at twelve.[15]

With respect to young persons and homosexuality, a tradition exists in Western culture, extending as far back as fifth century B.C. Athens, in which it was appropriate for adult men to court males between the ages of thirteen and eighteen.[16] Historical accounts of Western sexual practices and twentieth-century ethnographic accounts confirm the persistence, and often the social legitimation, of such relations.[17] Equally, of course, such relations received social disapprobation and legislative sanction. Our point here is that views about age of consent and homosexuality are hardly fixed, objective, or naturally mandated, but are appropriately the subject of public debate and adjudication. As before, we underscore the importance of a reasoned climate of debate.

The issue of homosexuality is not only directly relevant to the case of Sharpe (and others to whom we've referred), but also, as we'll show in the following chapter about the crafting of the child pornography legislation, issues of sexuality, and particularly homosexuality, were inextricably entwined with a variety of concurrent and related legislative initiatives and judicial decisions.

It's been cogently argued that "homosexuality" is a "socially constructed" phenomenon.[18] This refers to the historical development of "homosexuality" as a set of ideas, as a social ensemble represented by various "gay communities," and as a possible individual identity, as distinct from a longer history of merely same-sex sexual practices that we now describe as homosexual. The newness of this social construction can be seen in the increasing social tolerance of homosexuality in North America, which is recent enough to be a matter of living memory. Even that increased acceptability is largely confined to behaviours that are described as "virtually normal," and other forms of homosexuality remain controversial.[19]

If the conceptualization of homosexuality (as distinct from its "reality") is socially constructed, so is that of "child abuse," as philosopher and medical historian Ian Hacking shows. By the 1990s, child abuse had assumed a central place in the array of social problems confronting us, and its incidence was reportedly epidemic.[20] The prominence of the problem of child abuse would provide one of the motives for trying to do something about it, such as cracking down on child pornography. Our interest is in identifying the social forces that came together to create that urgent prominence, and to touch on the question of whether the range of acts that the concept came to embrace is justified, and therefore, whether the degree of public alarm that was generated is warranted.

Child abuse, "as a way to describe and classify actions and behaviour, came into being in discussions and observations that took place in Denver, Colorado, around 1960," Hacking reports.[21] The immediate stimulus for this redescription of various events, now seen to be related, came from a group of pediatricians who noticed repeated injuries to small children, including bone fractures, that may have been caused by parents beating up their babies.

The concept quickly took root in North American consciousness, supplanting the Victorian-era notion of "neglect" of children. Hacking traces its rapid development and changing meaning, from its origins as a pediatric concern through its crystallization in the notion of "the battered child syndrome" to the creation of "knowledge" about child abuse that invoked a much larger "conceptual, analytic frame of this newly noticed kind of human behaviour." So, for example, we soon had the maxim "Abused as a child, abusive as a parent." Hacking makes the point here, as elsewhere in his discussion, that he is not saying a particular proposition is false, but rather that often "the grounds for accepting the proposition as true had little to do with evidence."[22]

If battered child syndrome as a concept was first applied to babies three years old and under, it soon was viewed "as only a sub-class of the 'real' kind, the abused child." In the 1960s, child abuse and neglect meant physical abuse. "Sex was peripheral or absent." But not for long. Many institutional authorities knew, of course, that physical abuse and sexual abuse often occurred in the same households. In the early 1970s, Hacking notes, American feminists publicly joined them, further remoulding the idea of child abuse. By the late 1970s one could find articles in popular feminist publications with such headings as "Incest: Child Abuse Begins at Home." Despite the stereotypical image of pedophile molesters preying on boys, "a welter of otherwise discordant figures," Hacking notes, "confirms that men sexually abuse girls in their families far more often than anyone abuses boys." It was left to feminist analysts to vigorously address a previously ignored social situation.

While the expansion of a category can be helpful in bringing to public attention previously hidden or unreported events, there's also the problem of the inflation of a category. Certainly, one of the effects of the establishment and expansion of a category, as Hacking points out, is that it adds a "moral weight" to the acts, such that "child abuse became the worst possible vice." Eventually one would encounter, in formal legislative testimony, characterizations of child abuse as expansive as "anything that hinders 'the optimal development of children to which they should be entitled,' regardless of its cause."[23]

Hacking's discussion is not intended to deny the reality of child abuse, but rather to explore the history and effects of an expanding concept in the course of a broader discussion examining the usefulness of social constructionist methods. A good deal of what he observes about child abuse is relevant to the category of child pornography.

If Hacking is primarily concerned with examining the social construction of the category of child abuse, Wendy Kaminer offers a sharply critical analysis of a large range of behaviours, of which child abuse is a part, in relation to what she perceives to be a "rise of irrationalism" in North American societies. Kaminer identifies several social groups that converge, for the most part unintentionally, and whose various ideological concerns come together to produce a particular social climate or public mentality. Among them: religious fundamentalists, "family values" proponents, ultra-conservative politicians, some branches of the feminist movement, therapists, "recovery" movement leaders, victims' and survivors' groups, and the like.

Once these various views and agendas are synergized, Kaminer argues, categories that once may have been useful can become inflated beyond recognition and result in bizarre excesses; worse, the arguments and methodologies of such proponents are often, according to Kaminer, "profoundly irrational." Increasingly, a zealous ensemble emerges that "seeks truth not in debate but in revelation. It values bolstering people's self-esteem over challenging their ideas. It assesses proposed truths partly by the passion with which they are held and partly by their alleged therapeutic effect."[24]

Kaminer cites a variety of excesses, including claims of satanic ritual sexual abuse, multiple personality syndrome, recovered memory and "past life regression" therapies, and the sexual harassment policies that resulted in widespread "speech codes" on university campuses in the 1990s.

For example, as Hacking remarks about claims of satanic ritual abuse (SRA), "undoubtedly the idea of SRA is a real idea, perhaps a very bad idea." But in contrast to the reality of child abuse, "the most systematic and exhaustive official investigation of SRA that had been conducted anywhere . . . found that none of the charges was substantiated by any evidence whatsoever."[25] Nonetheless, Kaminer adds, "70 percent of people surveyed by *Redbook* [magazine] in 1994 – believed in the existence of abusive satanic cults."[26]

What distresses Kaminer about various recovery movements, including those devoted to child abuse, "has been the virtual sanctification of individual testimony of abuse. 'Believe the women' and 'believe the children' were rallying cries for followers of recovery, including many feminists, who were convinced that incest and other forms of child abuse and family violence were practically ubiquitous. If you questioned a self-proclaimed victim, or tried to reason with her, declining to presume that her story was true, you were likely to be accused of collaborating in her abuse."[27]

Kaminer's purpose "is not to minimize the problem of abuse but to point out the irrationalism" of many aspects of its identification and treatment. At times in the 1990s, Kaminer notes, sexual and personal harassment simply became "making someone feel uncomfortable," and "to anti-porn feminists, pornography *was* violence against women, not just an image of violence. Questioning the effect of pornography, or asking for proof of it, was a callous breach of etiquette."[28]

Similar unexamined claims apply directly to the issues at hand. It was often claimed, in testimony to the legislative committees considering Canada's child pornography legislation in 1993, that abused children were invariably "scarred for life." Whether that's true or not wasn't demonstrated, but belief in the claim would certainly have an impact on the people crafting a law that, among other things, turned on a notion of "anticipated harm."

As Kaminer notes about the U.S. First Amendment, and as we note about the corresponding Section 2 of the Canadian Constitution, if such constitutional provisions for freedom of thought and expression "didn't protect speech that many people find offensive, we'd have relatively little need of them . . . Freedom of speech rests on the recognition that words are not acts and the state need not and must not protect us from them – as it protects us from criminal behaviour. Of course, in some marginal cases, action – like nude dancing – is a form of expression, and words – such as a verbal agreement to kill someone – are subsumed in a criminal act. But in most cases the distinction between speech and action, like the distinction between thought and deed, is sufficiently clear."[29]

The anthropologist Hugh Brody tells an anecdote that illustrates the divergences not only of public mentalities, but of assumptions about such states of mind. On arriving at a small settlement in the Canadian Eastern Arctic, Brody was told by local white administrators of a case that had created "a terrible conflict with the [Inuit] people." A white schoolteacher had apparently sexually molested several boys in the school. He was eventually charged and removed from the community by the

RCMP. Brody was also warned by the white administrators of the depth of indignation about the affair on the part of Inuit families, and was persuaded that "the subject was one to be avoided and that the community would nurse for all time an undying grudge against the disruptive immorality of southerners."[30]

But after he'd been in the community some time, Brody "took courage and asked the fateful question" about the homosexual teacher and his removal from the community. "Yes, came the answer, that was a very bad thing . . . The bad thing was the way the teacher left – suddenly taken away by the police. The Whites had been terrible in the way they behaved."

Brody asked what should have been done about it. He ended up talking with several other Inuit families about the matter, including, as he later learned, three fathers of boys who had been involved. All of them said more or less what the first man told Brody, namely, "He should not have been sent away at all. Instead, he should have had a meeting with the Inuit, and we would have told him, 'We like you very much and we think you are a good teacher for our children but we do not like you making love with them. So, please stop doing that.'"

This episode displays a tone of public discussion devoid of histrionics, one that would be helpful to thinking about such issues as child pornography.

In contrast to the public image of Robin Sharpe that developed in the course of judicial events, shaped by media sensationalism and public histrionics, Sharpe in fact is a man in his mid-sixties, a retired city planner, the divorced father of two children (who continued to be supportive of him), a man who had "come out" as a homosexual in his late thirties, a writer who had a degree of recognition – independent of his pornographic writings – in the Vancouver literary community, and something of a political activist around the issues of drug legalization and free speech. Perhaps most important, Sharpe was someone who, between his initial arrest and his eventual appearance in B.C. Supreme Court in November 1998, had turned himself into a "jailhouse lawyer" capable of conducting his own initial defense.

There's a maxim in the legal community that someone who defends himself or herself "has a fool for a client." While that may be true in most instances, in this case, if the client was foolish, he at least had an advocate who was demonstrably no fool. Sharpe, a man of modest means living on a small pension, had initially engaged the services of qualified lawyers. However, when it became clear that they were prepared to do little more than arrange a plea-bargain deal if Sharpe would agree to plead guilty, he dismissed them.

While Sharpe may have thought himself "incredibly stupid" to have taken the materials he did across international borders, he did not think himself necessarily wrong, either morally or constitutionally, to create and possess such materials. From the beginning, he considered the possibility of mounting a constitutional challenge to the child pornography law, so now he tried to find lawyers and organizations that would take on a constitutional challenge to the law, but he was unable either to secure their support or to afford them.

Between his arrests and his February 1999 preliminary hearing, Sharpe did considerable reading in case law relating to child pornography cases. He studied the transcripts of the legislative proceedings leading to the passage of the child pornography law and learned something about the current state of sentencing jurisprudence. As well, he did a good deal of informal theorizing about the issues and firmed up his own constitutional position on the matter.

Also prior to the preliminary hearing, Sharpe had a brief pre-trial conference before a judge, where he discussed legal representation arrangements with the prosecutor Terry Schultes, whom Sharpe found consistently helpful in providing assistance on legal procedures involved in the task of representing himself.

The preliminary hearing – to decide whether there was sufficient evidence to proceed to trial – began on February 11, 1998, in Surrey Provincial Court before Judge R.D. Miller, nearly three years after Sharpe's initial arrest. The Crown called half a dozen witnesses, including Detective Waters, and entered over a hundred exhibits. The judge determined that there was sufficient evidence to proceed, a date for trial was set, and Sharpe was now formally charged with four counts of violating the child pornography law. He was accused of –

1. on April 10, 1995, in Surrey, B.C., having "in his possession for the purpose of distribution or sale, child pornography: computer disks containing a text entitled *Sam Paloc's Flogging, Fun and Fortitude*";
2. on April 10, 1995, in Surrey, having "in his possession child pornography" (the computer disks, and other writings and photographs);
3. on May 13, 1996, in Vancouver, having child pornography in his possession for the purpose of distribution or sale; and
4. on May 13, 1996, being in possession of child pornography.

That is, he was charged with possessing child pornography with the alleged intention of distributing or selling it on two separate occasions, and on those same two occasions, he was charged with simple possession of child pornography, including "books, manuscripts, stories and photographs."

The advantage of the preliminary hearing for Sharpe was that it gave him the opportunity to hone his skills in the art of cross-examination. In dealing with both Waters, a twenty-two-year veteran of the police department, and other witnesses, Sharpe concentrated on establishing grounds for a possible subsequent challenge to the search warrant of his apartment. As he quickly learned, legal proceedings almost invariably feature moments straight out of the Keystone Kops.

For example, when cross-questioning police constable Mac-Donald, who had requested the warrant for Sharpe's 1996 arrest on the grounds that he wasn't sure where the wanted man was living, Sharpe asked the police officer why he hadn't simply looked in the telephone book.

The police officer replied to the court, "Quite frankly, Your Honour, I never looked in the phone book."

Did MacDonald not find phone books reliable? asked Sharpe.

"They are an aid to an investigation, Your Honour. That is correct," deadpanned the officer. (Sharpe was trying to show that the warrant was unnecessary, since he was easy to find. If he could have proved the warrant was wrongfully acquired, the second set of charges would have been thrown out, but he was unsuccessful.)

The one concrete accomplishment of the preliminary hearing, from Sharpe's perspective, was getting the Crown's agreement to move the trial to Vancouver.

However, as the trial got underway, Sharpe made his counter-move, filing a constitutional challenge to the child pornography law. Since disputed legal questions must be heard and decided upon before the trial can proceed to a determination of someone's guilt or innocence, a special hearing – known in legal terminology as a *voir dire*, a trial within a trial – was set in order to determine the status of the law.

It began November 9, 1998 (and would run for seven sessions, to the end of the month), and was held before Justice Duncan Shaw of the B.C. Supreme Court, at the B.C. Courthouse in downtown Vancouver. The *voir dire* began with the reading of the four charges against Sharpe. Schultes acknowledged that Sharpe had filed a proper notice of a constitutional question, the technical requirement at that time for mounting a challenge to the law, and the hearing turned to the legal issues.

The case was a relatively straightforward one. Sharpe was challenging two sections of the child pornography law – Section 163.1(1)(b), which prohibits "any written material or visual representation that advocates or counsels sexual activity with a person under the age of eighteen years" that would otherwise be a crime, and Section 163.1(4), which prohibits simple possession of child pornography – on the ground that they violated one of the fundamental provisions of the Canadian Constitution, namely, Section 2 of the Charter of Rights and Freedoms, which provides that "everyone has the following fundamental freedoms: . . . (b) freedom of thought, belief, opinion and expression, including freedom of the press and other media of communication."

Schultes conceded that the child pornography law infringed on the constitutional freedom of expression provisions, but claimed that the legislation was "saved" by virtue of Section 1 of the Charter, which says that "the Canadian *Charter of Rights and Freedoms* guarantees the rights and freedoms set out in it subject only to such reasonable limits prescribed by law as can be demonstrably justified in a free and democratic society." That is, a citizen's right – in this case – to freedom of speech can be curtailed if the limitations are "reasonable," lawful, and can be "demonstrably justified" within the norms of a democratic society.

Sharpe's case was certainly not the first to turn on whether or not an admitted constitutional violation could be "saved" by Section 1. What's at the heart of such Section 1 debates – and what makes the Sharpe case part of that debate – is the question of whether there are some social "goods" in such urgent need of being protected that it's justified to limit our most fundamental freedoms as the best means of achieving those social objectives.

In addition to the exhibits presented at the *voir dire*, the Crown called nine witnesses, while Sharpe, primarily for lack of financial resources, called none. The Crown's two star witnesses were Detective Noreen Waters and Dr. Peter Collins, a forensic psychiatrist who works for the Clark Institute in Toronto, the Ontario Provincial Police, and a variety of other institutions. Dr. Collins was introduced into the proceedings as the state's expert witness on the question of harm caused by child pornography. In the following chapters, various judges will be commenting on the claims of such experts. The question of harm, or anticipated harm, caused by child pornography is, obviously, a complex matter, as well as a controversial one. Certainly it's one of the issues central to cases like this one. Rather than attempting to adjudicate the debate within the field of social science about harm in relation to child pornography, our concern will be with the weight various judges involved in the case gave to the harm claims of expert witnesses, and how that weighting affects their judgment about constitutional questions in relation to the child pornography law. Sharpe himself conducted extensive cross-examinations of the Crown witnesses, and proved to be a more than adequate representative of his own interests.[31]

On November 26, 1998, the *voir dire* in the case that would be known as *R. v. Sharpe* concluded, and Justice Shaw retired to his chambers to consider his ruling. On January 15, 1999, he returned to court to deliver a startling and controversial decision. In order to make sense of that decision, it's first necessary to examine the child pornography law that was crafted in 1993 by the government of Conservative Prime Minister Brian Mulroney and two of his ministers of Justice, Kim Campbell and Pierre Blais.

CHAPTER TWO

The Making of the Kiddie Porn Law

Canada's child pornography law was far more a product of political expedience than pressing national need or even a desire to protect children from exploitation and abuse. What's more, although the proposed law received the assent of all political parties in the Canadian House of Commons, it was primarily designed to address the political needs of an ideologically fractured Progressive Conservative Party as it neared the end of a long period of tenure in government.

Naturally, the motivation behind the "kiddie porn" law doesn't at all vitiate the virtue of such a law, but it will help to explain some of the anomalies of the legislation that would eventually face a constitutional challenge in the courts.

Since the story of the crafting of the kiddie porn law has not been told before, it will be useful to set its creation within the larger context of the situation of the Canadian government – and especially the activities of its Department of Justice – during the period from 1988, when the Tories were re-elected to a second successive term in government, to 1993, when the kiddie porn law was frenetically enacted just months before the country went to the polls again.

In a February 1990 cabinet shuffle, less than a year and a half after Prime Minister Brian Mulroney's re-election, an unusual politician from British Columbia was appointed as the first woman to hold the powerful post of minister of Justice. For the then forty-four-year-old Kim Campbell, the promotion from a junior ministerial portfolio to minister of Justice and attorney general of Canada was but the latest step in what was truly a meteoric political career.[1]

Born into what would become a family of lawyers, beginning with her father George Campbell and eventually including herself and her sister, Campbell quickly embarked on what became a litany of achievements. At Vancouver's Prince of Wales High School, she was the first female elected president of the student council. She won first-class standing in her University of British Columbia Honours B.A. in political science, did equally well in graduate studies, and was awarded a Canada Council Doctoral Fellowship to the London School of Economics. There she studied under noted Sovietologist Lionel Shapiro, travelled to the Soviet Union in 1972, and wrote a dissertation on the role of political change during the period of de-Stalinization.

After teaching political theory in the B.C. post-secondary system for five years, Campbell entered law school in 1980, and in the same year was elected to the Vancouver School Board. Representing the conservative Non-Partisan Association party, she eventually became chair of the school board while articling with and joining the Vancouver law firm of Ladner Downs. Even beyond professional and political attainments, Campbell was quickly marked as an intellectual who comfortably quoted Edmund Burke or alluded to Tolstoy's *Anna Karenina*; she played the cello; she spoke some Russian, German, French, and, as observers noted, "all too candidly, English."[2]

In the mid-1980s she became an adviser to British Columbia premier Bill Bennett. When he stepped down in 1986, Campbell ran as a longshot candidate in the ensuing leadership race of the right-of-centre Social Credit party, and although she finished far back in a contest won by former MLA Bill Vander Zalm, she coined a phrase that was to haunt the enthusiastic but intellectually lightweight new premier: "Charisma without substance is a dangerous thing."

In the 1986 provincial election she won the Vancouver–Point Grey seat for Social Credit, but Premier Vander Zalm froze her out of his cabinet. In 1988, when the Supreme Court of Canada's decision in *R. v. Morgentaler* struck down the country's abortion law as unconstitutional, Vander Zalm unilaterally announced that he would withdraw all funding for abortion, and Campbell condemned the premier's view as a "narrow, bigoted opinion."[3] Vander Zalm's attempt to stop abortion funding was successfully challenged in the courts by the B.C. Civil Liberties Association, and the fundamentalist Catholic politician was forced to back down.

With little future in the Vander Zalm government, Campbell left the provincial caucus and gained the Tory nomination in the federal riding of Vancouver Centre after Conservative MP Pat Carney resigned the seat (Carney went on to become a member of the Canadian Senate). Campbell then upset national New Democratic Party president Johanna den Hertog by less than 300 votes in the 1988 federal election – a battle in which a Conservative-sponsored free trade agreement with the United States was a major issue. Campbell's feisty campaign performance – a repeated video clip caught her shouting "What are you afraid of?" at an anti–free trade heckler – led to her prompt appointment to the junior cabinet post of minister of state for Indian Affairs in January 1989, and just over a year later she became minister of Justice. It would not be the end of what journalists described as Campbell's "rise and rise."

Apart from Campbell's seemingly consistent political luck and her undeniable intelligence, there were a number of hard-headed practical reasons behind Mulroney's choice of an articulate woman for the Justice ministry. The prime minister's overriding internal political concern was maintaining the unity of a fractious government caucus. Although Mulroney had won a comfortable, if not massive, second-term majority in 1988, by the time of Campbell's appointment it had been eroded by the defection of Quebec MP Lucien Bouchard and a few of his colleagues, who formed the new parliamentary Bloc Québecois. Worse, the Tory majority was not only threatened by further Quebec nationalist defections, but also by a restive right-wing Conservative group of about twenty-five to thirty MPs, known as the "Family Caucus." Certainly, the desire to ideologically satisfy MPs who held a balance of power within the government proved to be a crucial factor in driving child pornography legislation.

Of the specific matters that made Campbell's appointment attractive, there were, first, two issues on the Justice agenda, both relevant to women, that were potentially divisive (within the Conservative Party, as well as more broadly) and that would be difficult to steer through parliament. Second, there were pressing government concerns – especially with respect to national unity and a large deficit that precluded vote-garnering spending measures – that meant the Justice ministry was likely to be the focus of public and media attention even beyond its normal prominence as a powerful government agency. Making law is something that even a financially impoverished government can afford.

Of the two Justice issues, one was a proposed abortion law to replace the statute struck down by the Supreme Court in 1988, which Campbell inherited from her predecessor, Doug Lewis. The main feature of this moderate, but contradictory, bit of legislation was to recriminalize the act of abortion, while providing such broad exemptions from its sanctions as to ensure the legality of virtually every abortion sought.

The other issue was reform of the country's gun control legislation. A significant public desire for stronger gun control laws had developed in the wake of the murder in 1989 of fourteen women students at an engineering college in Montreal. The "Montreal Massacre," as it came to be called, had taken on the profile of a women's issue not only because all of the victims were women, but also because it was the stated intention of their deranged murderer to kill them as a blow against feminism.

Both of those issues posed political problems that might be eased by a woman appointee. A proposal for any abortion law was bound to draw criticism from feminists already suspicious of the Conservative social policy agenda. The suspicion was augmented by the presence in Tory ranks of the Family Caucus, which had organized itself into a distinct body within the government, with its own meetings and agenda (including opposition to abortion). Having a moderate abortion bill shepherded by a woman minister with proven feminist credentials on the issue might ease its passage and deflect external criticism.

Gun control, on the other hand, posed an internal dilemma because many of the government MPs represented rural constituencies in which firearms were widely used for hunting and recreational target-shooting purposes. Again, a woman minister might succeed in moderating some of the predictable conflict. If there was to be new gun control legislation, it would be more awkward for the Family Caucus to attack a woman minister advancing it, particularly when she would be perceived as channelling the political forces created by the Montreal Massacre.

Avoiding divisiveness on such contentious issues was important to the prime minister's major national political commitment, namely, a resolution of the historical Quebec question. It was an issue that had preoccupied him during much of his first term and would again absorb considerable government attention in the latter half of his second term.[4] Appointments such as Campbell's to the Justice ministry were part and parcel of an intricate and fragile political web, whose weaving combined strands involving national political objectives with those of the internal politics of the governing Conservative Party.

The identification of Kim Campbell as the right woman in the right place at the right time was not, however, as straightforward as it seemed. First, although Campbell was married, she was hardly a role model for "REAL Women" (the name of a conservative women's group), given that she was childless and was about to see her second marriage end in divorce. Second, Campbell's views on a range of social questions, specifically those involving sexual justice, placed her in the tradition of "red Toryism," far from the positions of the Family Caucus, which was ideologically allied to the moral perspective of Christian fundamentalism.

Third, and perhaps most important practically, Campbell represented a riding that had a large, politically active population of homosexuals who were in the midst of a terrible struggle with the AIDS epidemic. The Family Caucus was as preoccupied as its brethren in the Republican Party of the United States with the need to identify and block the "gay agenda" to normalize homosexual "lifestyles." Campbell, conversely, was committed to a long-scheduled reform of the Canadian Human Rights Act, which would include "sexual orientation" among its specifically prohibited grounds of discrimination, a reform that the Family

Caucus vowed to oppose and which would place it on a collision course with Campbell's personal political interests.

Finally, Campbell was seen by the Family Caucus as too closely allied to the views of her chief bureaucrat, the deputy minister of Justice, John Tait. Tait was a distinguished Ottawa mandarin, but he was associated, in the minds of many in the Family Caucus, with what they perceived as the pro-gay bias of the Justice department. The effect of this alleged bias was seen in two ways – first, in the advice it offered to the government (e.g., that continued discrimination against gays in law and policy was unconstitutional); and second, in its failure to contain the legal advance of gay rights in courts, often losing cases that the Family Caucus thought it should have won easily.

In any case, Campbell set to work putting together a team of legislative advisers, schooling herself in the administration of the vast ministry to which she had been named, and defining her priorities. In her first ministerial posting to Indian Affairs, she had approached a senior civil servant and asked him to tutor her on the actual workings of government. She stuck with the lessons for a year, dubbing her civil servant tutor "Sir Humphrey," a reference to the Machiavellian bureaucrat from the *Yes, Minister* British television series. Now, in Justice, she made similar tutelary use of her experienced deputy minister, John Tait.

The overall direction set by Campbell for her ministry was, as she later explained, defined by "three priorities: protection of society, fairness in the relationship between citizens and government, and inclusive justice."[5] The notion of "inclusive justice," which meant opening the department to absorb new ideas from outside the system so as to reflect the concerns of previously marginalized segments of society, would become the slogan of her tenure as minister. Her legislative agenda would be driven by this notion, but also by the practical requirement to respond to a series of important decisions by the Supreme Court of Canada.

For her legislative team, in addition to Deputy Minister Tait and the corps of lawyers under his command, Campbell also relied on Richard Clair, Peter Lugli, and later, Marianne Campbell (no relation) from her personal staff. Finally, her legislative group was completed when Deputy Minister Tait hired John Dixon, a former president of the B.C. Civil Liberties Association and an academic in the philosophy department of Capilano College in North Vancouver, B.C. Dixon, who had no political affiliations, served as a special adviser to Tait, but Tait used him to directly support the minister, hence bridging the divide between elected and unelected government officials.

When Dixon began work in the Department of Justice in January 1991, his very first communication from his minister concerned pornography. He received a note from Campbell on Privy Council stationery, directing him to prepare a rationale for pornography legislation that would turn on the conflict between individual expression rights, which protected various forms of sexual representation, and the equality rights of women as a group. Dixon turned over the note, wrote his first two words of advice – "No, Minister" – and sent it back to Campbell. Though his reply offered a humorous turn on the *Yes, Minister* model, Campbell's note would prove to be portentous.

It was no accident that Campbell was concerned with the pornography issue. For the previous two decades, intellectual North America had been preoccupied with "porn wars" that divided venerable allies – feminists and civil libertarians – into opposing philosophical and legal camps.[6] Campbell had read widely in this area and had a natural interest in using her new role to respond to and advance the feminist agenda. Besides, this was an area in which there was an intriguing correspondence between the interests of women and the concerns of the moral and religious Right, as exemplified by the Family Caucus in her party. Women in the United States had already discovered – often uneasily – a common cause with Republican Party exponents of traditional "family values." This group had never faltered in its war against "dirty" books and pictures, and rather enthusiastically welcomed women joining it in its tireless struggle for "decency."

Such an alliance was inherently unstable, however. Where the Right held to a notion of morality that claimed to discover a perfect and inviolate coincidence between the boundaries of heterosexuality and decency, this moral revelation was not shared by the majority of feminists, whose inclusive philosophy had led them to a liberal acceptance of the many lesbians in their ranks. Besides, feminists attacked pornography on the modern legal basis of the alleged social scientific evidence of the harm it caused women, while their allies on the Right stuck to the older position that "filth" should be expunged on the simple ground of its immorality.

Campbell saw all of this, but was still intrigued by the potential of legislative initiatives on the porn front. For one thing, as we've already noted, she faced a very specific political problem in the form of the Family Caucus, and she needed to solve that problem as a condition of advancing her full legislative agenda. Could the smouldering pornography issue provide some badly needed common ground for her with the Family Caucus? Could well-conceived legislation in this area offset some of the unavoidable divisiveness guaranteed by the Justice agenda?

Along with Campbell's own interest in the pornography question, there were also institutional pressures for attention to the issue. Although the government had tried and failed, as recently as 1988, to pass new pornography legislation, commitment to such legislation was still alive in various governmental quarters. As well, a June 1990 report on child sexual abuse by Rix Rogers, a special adviser to the minister of Health and Welfare, had recommended "that the federal minister of justice introduce legislation that will address the protection of children from the harmful effects of pornography."

It was not an accident that Campbell's initial memo to her adviser directed him to look at pornography law in terms of a conflict between individual and group rights. The most prominent anti-pornography feminist thinker – and the one who pioneered a legal approach to anti-porn sanctions based on a notion of the collective or group rights of women – was an American law professor, Catherine MacKinnon.[7] Among other things, MacKinnon was providing advice to an important group of Canadian women lawyers, the Legal Education and Action Fund (LEAF). LEAF had intervened in several judicial actions, the most significant of which was the pending case (to be heard in June 1991) of *R. v. Butler*, in which the Supreme Court of Canada would determine the constitutional validity of the country's obscenity law and, equally important, the grounds on which it would be upheld or struck down.

There were two other reasons for Campbell's and, as well, Deputy Minister Tait's interest in the line of argument about collective rights. The first had to do with the issue of national unity. There was a perceived need for a creative approach to reconstituting the country, and the current thinking in Ottawa leaned towards some form of "asymmetric federalism" in which different rights and powers would be conferred on different provinces on the basis of their distinctive needs within Canadian confederation. If Catherine MacKinnon provided a "group rights" approach with respect to women, there were similar theorists about, such as Canadian philosopher Charles Taylor and a contingent of political thinkers interested in "communitarianism," who were being eagerly read in the Justice department for what they had to say about federalism.[8]

The idea was that the "collective rights" notion might provide some intellectual ground that could be used to balance the emphasis on individual equality rights in the Charter of Rights and Freedoms. The question at issue was: What does the constitutional principle of equality under the law demand? Does it bar the "unequal" treatment of different provinces, as contemplated in asymmetric federalism? Perhaps not, went the thinking of some analysts. Perhaps the equality guaranteed in the constitution could be interpreted or extended to include a range of group or collective rights, as was already explicitly the case in terms of aboriginal rights and some language rights.

Beyond this philosophical interest in group equality rights, the Department of Justice had a second and more pragmatic interest in such rights, stemming from its practical experience with Charter litigation. Justice lawyers were responsible for representing the Government of Canada in all lawsuits, and they were becoming swamped by Charter challenges to laws and policies of the government. Perhaps, suggested some lawyers within Justice, setting group rights against individual rights might relieve the pressure. After all, it might be argued that the laws and policies of the government were a means of securing the most general interests and public goods of Canadians. What better way to characterize those general interests and goods than as what Canadians as a collectivity have the right to expect from their government? If individual rights were being advanced to trump, or override, law and policy, one way to protect the government's agenda might be to promote law and policy to the status of group rights. This would give Justice a new range of legal weapons to deploy in defense of its clients, and might provide a means to contain and control the seemingly open-ended threat of Charter challenges to government action.

Thus, Campbell set her advisers on a two-track course to develop the thinking of the Justice department about both collective rights and pornography legislation. For the next few months the ministry was preoccupied with a directive that was hardly going to be diverted by a "No, Minister" quip.

If a minister insists on new legislation, the job of advisers is to provide her with advice on how to get it. To that end, on February 14, 1991, Campbell received a memo that offered three suggestions.[9]

The first suggestion was a quite modest proposal to "redraft the obscenity provisions to reflect the advancement of post-Charter law and clean up the anachronisms." For example, there was still a clause in Section 163, the obscenity law, which prohibited "crime comics" that depicted "pictorially, the commission of crimes, real or fictitious," so that, technically, it might be a crime to sell the well-known Walt Disney Studios–produced "Scrooge McDuck" comics because they contained pictorial depictions of crimes committed by cartoon characters called the "Beagle Boys." This clause went back to the 1950s, when a flurry of interest in "juvenile delinquency" posited the view that there was a causal connection between crime comics and youth crime.

The memo also proposed, in the first suggested course of action, that a new law could "hive off simple depictions of intercourse as falling outside the offence. Customs is currently seizing descriptions and depictions of anal intercourse, against the insistent advice of Justice Department lawyers that this runs against the case law . . . This leads to really awful discrimination against gay literature and erotica." Indeed, the controversy over the "prior restraint" censorship practices of Canada Customs – seizing suspected obscene materials destined for the Canadian market – had already reached the point where a Vancouver gay and lesbian bookstore, Little Sister's, had begun a constitutional challenge to the statutory powers given to Canada Customs.[10]

A second suggestion proposed to tackle a more fundamental issue by distinguishing "between description and depiction, between text and pictures, separating the textual as outside the range of the obscenity provisions." Such a move would finally settle the longstanding and never more than half-clarified question about writing and obscenity. Rather than trying to determine whether a piece of writing containing sexual representations was a work of literature or not, the law could simply declare, in effect, that written erotica doesn't cause harm in any legal sense.

"This would go a long way," argued the memo, "to focussing the offence on the sorts of pictorial representations that some people believe (against all available evidence . . . but let that pass) incite persons to criminal sexual acts. Nobody can reasonably construct a case for text as either effrontery (you have to make a specific personal effort called reading to unleash its force upon yourself) or incitement (too much room for the intermediation of reflection). So this would be a huge step towards bringing the obscenity provisions into some sort of conformity to common sense . . ." The very language of this proposal, with its broad-brush sarcasm, stands as an indicator of the critical attitude of many Justice officials about the intellectual gaps and outdatedness of the existing obscenity provision.

But it was the third suggestion that caught Campbell's attention. This was a proposal to "create a new sub-section of the obscenity section to capture the making, distribution, and possession of photographic kiddie porn." The new idea here wasn't the notion of prohibiting child pornography – that was already in the law, as we've noted above – but rather the idea of making simple possession of child pornography a criminal offence. "The reasoning here, with respect to possession," said the memo, "is that in order to make a photograph of the sexual use of a child, the sexual use of a child must actually be contrived in the real world," and such use of a child was already a crime (unlike the sexual activities of consenting adults in relation to their photographic representation).

"Thus, there is a symmetry between the photographic representation of the sexual use of children and stolen property," the memo suggested. "So we should prohibit even the possession and enjoyment of kiddie porn for the same reasons we prohibit the possession and enjoyment of stolen property: because by so doing we attack the possibility of profiting from criminal wrongdoing. The offence could be charged on the presumptive evidence that the photographs were of children. The defence would then be that you could show that they were not, in fact, children."[11]

It was this suggestion that Justice Minister Campbell decided to pursue, announcing in the Commons in late May 1991 her general intention to introduce a child pornography law. Both the minister and her deputy were attracted to the idea of a new censorship law that would appeal to the "moral right wing" (especially the Tory Family Caucus) and that would also be endorsed by civil libertarians. It was the sort of "win-win" move that both politicians and statesmen adore. Thus, the Canadian kiddie porn law was conceived – although its actual birth was a considerable way off.

As the option of a child pornography law advanced to the stage of a public commitment, advice on the group rights approach was provided in a series of memos, culminating with one on March 14, 1991, that took up the question of whether Canada's individual equality rights were an obstacle to developing policies that addressed national collective interests.[12] At this point the collective rights route was rejected. The bottom line was that "beyond the extent to which some such collective rights (as in the case of aboriginal and language rights) are already entrenched in our Constitution, it would be legally and philosophically awkward, as well as politically dangerous, to attempt to fashion a much more expansive and ambitious role for them." The reason for rejecting a more "ambitious" role for such collective rights had to do with the danger of unleashing genies from bottles.

Positive rights (as contrasted to negative ones), went the argument, are extremely difficult for courts to adjudicate. It's far easier to tell a government to stop doing "x" (as in the Supreme Court abortion decision, where the court told the government to stop relying on overly restrictive therapeutic abortion committees) than to tell a government what it should do.

Further, group rights bring large, organized forces into the policy-making arena with the potential to acquire equally large, novel powers. A notion of "inclusive justice" that brought previously unrecognized groups to the table for genuine consultations was one thing; carving their powers into constitutional stone was another. Self-consciously creating a big role for positive group rights in the scheme of governance could set loose new powers and players that might undermine the authority of the courts as they got more involved in policy adjudication, and could potentially render government itself irrelevant as just one more player in a court-adjudicated policy area. While those were the very reasons that some people supported group rights as a broadening of democracy, it was this argument that quickly cooled the fervour of group rights enthusiasts inside government. In any case, it was argued that collective interests (as distinct from rights) could be accommodated without the necessity of entrenching collective rights.

That left the question of whether equality rights would get in the way of policies accommodating collective interests. The principal constitutional passage embodying equality rights is Section 15 of the Charter of Rights and Freedoms, which says, "Every individual is equal before and under the law and has the right to the equal protection and equal benefit of the law without discrimination and, in particular, without discrimination based on race, national or ethnic origin, colour, religion, sex, age or mental or physical disability." (This concept of a list of prohibited grounds for discrimination will crop up later when we examine the proposed "sexual orientation" amendment to the Canadian Human Rights Act.)

In the March 14 memo that concluded the exploration of a group rights concept, the main point made was that judicial interpretations of the individual equality rights of Section 15 were narrowly enough focussed that Section 15 was unlikely to be an obstacle to "differential treatment of regions or groups that differ in ways relevant to the interests of Canada as a whole." Or to put it more plainly, the government could make laws addressing the special needs of regions and groups (such as the province of Quebec or aboriginal people) without having to worry that an individual (Albertan or Caucasian, say) would drag it to court complaining that he or she had been discriminated against (as an Albertan or as a "white" person). "It is clear," urged the memo, "that Canadian courts would never entertain a section 15 suit which challenged the system of transfer payments used in our country to partially equalize economic benefits. It is not that they would accept it as an instance of unequal treatment and then justify it as a reasonable infringement of section 15; [rather,] it would never be accepted as an instance of inequality."

As we trace the paper trail that led to the child pornography law, we want to make a couple of observations about the character of these documents and about rights as a general topic. In a sense, this memo and others similar to it are reminders about why we have democracies in the first place. Since we're addressing what is finally a rather esoteric, though not at all unimportant, bit of constitutional law, it's worth recalling that the reasons we're debating such questions have as much to do with democracy itself as they do with the intrinsic interest of the disputed legislation we're examining in such detail. The reason for underscoring this point is that opponents of challenges to the child pornography law will insist that the issue at stake is a simple and detachable question of the protection of children, and that claims about more encompassing democratic perspectives are irrelevant and diversionary.

The one thing to anticipate regarding rights generally, as this memo and subsequent ones about the child pornography law make clear, is the delicate interplay between rights and interests that is central to deciding how we live together in a democracy.

So, on the one hand, while rights are vitally important, "no right is absolute, and some rights are more important than others." Just to take an obvious example of the hierarchy of rights offered by the March 14 memo, while "the enjoyment of private property is an important common law right with or without Charter [recognition], this right must give way in some circumstances (such as, for instance, a case involving restriction of access to a private tennis club) when it conflicts with the human right to be protected from discrimination on the basis of race."

That is, there are clear instances where, in the hierarchy of rights, a right to racial equality takes precedence over a lesser right that's being used to deny the higher one.

On the other hand, as the memo argues, and as will be relevant in the Robin Sharpe case, "even the fundamental freedoms may not trench upon the most substantial and compelling public interests. Our commitment to a principled protection of a range of individual prerogatives . . . is grounded in our commitment to self-government and – by extension – our commitment to [a] distinctive moral/political culture that . . . depends upon reposing the ultimate source of political authority in the citizenry. But this means that the principled commitment to the protection of individual rights flows from a more primitive, fundamental, and more important commitment – our commitment to the creation and protection of a particular form of human community – and hence rights claims that threaten vital collective interests threaten the very basis of their continuing effective existence and are justifiably limited on such grounds." Of course, this is the very argument that will be used by proponents of group rights seeking to justify the infringement of individual rights when it comes to pornography issues. Our point is that it is exactly this tension upon which the deliberations of governments and courts will turn in deciding how to resolve such issues.

If Justice Minister Campbell could be persuaded that collective rights were too practically cumbersome and too intellectually insubstantial to pursue (and that, in any case, individual rights weren't a bar to accommodating group interests), the same was not true of pornography. The idea of a pornography initiative was now on the table.

However, from the point of view of her advisers, there were

considerable problems. First, the existing obscenity provisions of the Criminal Code (Section 163) very clearly covered child pornography. Indeed, there were no decisions extant in any Canadian court that threw any doubt whatsoever on the proposition that pornographic materials involving the use of children would be viewed as the most serious form of obscene expression targeted by the Criminal Code. Second, there was no child pornography controversy abroad in the land, crying out for legislative clarification or governmental response. Child porn was, simply and unequivocally, obscene, and anyone making, distributing, selling, or publishing it would be subject to prosecution wherever and whenever they were detected in Canada.

Finally, there was the crucial related matter of the extreme rarity of child pornography. In 1991 there was virtually no market in child pornography in Canada. At least, there was none that could be detected by officials in the research division of the Department of Justice, who had been charged with the task of going out and finding it. Campbell's advisers met with those officials, who reported that among the very few instances of child pornography found in Canada, the greatest number of them came from misdirected mailings by the U.S. Postal Service as part of an American sting operation against kiddie porn. That is, what market there was in Canada had been inadvertently created by U.S. authorities.

A Justice department study dutifully documented all of this, notwithstanding occasional counterclaims by Canadian police officials that kiddie porn was indeed a problem.[13] For example, in an almost five-year period between 1986 and 1990, only 1.3 percent of more than 38,000 seizures of pornographic material by Canada Customs involved child pornography. Similarly, statistics for Customs' seizures in Ontario from 1987 to 1989 showed that child pornography accounted for only 0.5 percent of some 6,500 "enforcement actions." The marked increase in the availability of child pornography as a result of Internet technology developments had not yet occurred. For the moment, however, there wasn't compelling evidence that there was a genuine need for legislation.

If a principle of sound government is that law should only be enacted when there is real need, then contemplating unnecessary legislation brought with it the danger that the expansion of legislative activity and the multiplication of statutes could damage both the administration of laws and respect for them. Further, if a criminal law had no real target, the danger increased that its impact would be on the wrong people. Such a result in the criminal law context is called injustice.

While the child pornography law was in its embryonic stage, the Justice ministry was engaged in a range of other issues, including one involving literal embryos.

As justice minister, Kim Campbell was expected to guide through Parliament a proposed abortion law that had been drafted by her predecessor, but she had little enthusiasm for the task. "I had taken the position that I was not uncomfortable with the absence of a law," she notes. "However . . . I had also said I would not object to a law that simply confirmed the status quo, which was that the decision was one for a woman and her doctor to make."[14]

Similarly, while Prime Minister Mulroney did not have a strong personal attachment to the abortion issue, he did have a strong political interest in dealing with abortion in such a way as to inflame neither his right wing nor so-called New Conservatives, who tended to be more urban, less religious, and more highly educated than the classic version of Conservatives. The newer brand of conservatism tended to focus on fiscal issues rather than social ones, and to be "softer" or more permissive on issues of sexual morality.

In an effort to blunt the potentially divisive legislative effort, Mulroney assigned the task of drafting a new law to a committee of ministers. When that failed he took the novel step of creating an all-caucus committee to prepare draft legislation. The committee produced a compromise that appeared to take into account the internal dynamic of the Conservative Party. "Procuring an abortion" would remain a criminal offence, inscribed within the Criminal Code of Canada, as it had been prior to the *Morgentaler* decision. However, a complete defence would be available where, in the opinion of a licensed physician, the abortion was necessary for the physical or psychological health of the woman seeking it.

The proposed law "was worded as a prohibition," Campbell observes, "but the area of prohibited conduct was extremely narrow . . . What was primarily rendered illegal by this bill was abortions performed by someone who was either not a doctor or not acting under the direction of a doctor." The bill was intended to satisfy "pro-life" conservatives that abortion was not "just another health issue," but a criminal offence, while appeasing "pro-choice" proponents with a scheme that effectively ceded governance of abortion to women and medical professionals. It was a compromise that Campbell could live with in good conscience, because it "would make it difficult for provinces to treat abortion as a non-essential procedure" and thus attempt to limit access to abortion, as B.C. had tried to do.[15] The reason for this was that the constitution gave the federal government exclusive jurisdiction to make criminal law, and making abortion a crime effectively ruled out provincial measures. Minimally, the new law would remedy the situation leaving the country with no legislative guidance on the question of abortion, as had been the case ever since the *Morgentaler* decision struck down the previous law.

Nonetheless, it didn't require any extraordinary mental effort to see that there was something contradictory about a law that criminalized a particular act and simultaneously exempted almost all instances of the act from prosecution. The proposed law received criticism from all sides. Pro-life commentators quickly condemned the legislation on the grounds that the retention of the criminal offence was no more than empty symbolism. On the other side, pro-choice leaders were furious at the "recriminalization" of abortion, making women subject to the stigmatizing force of a criminal prohibition. Far from seeing this as mere symbolism, the pro-choice camp saw the retention of the offence as an insufferable, regressive insult to women. While many moderates were satisfied that the proposal was an ingenious, appropriately Canadian compromise, even some people in the middle found themselves uneasy, viewing the compromise as more disingenuous than genuine.

In the final analysis, the crucial opposition to the legislation came from physicians themselves. Perhaps the doctors had been unwisely neglected by government trouble-shooters sent out to soothe various sensibilities. In any case, physicians were the one group of professionals that saw themselves exposed to the risk of some form of prosecution for offending the criminal prohibition, and though their concerns were probably legally groundless, their opposition would be telling on legislators.

Campbell succeeded in securing passage of the abortion bill in the House of Commons by a narrow seven-vote margin, but approval by the Senate promised to be more difficult. There was considerable behind-the-scenes manoeuvring as the Government Whip calculated that the bill would pass if every Conservative senator in support of the measure attended and voted for it, and if those Tory senators chary of the proposition simply agreed to absent themselves rather than register opposition. Senator Pat Carney, the former MP whose Vancouver Centre riding was now represented by Campbell, was one of those expected to be absent. Instead, at the last moment she turned up at the end of January 1991 and cast a deciding vote against the bill, resulting in a tie vote that, by Senate rules, defeated the bill. As Campbell later delicately put it, "My relationship with Pat became strained after what I considered her breach of caucus collegiality."[16]

The net political effect of the defeat of the abortion legislation was the embitterment of the Tory Family Caucus. While it had attacked the bill as inadequate throughout the legislative process, in the end it hungered for the "half a loaf" consolation the bill could have provided. Ironically, though they had wanted the defeat of the bill, its actual failure left Family Caucus members feeling tricked by the liberal wing (represented by feminist Carney) of their own party. It was perhaps not entirely coincidental that Justice Minister Campbell set her advisers to work on pornography legislation hard on the heels of the defeat of abortion recriminalization.

In the longer run, no succeeding government introduced any further abortion legislation, and Canada has managed to live for a dozen years as one of the few countries without any criminal law whatsoever respecting abortion, while at the same time providing abortion as a normal medical service. Although Canada has a high rate of abortions relative to births, if one doesn't regard abortion itself as morally catastrophic, the lesson seems to be that the absence of a law where there's no pressing need for one is not a harbinger of widespread societal disruption, and that even some difficult problems can be managed by self-governance at the level of civil society. Or to put it less formally, the claim that women, individually and collectively, could decide for themselves what to do about abortion has proven itself to be sound.

The Justice ministry had plenty of other things to attend to during 1991, including the complexities of designing and passing gun legislation, developing amendments to the Canadian Human Rights Act that would prohibit discrimination against gays, and putting into practice its commitment to "inclusive justice" by hosting two major conferences – one in summer 1991 on women and the law, and a second in the fall to consider aboriginal justice issues. At the same time, the department was busy fielding lawyers to represent the government in a variety of court cases, the most important of which was *R. v. Butler*, heard in June 1991, to determine the constitutional status of the obscenity law.

However, it was another Supreme Court of Canada decision, in *R. v. Seaboyer*, that made the most pressing demand on the Justice ministry that year. In fall 1991 the court struck down the "rape shield" law, a statute that barred those accused of sexual assault from introducing evidence of "previous sexual conduct" involving the alleged victim and any person other than the accused, unless the sexual conduct occurred at the time of the alleged assault.

The rape shield law struck down by the court was hardly a radical bit of legal protection for women. The Canadian Criminal Code, until the early 1960s, would not accept an uncorroborated complaint of rape or indecent assault if the complainant was not of "previous chaste character." One of the principal lines of defence for an accused, if the assault was proved and there was clearly no consent, was to introduce evidence that the complainant was not of chaste character. Courts found that it was not even necessary to show that the complainant had had previous intercourse with other men; mere "lewd conduct," such as inappropriate speech in a public place, could discredit a sexual assault complaint in court by demonstrating a lack of necessary chastity.

Though the rape shield law had been designed to repair egregious excesses of sexism in the law, there was some question about whether it went too far in restricting a relevant defence to charges of sexual assault. In the case of Seaboyer, his "previous sexual conduct evidence" involved a claim of consensual sadomasochistic sexual relations between the complainant and another man on the previous night. So even though the evidence went directly to the source of physical marks that the Crown had introduced as corroborative of the complainant's allegation, the trial judge disallowed it on rape shield grounds. The Supreme Court of Canada struck down this shield as overbroad.

Campbell quickly mobilized her ministry to draft a new law and held an unusual set of consultative meetings with feminist organizations across the country. The initial consultations proved disappointing to Campbell, who was opposed to "leaving the courts to work out a new approach to the admissibility of evidence in cases of sexual assault," since that "would turn victims into jurisprudential guinea pigs and discourage the reporting of sexual offences."[17]

Instead, Campbell forged ahead, securing approval from cabinet in November 1991 to draft amendments to the Criminal Code for a new rape shield law that included a revised definition of consent, restrictions on the defence of honest belief in consent, and a preamble. "It is unusual for criminal statutes to have a preamble," as Campbell notes, "but since the courts cannot consider the parliamentary debates in interpreting legislation, this was a way of ensuring that the social circumstances in which the bill was drafted would be considered by a court in the event that its constitutionality was challenged."[18] Although many in the legal profession derided the preamble as empty of political force, it was one of the things that feminist leaders found important and engaging when they met with Campbell in late November 1991, and which secured their participation and support when the minister introduced the bill in the House of Commons in December 1991. Unsurprisingly, neither the preamble nor the substance won any points for Campbell with the Family Caucus, which regarded it as a deplorable instance of "political correctness."

In the end, Campbell succeeded in producing a new rape shield law that, though perhaps slightly more porous than the previous one, included "a reaffirmation of the principle that evidence of a complainant's prior sexual activity is admissible only when it is specific and relevant to an issue to be proved in a trial, and where its value is not outweighed by the danger of unfair prejudice."[19]

By summer 1991, enthusiasm for a child pornography law – even one narrowly focussed on a possession offence where sexual representations involve the illegal sexual use of real children – had reached such a pitch within the ministry that some of Campbell's advisers were moved to reiterate their misgivings.

A memo sent to Campbell and Tait on July 16, 1991, presented the most extended and sober argument against the wisdom of kiddie porn legislation yet heard.[20]

Interestingly, the overt focus of the memo was not on principle – it conceded that there was "no good principled (i.e., civil libertarian) argument against" the sort of kiddie porn legislation being contemplated – but rather on policy considerations. "It would be a policy mistake to introduce new law targeting kiddie porn," the memo said in a prefatory summary. "The harm is virtually non-existent in Canada, [there is] no large constituency actively demanding legislative action, and in this environment the initiative could a) possibly encourage abusive enforcement tactics; b) possibly harm our efforts to include 'sexual orientation' in the Canadian Human Rights Act, thus angering gays; c) possibly divide and consequently anger the feminist movement; d) raise an issue which could prove divisive for the government while at the same time exposing it to charges of opportunism."

Though the July 16 memo concentrated on the question of whether proceeding with kiddie porn legislation was a good policy idea, it also offered a compelling argument disposing of possible civil libertarian objections to such legislation.

"Virtually everybody regards the sexual abuse of children as desperately and completely wrong, and that photographic depictions of such abuse should be absolutely prohibited," the memo observed. "Prohibitions on making and distributing are in place (in the form of the present law, which does not distinguish between adult and child porn), but it is reasonable to consider going further with kiddie porn, and making even simple possession an offence."

But what about the qualms of civil libertarians worried about infringements on free speech? "Kiddie porn cannot legitimately shelter" under the section of the Canadian Constitution guaranteeing free speech, the memo asserted. It recognized that "freedom of expression protections of a democracy have a political purpose." Simply put, if the people are to rule, they need the broadest intellectual rights possible to deliberate and judge public matters. "It is for this reason that the expression rights must extend their protection to the obscene, because sexual mores and possibilities are of great social and political moment, and easily fit within the ambit of 'the ruler's agenda.'" Indeed, it was for that reason that Campbell's advisers had been studying the possibility of revising the obscenity law to remove its moralistic anachronisms and to ensure that it didn't unnecessarily infringe on free speech.

All that was well and good, "but what about forms of expression that are made through the contrivance of a criminal act?" What's more, what if there is a commerce in such expressions, the profits of which motivate the crimes? Since Canadian society "regards the sexual use of children as a crime, and any photographic record of the sexual activity of children which is offered for sale may, on the face of it, be fairly considered to have been made with a view to its value in trade," a possession offence had obvious relevance to combatting such traffic. The memo emphasized "the photographic element, because it is not true that a drawing, painting or written account of the sexual use of children must involve their criminal use." This is one of the crucial distinctions of our own argument about how to construct an appropriate child pornography law, and we'll continue to reiterate it throughout our account.

The July 16 memo repeated the analogy (presented in the February 14 memo) between stolen property and kiddie porn in justification of a possession offence. But here the memo took into account potential civil libertarian objections, admitting that "there is an important asymmetry between stolen property laws and kiddie porn laws: the expression rights are more fundamental than property rights," therefore there must be more caution in infringing them. "Ought we to forgo kiddie porn laws on principle?" No, said the memo, "for two reasons."

The first reason is "the very great importance of the good aimed at." Since the sexual abuse of children is a serious criminal offence, and one that is difficult to detect and punish, photographic images of such abuse provide "an opportunity for the state to attack" the abuse itself, albeit indirectly. Second, "little or no danger is posed to the expression rights if the definition of kiddie porn is limited to photographic images. The purpose of the expression rights centres on the deliberative function and prerogatives of the ruling people." While there were many legitimate questions to be asked and answered about children and sexuality, "all of these questions – which raise important policy considerations – can be posed and discussed without resort to the use of photographic images . . .

"When these two considerations – the importance of the good, and the correspondingly slight threat to civil liberties – are joined," this section of the memo concluded, "there is a good case for over-riding the expression rights in the specific and limited case of photographic images of the sexual use of children, given that those images are made possible by the contrivance of a criminal act for that purpose."

The memo then turned to its ostensible main purpose: presenting policy arguments against a new kiddie porn law. We say "ostensible main purpose" because while the memo made a best effort to persuade the minister that it wasn't good policy wisdom to go ahead, it seems fairly clear that there was recognition that the momentum for a law was too far developed for dissuasion to have a chance, and that the real strategic intent of the memo was to reiterate the importance of keeping the bill narrowly focussed if the support of civil libertarians was to be maintained.

Nonetheless, the policy objections are germane and proved to be all too relevant once the kiddie porn law moved farther along the legislative pipeline. Once more, the memo noted that "there is virtually no commerce in kiddie porn in North America, and new law may encourage new abuses on the part of law enforcement authorities. All recent (last decade) studies of kiddie porn have turned up the rather startling finding that it is virtually non-existent" as a commercial market (though there is some non-commercial "trading" of such images). The memo here cited the

U.S. postal authorities' sting operation as an example of enforcement abuse.

Second, while "the idea of a surgical strike on kiddie porn" may be attractive, "it may not be easy to control the agenda. Once we announce one form of stiffening of the law, we will be drawn into uncomfortable debate concerning neglect of other forms of porn." For example, what if enthusiasts began demanding a possession offence for adult porn, where the sexual representations are not a dedicated element of a criminal offence, as they are in kiddie porn?

Third, there was the problem of gay constituents, an important group of people in Campbell's own riding. "We are entering a very delicate stage in our efforts to include sexual orientation in the Canadian Human Rights Act," noted the memo. "The set of those who will oppose such an initiative closely corresponds to the set of those who want more far-reaching pornography laws." Wouldn't the introduction of new kiddie porn legislation "stir up this group"? Since Family Caucus types firmly believed that "gays are specially liable to sexual abuse of the young," there was good reason to anticipate that a kiddie porn debate "will work against us on sexual orientation, and offend gays, who will attack it as a cynical sop to the Right. If we are unsuccessful in including sexual orientation, gays may focus on the kiddie porn laws as showing that the government decided to opt for political advantage instead of making good on our promise to protect their rights." Finally, in terms of policy considerations, there was very little public demand for a legislative initiative, nor was pornography a current major agenda item for such organizations as the National Action Committee on the Status of Women. "Our mail on pornography is very small."

Balancing the pros and cons, the memo concluded, "While generally attractive, and consonant with freedom of expression principles, a legislative initiative attacking kiddie porn would not be a good justice policy at this time."

But it was indeed too late for such considerations. Campbell had already committed herself to child pornography legislation in the House of Commons, and although such promises were neither politically nor morally binding, she appeared determined to proceed.

Behind the scenes, there was a struggle over how to manage the development of a proposed bill on child pornography. Legislation is, officially, secret before it is tabled in the House of Commons for what's known as "First Reading." It is not, however, secret to other interested ministries and agencies of government. The standard legislative practice is to produce and circulate a draft "Memorandum to Cabinet" in order to benefit from the widest available range of expert advice and to provide a political "heads up" to ministers who may be called upon to comment when the legislation appears. Of course, once circulated in this way, a good deal of the content of a legislative proposal may "leak" out to the public.

Some of Campbell's advisers argued against the standard, informal practice on the grounds that it would inevitably create political pressure to "toughen and broaden" the law in ways that had already been identified as unwise. But other advisers in the Justice department continued to press for a stronger law, even after the minister was settled on the shape of the possession statute. The quarrel, broadly speaking, was over the definition of "child" and the forms of expression material covered by the law.

Since these issues will resurface throughout the debate on the law, this is a suitable place to introduce the contentious question of the definition of a child. While everyone agrees that children should be protected from sexual abuse, there is considerable disagreement – as reflected in the internal and ongoing Justice department debate – over the age at which children become capable of meaningful consent to sexual activities. That the concept of "age of consent" is far from settled is reflected in a bewildering snakes-and-ladders set of definitions contained in the Criminal Code.

The basic age of consent in Canada, which, as we noted earlier, was established more than a century ago, is set at fourteen. Sex with persons under fourteen is generally illegal, certainly for adults, although there are some definitionally complicating age provisions for both sex between children and between children and adolescents. For example, if someone aged twelve or thirteen makes a sexual complaint, the accused cannot offer the defence that the complainant consented to the activity unless the accused is twelve years or older but under the age of sixteen, or is less than two years older than the complainant, and in neither case is in a position of trust or authority towards the complainant. Further, no person aged twelve or thirteen shall be tried for offences under the "sexual touching" sections of the Criminal Code unless that twelve- or thirteen-year-old is in a position of trust or authority towards the complainant.

Canada also has an intermediate category of "young persons" – people aged fourteen to seventeen years inclusive – who are protected from certain forms of sexual exploitation at the hands of adults. While no adult may, under any circumstances, legally engage in sexual relations with a person under fourteen, adults may legally engage in sexual relations with young persons between the ages of fourteen to seventeen inclusive if, and only if, the adult is not in a position of authority or trust with respect to that person, and as long as the adult does not attempt to secure the consent of the young person by means of any commercial inducement (as in cases of youth prostitution).

Finally, there is an additional complication that, practically speaking, differentiates between heterosexual and homosexual relations. It's a criminal offence to engage in anal intercourse with any person, other than one's spouse, under the age of eighteen. Thus, by implication, the age of consent for homosexual relations is four years older than that for heterosexual relations. Unqualified competence to choose to engage in sexual relations with another person, therefore, only begins at the age of eighteen.

It's easy to see, given the above, and taking account of variable ages set for such activities as voting, drinking, and obtaining a driver's license, why the definition of a child for the purpose of child pornography legislation is a legitimately contentious issue. If the definition was set at the age of consent for heterosexual relations, those on the Right would likely attack the statute as offering children insufficient protection. On the other hand, if the definition was set at the age of consent for homosexual relations, it would be attacked by civil libertarians and those on the cultural Left as unrealistically high. For example, many of the most photographed models in fashion and women's magazines are between fifteen and seventeen years old and are neither represented as, nor considered to be, children.

One final introductory consideration about age, although it was seldom discussed in government circles, concerns youth sexuality itself. An obvious anomaly that flows from setting the definitional age at eighteen is that while it would be perfectly legal for two sixteen-year-olds to engage in sex, if they made a photographic representation of that sexual engagement they would be guilty of the offence of making and possessing child pornography. The notion of an act itself being legal, but its mere representation being a crime, appears to be a blatant distortion of both common sense and law. It's that sort of anomaly that raises a question about the motivation of at least some of the proponents of such legislation. Is the aim to protect children or is it to expand the definition of a child in order to control the sexual activities of young people?

Disagreement about the appropriate age definition for the kiddie porn law continued to be a central obstacle to crafting the law. While the minister and deputy minister had informally indicated that they would be reasonably happy with a compromise age of sixteen, influential officials within the Justice department continued to disagree. They would find outspoken allies both inside and outside government.

Even as the ministry focussed on other issues in late 1991, the debate about child pornography legislation simmered. A November 7, 1991, memo reported on the latest meeting of Justice officials reviewing the child pornography file.[21]

By then, ministry officials were considering the possibilities of a linkage between child pornography legislation and planned amendments to the Canadian Human Rights Act to explicitly include homosexuals under the act's protection. The meeting quickly devolved into another discussion about the pros and cons of the kiddie porn law. Before offering the minister any arguments for or against the law, the memo reiterated that "we are all firmly of the opinion that any legislation should be strictly limited to photographic depictions of the sexual use of children."

The pros and cons were, by now, fairly familiar. On the plus side were —

1. the virtually unanimous public abhorrence at the sexual use of children and the photographic representation of such use, and the facts that
2. a possession offence likely would be accepted by proponents of civil liberties in the name of the good that would be accomplished,

3. the proposed possession offence would reduce the incentive to produce child porn,
4. a law strictly limited to photographic media would engender only marginal opposition,
5. such legislation would raise the government's "profile as guarantors of decency," and
6. "all of the above might help set the stage for the successful negotiation of sexual orientation inclusion by convincing conservative parliamentarians that we are morally 'on side'."

On the negative side:

1. the fact that there was little "market in child porn in Canada (as per Justice Department studies) . . . is bound to come out,"
2. even a narrowly focussed bill would almost certainly produce an unwelcome widening debate on obscenity, and
3. such a "loss of control of the agenda" would produce division and opposition among feminists,
4. as well as gays, whose communities would be spotlighted "in a way that works directly against the ultimate object of the exercise."

The November 7 memo concluded, "There are no good principled arguments against child porn legislation that would absolutely prohibit even the simple possession of photographic representations of the sexual use of children. On the other hand, there is virtually no real mischief for the law to address; it will be extremely difficult to control the porn agenda once it is opened at any point; and the process may make it more difficult to advance gay rights."

While the ministry was still far from a consensus on child pornography legislation, in February 1992 the Supreme Court of Canada rendered a landmark decision on the constitutionality of Canada's existing obscenity law. The case, *R. v. Butler*, which was heard in June 1991, was the first major Charter test of pornography in the country, and the judgment would have far-reaching consequences, substantially affecting the course of all subsequent debate about the censorship of obscenity, as well as the child pornography legislation.

The decision unanimously upheld the central provision of the existing law, Section 163, which decrees that "any publication a dominant characteristic of which is the undue exploitation of sex, or of sex and any one or more of the following subjects, namely, crime, horror, cruelty and violence, shall be deemed to be obscene." The decision also explicitly and repeatedly declared that any representation of sexual activity involving actual children in its production is obscene. This meant that only an extension of criminal prohibition to include simple possession of child porn would represent a legislated advance on the case law.

The reasons for judgment make the *Butler* decision – whether one approves or deplores it (we're in the latter camp) – a vital one for the crafting of the kiddie porn law, which was conceived as simply an extension of Section 163.[22] First, we'll provide a bit of historical context concerning Canadian pornography law; then we'll look at what the court decided and why; and finally we'll offer our criticisms.

"As in many other countries, initial attempts to regulate sexually explicit materials in Canada stemmed from traditional notions of government responsibility for societal decency and morality," legal scholar Jodi Kleinick observes in her review of the *Butler* decision. It's a tradition that goes all the way back to mid-seventeenth-century England. In twentieth-century Canada, moral standards changed gradually but dramatically. Before the Second World War, the general view of pornography, consistent with that of the other major Western democracies, was that graphic or textual representations of sex, or even frank discussions of it in a publication, were obscene because they were immoral. Although an otherwise obscene publication might be "redeemed" if its sexual content was coincidental to some more acceptable purpose, for the most part it was not thought either politically or legally necessary to go beyond the identification of a publication as immoral in order to establish its obscene nature and justify its censorship. If it was about sex, it was dirty.

The "archeological" remnants of this idea can be seen in the Criminal Code of Canada, where the obscenity provisions are still posted under the heading "Offences tending to the corruption of public morals." That is, the obscenity provisions sit squarely within the section of the criminal law that literally codifies the sexual morality of Canadian society.

However, after the Second World War a series of court decisions and parliamentary initiatives showed the judiciary and legislatures moving away from the standard that had been set by a nineteenth-century English case, *R. v. Hicklin*, where the test for obscenity was "whether the tendency of the matter charged as obscenity is to deprave and corrupt those whose minds are open to such immoral influences." Legal and legislative thinking turned towards the liberal principles that British political philosopher John Stuart Mill enunciated in his classic *On Liberty*. The core of Mill's principle of liberty was that the only legitimate reason for which a state could limit the freedom of one of its members was to prevent harm to others. This principle, in its turn, is grounded in the more general principle of utility, which held that actions or laws were good insofar as they produced the greatest amount of happiness for the greatest number of people.

On Liberty develops a comprehensive argument that there are very few forms of human freedom more conducive to the production of human happiness than the freedom of what Mill called "thought and discussion." So if there was to be censorship, or interference with the thought and discussion of the citizenry, there must be a justification of such censorship in terms of showing an actual harm to others – harm that, if censorship took the same view as the rest of the Criminal Code, would eventually be defined as direct and measurable, rather than indirect, such as the harm caused by mere offensiveness.

Notions such as these, along with the American tradition of free speech rooted in "natural law," provided the intellectual underpinnings of the expression rights entrenched in Canada's 1982 *Constitution Act*.

Even before that, the accelerating sexual liberalization of Western cultures had an impact on Canadian obscenity standards. Discussions in the Canadian Senate in 1952 led to a series of recommendations that resulted in the House of Commons establishing a new standard in law in 1957: that obscenity is "any publication a dominant characteristic of which is the undue exploitation of sex, or of sex and any one or more of the following subjects, namely, crime, horror, cruelty and violence . . . " This became the core of Section 163 of the Criminal Code.

The new definition raised an obvious question. How do we tell whether the "exploitation of sex" in a publication is "undue"? The measure that Canadian courts developed is what's known as the "Canadian community standard of tolerance" test. In this test, the courts measured a purportedly obscene publication against what the Canadian community, taken as a whole, would "tolerate" – not what it would tolerate seeing or reading itself, but what it would tolerate others seeing or reading. As Chief Justice Brian Dickson put it in a 1985 case, *Towne Cinema v. R.*, "It is a standard of tolerance, not taste, that is relevant. What matters is not what Canadians think is right for themselves to see. What matters is what Canadians would not abide other Canadians seeing because it would be beyond the contemporary Canadian standard of tolerance to allow them to see it." Further, as Justice John Sopinka wrote in the *Butler* decision, "It is the standards of the community as a whole which must be considered."

There are several obvious difficulties with this test. First, if the court is to adopt the perspective of the "Canadian community as a whole," there's the logical conundrum of who, precisely, are the "other Canadians" whose reading and viewing habits will or won't be tolerated. Isn't the notion of the "community as a whole" merely a means of imposing the "tyranny of the majority"? Second, how is a court to determine what the Canadian community standard of tolerance is? The tolerance test was declared to be "objective" and so easy to apply that there was no burden on the Crown to advance any evidence concerning it. But how is the obvious subjectivity of a test of "taste" escaped when the issue is rephrased as one of "tolerance," given that tolerance and intolerance are notoriously matters of taste rather than the product of some dispassionate deliberative process? Further, if the court isn't to make use of some social science or public opinion poll measure of tolerance, won't the "objective" judgment of the community standard simply be a guess?

As if the fundamental concept isn't muddled enough, there's an even larger difficulty. The notion of tolerance evolved as a sort of halfway house between "taste" and "harm." But once rights have been entrenched in a constitution, as happened in Canada in 1982, how can they be subjected to the whims of tolerance? That was exactly the problem Justice Bertha Wilson foresaw in the *Towne Cinema* decision, referred to above. She wrote, "The test of the community standard is helpful to the extent that it provides a norm against which impugned material may be assessed, but it does little to elucidate the underlying question as to why some exploitation of sex falls on the permitted side of the line under [the obscenity law] and some on the prohibited side. No doubt this question will have to be addressed when the validity of the obscenity provisions of the Code is subjected to attack as an infringement on freedom of speech and the infringement is sought to be justified as reasonable."

As feminism matured into a political movement during the 1970s, thinkers such as Catherine MacKinnon also anticipated this difficulty. The solution developed by anti-pornography activists was not to deny Mill's principle that the only justification for state interference in individual free speech was harm to others, but to turn the harm principle back on its proponents. Calling upon the resources of the developing social sciences, feminist theorists advanced the view that the harm done by obscene publications was the incitement of men to the commission of criminal sexual assaults on women.

If it turned out that a notion of direct and measurable harm couldn't be fully supported by social science findings, anti-porn theorists offered an alternative approach that invoked the equality rights guaranteed by Section 15 of the Charter. This approach can be clearly seen in the intervenor's brief submitted in the *Butler* case by the feminist Legal Education and Action Fund. LEAF introduced the idea, inspired by Catherine MacKinnon, that the harm caused by pornography should be determined by asking what effect its existence has upon women's rights to equal treatment before the law. In this way, the legal question becomes an issue of balancing one right – freedom of expression – against another Charter-protected right, the Section 15 right to "equal protection and equal benefit of the law without discrimination."

This radically alters the problem of attempting to justify the limitation of the fundamental right of freedom of expression solely on the basis of evidence that pornography causes men to commit criminal acts of sexual aggression. The old approach pitted a right against a public interest, and the status of that interest was problematical in that there was no objective proof that pornography caused – in the strong sense of "incited" – men to commit acts of violence against women. The new approach recast the pornography issue as one of "sexual discrimination against women." But whatever the approach - social-science-supported proof of harm or an interpretation of equality rights – feminist thinking was underwritten by a long-held tenet of belief summed up in the slogan "Porn is the theory, rape is the practice."

At this point, along came Donald Butler. He was the owner of Avenue Video Boutique in Winnipeg, Manitoba, a shop that sold "hard core" videotapes. On August 21, 1987, police raided Butler's shop and he was charged with numerous counts of violating the obscenity law. Butler was subsequently convicted by the Manitoba Court of Queen's Bench, and that decision was reinforced by the Manitoba Court of Appeal, which dismissed Butler's appeal of his conviction. Both of the lower courts considered the question of the obscenity law's possible infringement of free speech rights, and the corollary question: If free speech was infringed, could the infringement be justified under Section 1 of the Charter (which says that rights and freedoms are subject to "reasonable limits prescribed by law as can be demonstrably justified in a free and democratic society")? While the trial court decided that the infringement of free speech could be justified under Section 1, the Manitoba Appeal Court went further and ruled that the porno tapes at issue were not protected by freedom of speech and, therefore, there was no need to consider whether an infringement of freedom could be "saved" by Section 1.

Some four years after Butler's initial arrest, the Supreme Court of Canada "seized the opportunity to address the three main questions that have arisen in the obscenity debate since the Canadian Charter of Rights was enacted: first, whether Section 163 infringes on the right to free expression under Section 2(b) of the Charter; second, which approach should be used to determine whether a particular publication is obscene under the statute; and finally, whether Section 163 is a reasonable and demonstrably justified limitation on freedom of expression under Section 1 of the Charter."[23]

Unlike the Manitoba Court of Appeal, the Canadian Supreme Court determined that pornography, even of a violent or degrading sort, is protected under free speech provisions because it "can convey, or attempt to convey meaning, and thus is not without expressive content."[24] Therefore, the court held that Section 163 infringes on the right of free expression and, consequently, must satisfy the requirements of Section 1 of the Charter.

Before deciding on whether the obscenity law is a justified limit on free speech, the Supreme Court of Canada offered a new interpretation of Section 163's core prohibition of "undue exploitation of sex." The judgment, said the Court, should not be made on moral grounds – and the community standard test should not be regarded as a measure of the community's moral tolerance – but rather on the basis of harm. The court defined "harm," in the context of obscenity, as meaning that exposure to the obscene material "predisposes persons to act in an anti-social manner as, for example, the physical or mental mistreatment of women by men, or, what is perhaps debatable, the reverse." The court admitted that "while a direct link between obscenity and harm to society may be difficult, if not impossible, to establish," nonetheless "it is reasonable to presume that exposure to images bears a causal relationship to changes in attitudes and beliefs."[25] In defining obscenity, the court concluded that the community standards and the harm-based approach "are necessarily linked, requiring lower courts to determine what the Canadian community would tolerate based on the degree of harm that may flow from exposure to these materials."[26]

The court further linked the community tolerance test and harm by providing an explicit measure in the form of a spectrum of "violence, degradation and dehumanization." The stronger the inference of a risk of harm, the less the likelihood of tolerance. Applying this measure, the court concluded, "The portrayal of sex coupled with violence will almost always constitute the undue exploitation of sex. Explicit sex which is degrading or dehumanizing may be undue if the risk of harm is substantial. Finally, explicit sex that is not violent and neither degrading or dehumanizing is generally tolerated in our society and will not qualify as the undue exploitation of sex unless it employs children in its production."[27] Thus, if material "is perceived by public opinion to be harmful to society, especially to women," that is sufficient for finding the material, through the community tolerance test, to be obscene.

After establishing its new interpretation of obscenity and harm, the court turned to the Section 1 question and held that Section 163 is a justified limitation on freedom of expression.[28] The court concluded both that the objective of Section 163 was sufficiently pressing and substantial to warrant a limitation on the right to free expression, and that the infringement on free expression was "proportional" to the good sought by the limitation. The most important conclusion of the court in its discussion of Section 1 was that "the harm caused by the proliferation of materials which seriously offend the values fundamental to [Canadian] society is a substantial concern which justifies restricting the otherwise full exercise of the freedom of expression."[29]

At the heart of the *Butler* decision is a notion of harm – one that will be relevant, if not central, to the kiddie porn law and the constitutional challenges to it. Both the concept of harm and the means for determining its presence, as interpreted by the Supreme Court, are highly unusual.

As noted above, the Court found that "while a direct link between obscenity and harm to society may be difficult, if not impossible, to establish, it is reasonable to presume that exposure to images bears a causal relationship to changes in attitudes and beliefs." Jodi Kleinick and other observers agree that "causation is an essential element of any harm-based rationale calling for suppression of expression," but then go on to wonder whether it is indeed "reasonable to presume" that there's a tight causal fit between "exposure to images" and "changes in attitudes and belief" that cause harm.[30]

Kleinick argues that the "burden of demonstrating the existence of a causal relationship" rests on the state, and "because actual harm is the *raison d'etre* of the harm-based approach to obscenity, the burden cannot be met if the causal link between the expression and the harm is presumed, if there is only a remote possibility that the harm will result, or if the harm is too indirect." That is, there are clear differences between notions of a) exposure to images directly causing acts, b) exposure to images causing changes in attitudes that may lead to acts, and c) exposure to images merely exerting an influence on beliefs. If harm is reduced to the latter, we are a long way from a notion of harm as direct and measurable damage to person or property.

The court conceded that the causal relationship between exposure to violent or degrading pornography and instances of harm is difficult, if not impossible, to establish, but then went on to simply presume causality. "To date, however," Kleinick points out, "there is no social science data that presents a sufficient basis for suppressing any form of pornography based on its effect on societal behaviour. In fact, the causal connection . . . has not been established and remains a matter of considerable debate." At this point in her analysis, Kleinick engages in a detailed examination of the social science research available, clearly demonstrating that even by the researchers' own standards, nothing close to a "causal" link has been established by laboratory experiments.[31]

To make matters worse, not only is there no evidence of the causal link between pornography and harm that would justify state interference with pornography, but the notion of harm that the Court relies on is a peculiar one that appears to lie between offensiveness and unsubstantiated perceptions of harm. It's unclear how such a notion could justify the suppression of a fundamental right.

That was the issue Justice Wilson was worried about when she wondered aloud whether it made constitutional sense to justify the censorship of speech by applying a test of community tolerance. If rights were, in the words of legal scholar Ronald Dworkin, to be "taken seriously," then the right to free speech must prevail over the interest of the majority in silencing speech it found disturbing or disgusting.

Of course, it is a kind of harm to be disturbed or disgusted, and this engages the considerations advanced by J.S. Mill in the theory of liberty that provides a foundation for the Canadian Constitution's notion of rights. Mill had a two-part argument against a notion of harm as psychological disturbance or offensiveness. First, there's the overriding importance of human liberty in which "absolute freedom of opinion and sentiment on all subjects" is a central component.[32] Second, Mill had a very specific idea of the forms of harm that should count against human freedom. He regarded sentiments or feelings or passions of disgust, dismay, discomfort and disapprobation as "contingent or constructive" harms – what we might call "indirect" harm – and he distinguished these from what he called "perceptible" harms, or what we would call "direct" harm.

So we have from Mill the following exegesis of his general harm principle: "But with regard to the merely contingent . . . injury which a person causes to society by conduct which neither violates any specific duty to the public, nor occasions perceptible hurt to any assignable individual except himself, the inconvenience is one which society can afford to bear, for the sake of the greater good of human freedom."[33] The reason for underscoring this point is because the elision of traditional or classic concepts of harm as "perceptible hurt" into much softer notions of feelings of alarm, disgust, or even discomfort is exactly what happened in the *Butler* decision.

To recapitulate: the Supreme Court of Canada justices understood that there were two serious and problematic questions in connection with the constitutionality of the obscenity laws. First, there was the embarrassing absence of any scientific proof that pornography caused men to harm women; and second, the common law application of the obscenity statute had coalesced around a community tolerance test that seemed to be a thinly veiled imposition of public morality rather than the application of any objective principle or rule.

In order to counter the criticism that there was no scientific proof of the harmful effects of pornography, the Court decided that harm could be assessed by reference to public tolerance. As for the subjectivity of the tolerance test, that could be remedied by providing something objective to tolerate, namely, the probability that a publication or other form of expression would cause harm. Even this probability was to be measured by nothing more than whether it was "perceived by public opinion" to exist.

A moment's consideration of the Court's reasoning makes its convoluted and circular character apparent. Given this, it might seem to make sense to simply dispense with the community tolerance test altogether – since it's not a real test and tolerance oughtn't to trump a right – and adjudicate obscenity cases on the basis of the court's determination of a risk of harm. However, the Court couldn't do that because such a simplification would open the door to an accused insisting that the Crown prove his expression "predisposes persons to act in an anti-social manner," i.e., that it causes harm, even indirect harm. But that is precisely what the recent decades of social scientific effort have failed to prove. So in *Butler*, the community tolerance test – reinforced with an equally scientifically unproven "degrading and dehumanizing" test – is retained to provide a refuge for the Court when challenged as to the evidentiary basis of its all-important adjudication of the harm issue.

As if all that isn't bad enough, there's the Court's reason for finding the suppression of certain forms of expression justifiable in a democracy: "The proliferation of materials which seriously offend the values fundamental to our society ... justifies restricting the otherwise full exercise of the freedom of expression." As constitutional scholar Ronald Dworkin remarks, "This is an amazing statement. It is the central, defining premise of freedom of speech that the offensiveness of ideas, or the challenge they offer to traditional ideas, cannot be a valid reason for censorship; once that premise is abandoned, it is difficult to see what free speech means."[34]

Or, as Kleinick puts it, "Freedom of expression must guarantee the right to hold and even advocate stereotypical notions about women, as offensive and false as they may be. If the Canadian Supreme Court allows suppression of speech whenever the speech leads to acceptance of undesirable beliefs or behaviour, section 2(b) of the Charter serves no purpose . . . Once society allows limits on expression merely because the expression negatively affects attitudes and reinforces stereotypes about groups, there can be no end to the invasion of the right to free expression."[35]

At the end of the day, the law of the land in Canada read that a sexual representation is obscene if it is perceived to cause bad attitudes about women that could possibly lead to bad acts. Given such shaky reasoning, it is little wonder that analysts like Kleinick would conclude that "morality is probably the *Butler* court's real justification for upholding Section 163," or that the authors of *Bad Attitude/s* would charge that "the *Butler* decision and its discourse of harm against women is really just sexual morality in drag."[36]

The *Butler* decision had an immediate impact upon the Justice department. The day after the Supreme Court's ruling upholding the federal obscenity law, the media eagerly sought out the Justice minister for her reactions to the judgment. Campbell praised the decision for balancing the need for society to protect itself from harmful varieties of pornography and the rights of those who want erotica available for their own purposes.

"The Supreme Court recognizes certain kinds of sexually explicit materials really do communicate a message that is inherently dangerous to women. On the other hand," said Campbell, the decision "is not a prudish view." Campbell also took the occasion to reannounce her intention to introduce a child pornography bill, hopefully by fall 1992.[37]

The fact that the *Butler* decision specifically mentioned child pornography was one of the factors that bore on the fortunes of the nascent child pornography legislation. The identification of pornography that "used children in its production," even if it had no elements of violence or degradation, was, in a sense, unwelcome to the Justice department because it meant that the Court had probably garnered a large share of the available political credit for protecting children. If a court that was seen as notoriously liberal by groups like the Family Caucus had certified the criminality of any publication involving the sexual use of children in its production, the government would have to go further if it were to gain any credit for itself. This confirmed the wisdom of crafting a statute making it an offence to merely possess, as distinct from producing or publishing, child pornography.

Given renewed impetus by the *Butler* decision, Justice officials focussed their energies on putting together the actual child pornography bill during March and April 1992. They wrestled with several key problems, the most important of which were age definitions, whether to include those "depicted" as children, whether to include a prohibition of written materials, and the absence of any pressing need for legislation. As noted earlier, Justice department research had failed to turn up a child pornography problem in Canada, and the government could be criticized for making empty political gestures with its criminal law-making authority. This was perhaps the least worrisome of the issues, since it could always be handled by simply insisting that numbers were irrelevant where the safety of children was involved.

The questions of age definition and the inclusion of written materials were more difficult, since both went to the political heart of the legislative enterprise. If the definition of "child" was set at the high end – eighteen to twenty years – it would be vigorously attacked as overbroad by the same civil rights and artistic groups that had successfully scuttled the attempted pornography legislation of 1988. Conversely, if the definition was at the low end of the scale – under the age of consent of fourteen years – it might serve to anger the groups, such as the Family Caucus, that the legislation was designed to please.

Similarly, if the legislative target was restricted to photographic and video representations of the sexual use of actual children, excluding works of the imagination not involving harm to children in their production (such as stories, essays, drawings, etc.), it would displease religious and "pro-family" groups as a weak gesture. But if works of the imagination were included in the legislation, a storm of protest could be expected from the cultural and political left. This political split held for the "depiction" issue as well. Those on the right would want a prohibition on child sex that was acted out or depicted by adult models, whereas those on the left would want such depictions treated as a form of expression and hence legitimately protected by the Charter.

How could the policy objectives of the legislation be balanced with the principles of the Charter of Rights and Freedoms? Or to put the problem another way, how could the government be seen to improve on the protection for children provided by the *Butler* decision while staying within the confines of the Constitution? Justice officials were still entangled in the search for this elusive pivot point months later.

A May 26, 1992, memo reported "two principal issues which require direction" from the minister before the draft could be finalized.[38] Before laying out the pros and cons of the unresolved issues, the memo reminded the minister that "this legislation was conceived, from the outset, as targeting the sexual use of children in the production of pornographic materials. The idea was to keep you out of the porn wars (divisive for women, poison for gays), out of the business of censoring ideas, and cleanly committed to the protection of children program. In order to control the agenda, and prevent being drawn into a debate over obscenity, we were to strictly limit our attack to the photographic representations of the sexual use of children."

The first of the two outstanding issues was: "How old are the children to be protected by this particular legislation?" The options available were fourteen (the age of sexual consent), sixteen, and eighteen (the age of majority). "Your staff strongly recommends the 16 years option, splitting the difference between the code demarcations of childhood and adulthood." The advantage of the compromise, in the eyes of Campbell's staff, was that it "keeps the legislation clearly focussed on children" and avoids confusion about identifying young adults. Its disadvantage, the memo recognized, was that various groups, including the Family Caucus, would prefer eighteen or even higher, and that the objection about age would "fold over into their general impatience with the limited scope and purpose of the legislation."

The second issue was: "Should we add to the basic offence (which is 'photographic or video materials in which a person who is under the age of 16 engages in or is present for explicit sexual activity') materials in which a person either appears to be under 16, or is depicted as being under 16?"

The recommendation was unequivocal. "Your staff advises against the depiction option, as drawing us out of the intended range of the legislation, and into the murky waters of censoring ideas." The memo insisted, "This is a children focussed initiative; it is not, strictly speaking, an expression crime provision."

At this point, the paper trail fades. The few additional documents relating to child pornography legislation merely reflect the frustration of a stalled debate within the ministry and don't materially advance the process. For Kim Campbell, that was it. The absence of a clear consensus within her department put plans for a kiddie porn law on the back burner, while the minister turned her attention to issues of more immediate import. To Campbell's credit, it can be said that she refused to sponsor legislation whose constitutional validity would turn out to be questionable.

If there was one justice agenda item that the minister was particularly committed to, it was the idea of amending the Canadian Human Rights Act (CHRA) to include "sexual orientation" among the prohibited grounds for discrimination. Both as a matter of political expedience (the minister represented a Vancouver riding with a significant proportion of gay voters) and as a matter of principle, equality rights protection for homosexuals preoccupied Campbell from the beginning of her mandate. Campbell's ultimately unsuccessful attempt to secure these protections in law served to further alienate the Family Caucus, and created a caucus unity problem of sufficient urgency to offset every objection to a new childpornography statute. If it is true that there is nothing so irresistible as a bad idea whose time has come, Campbell's determined attempt to protect gay rights is worth consideration as the last step in bringing the problematical child porn law to its crucial political moment.

By spring 1992, with gun control legislation passed and regulations for its implementation drawn up, the rape shield law reformed, and the pornography bill seemingly permanently stalled, Campbell once more turned her attention to the CHRA. "This issue had surfaced in the first Mulroney mandate," she recalls. "In 1985, a parliamentary committee . . . recommended sexual orientation be included among the forbidden grounds for discrimination in all federal law. The justice minister of the time, John Crosbie . . . committed the government to doing this. There had been a huge battle in the Conservative caucus," and action was indefinitely postponed.[39]

"Following a 1989 Supreme Court of Canada decision called *Andrews v. Law Society of British Columbia*," Campbell continues, "the federal government decided that sexual orientation should be treated as a prohibited ground of discrimination under the Charter. However, the Charter binds the actions only of governments, not private citizens or companies, whereas the Canadian Human Rights Act binds the federally regulated private sector, such as banks, railways and airlines. The bottom line for me was that the government was on record as being committed to making this change. I felt we had to act before another election. If we weren't going to fulfil our promise, we had better say so."[40]

As the internal Justice department memos of July 16 and November 7, 1991, demonstrate, Campbell made several efforts to introduce the CHRA amendments. For example, her efforts to table new legislation in October 1991 received a last-minute setback when the defense minister pointed out that the policy of the Canadian Forces was that homosexuals could not serve. Although the chief of the defence staff, General John de Chastelain, agreed to change the policy, a Conservative caucus meeting held just before the announcement was to be made produced such a "ruckus" by anti-gay MPs that the whole thing was put off. (Eventually the change was announced by de Chastelain, and unlike the concurrent situation in the U.S military, where a half-hearted policy of "don't ask, don't tell" about homosexuality served only to produce a seemingly interminable debate, the Canadian acceptance of homosexuals in the military ranks went off with surprisingly little controversy.)

The reason for emphasizing Campbell's persistence on the CHRA amendments is that later she would be criticized by both anti-gay politicians and gay rights proponents for her motives. It would perhaps be easy to join critics who accused Campbell of supporting sexual orientation solely as a matter of political self-interest, especially given our argument that the child pornography initiative was primarily a case of political exigency in the name of maintaining Conservative Party unity. But the popular, media-supported view of politics as no more than a game of power and opportunism, and the consequent demonization of government itself, is simplistically misleading, particularly in this case. Widespread cynicism notwithstanding, there are occasions when politicians take action because they actually believe it's the right thing to do. In this instance, there's evidence to support that unfashionable contention.

For one thing, Campbell decided to go ahead with the CHRA initiative in the face of opposition from the party's Family Caucus, and without offering the child pornography legislation as an ameliorating compensation. At various times during fall 1991 she met with Family Caucus MPs John Reimer and Benno Friesen in an unsuccessful bid to persuade them to moderate their views. It's true that Campbell eventually provided some compromise in the form of a definition of marital status to go along with the sexual orientation amendment, but that has to be seen as simply a recognition of her limited room to manoeuvre within the political realities of the Conservative Party.

Second, most of what Campbell has to say about the subject has the ring of authenticity. "During this period I was less shocked by the homophobia of MPs who I knew espoused fundamentalist religious doctrines," she writes, "than by the almost casual disdain in jokes and comments from people I had considered to be of moderate views. Perhaps I was more sensitive because it reminded me of the sexist humour that had once been considered acceptable in polite conversation. At a meeting of [cabinet's Planning and Priorities committee], as the chief of the defence staff and some others entered to brief ministers on the [gay] issue, there was some banter and Brian Mulroney joked,

'Well, at least they aren't holding hands.' This was greeted with great guffaws around the table . . . "[41]

The approach Campbell proposed in April 1992 "was to model our legislation on the Ontario Human Rights Code, in which sexual orientation was a prohibited ground of discrimination but a definition section put some limits on the interpretation." The principal limit was a definition of marital status as referring to relationships between people of opposite sexes. "I urged caucus to let me table the legislation before the summer. There were cases making their way through the courts related to the rights of same-sex couples and I warned my colleagues that if Parliament didn't say something on the issue, the courts would be making the law . . . In the end, I couldn't get the go-ahead . . . "[42]

For most of the summer and fall of 1992, the attention of Campbell, Prime Minister Mulroney, and much of the rest of the government was absorbed by the Charlottetown referendum, a national public vote on a complicated package of constitutional changes that sought to recognize Quebec as a "distinct society," provide aboriginal people with an "inherent" right to some form of self-government, and resolve the long-standing problem of Canada's appointed Senate. The referendum went down to an overwhelming defeat in October 1992, but its indirect consequences extended beyond the reiteration of the country's constitutional impasse. The debate itself contributed to Prime Minister Mulroney's already sagging personal ratings in public opinion polls, which had the obvious effect of requiring him to think seriously about stepping down as leader of the Conservative Party prior to the next election, which had to be held sometime in 1993.

By autumn 1992, the political situation had shifted in favour of the position Campbell had long urged her caucus to take on sexual orientation, and she launched one more effort to gain authorization to table her package of CHRA amendments – a package that included important measures in support of disabled people, as well as the familiar sexual orientation changes. Two critical events had transpired.

"The Ontario Court of Appeal had upheld a lower court's decision in a case called *Haig*," Campbell writes. The case involved Graham Haig, an Ottawa human rights activist, and Joshua Birch, a former Air Force captain who was forced out of the military when it was learned that he was gay. Haig and Birch went to court and won. "The plaintiff had argued that if sexual orientation is deemed a prohibited ground of discrimination under the Charter, then it is a denial of equal protection under the law to exclude that protection from the Canadian Human Rights Act."[43] In short, the Ontario Court said that sexual orientation protection should be "read in" to the CHRA, whether it was there in black and white or not.

The argument in *Haig* was relatively conclusive, but there was still enough legal manoeuvring room that Campbell could, if she chose, put the issue in limbo for a considerable time by following the normal government course in such cases of appealing the decision to the Supreme Court of Canada. A heated debate ensued within the Justice department, one that considered everything from Campbell's dual role as Justice minister and Attorney General (and thus responsible for appeals) to political calculations of public reaction. The consensus reached by Campbell and her advisers was a blunt injunction: "*Haig* should not be appealed."[44]

Campbell's decision to let the *Haig* ruling stand attracted little attention outside circles directly interested in the issue. While it didn't win Campbell any particular credit among gay constituents, nor did it endear her to the Family Caucus, nonetheless it was a telling moment of quiet inaction speaking louder than legislative words. Even Campbell's most vociferous parliamentary opponent, gay New Democratic MP Svend Robinson, recognized the move as "a major breakthrough," though he was also quick to remind everyone that the decision not to appeal was a "scathing indictment of the government's . . . betrayal of the promise it made to amend the [CHRA] act."[45]

A second and more immediate impetus to act on the CHRA amendments was provided by Conservative senator Noel Kinsella. After Campbell's confirmation that there would be no appeal in the Haig and Birch case, Kinsella immediately announced his intention to introduce a bill in the Senate that would add the words "sexual orientation" to the proscribed grounds of discrimination in the CHRA.[46]

Because Parliament would adjourn for Christmas on December 11, 1992, Campbell moved quickly to take the necessary steps for tabling the amendments. When the date for adjournment was moved up a day, Campbell had to short-circuit the process and ask government leader Harvie Andre to give parliamentary notice of the amendments even before she secured caucus approval. A worried Andre asked, "Are you sure you know what you're doing?" "Justice," Campbell quipped, before more seriously assuring him she realized that if the Conservative caucus failed to support the amendments, she would have no option but to resign.

The day before the CHRA package was to be formally introduced in the House, Campbell faced her caucus. She told them, "Tomorrow I am tabling a bill for the comprehensive amendment of the Canadian Human Rights Act," and then detailed what was in and out of the bill. "Sexual orientation" was in, exemptions for religious organizations were in, a marital status definition limited to heterosexuals was in, but any notions of including traditional definitions of "family" and "spouse" were out, given recent court decisions. As for the things the Family Caucus could reasonably hope to maintain, Campbell urged them to support the bill, arguing, "We cannot win these things by sending more lawyers to the courts. We must send law, and we must send it now."[47]

Campbell's presentation to caucus was bolstered by some public opinion research that showed 72 percent of Canadians, irrespective of geographical region or political party affiliation, didn't think people should be discriminated against because of their sexual orientation. The research also indicated that "the issue was simply not a vote driver, one way or the other."

"Up until that meeting, the prime minister had said nothing about the issue at caucus," Campbell later recalled. "This time, when he stood up to make his customary remarks at the end of the meeting, he referred to my presentation and asked, 'Who are these people, after all? They're our children, or somebody's children. They're our neighbours.'"[48]

On December 10, 1992, with caucus support in hand, Kim Campbell tabled the amendments to the Canadian Human Rights Act. For her, it was one of the prouder moments of her tenure as Justice minister. Ironically, it would also be her last action as minister, and an action without consequence.

Opponents on both the left and right offered little mercy to the minister of Justice. "On a day that should have been a day of celebration for the gay and lesbian community," said MP Svend Robinson, "I have to say I feel a sense of betrayal, of sadness that Kim Campbell and the Conservative government have effectively allowed the right-wing Family Caucus to write this legislation." Of course, opposition politicians are permitted a bit of critical hyperbole on such occasions (presumably Robinson didn't want to see the sort of legislation that the Family Caucus would actually have penned, given the opportunity), but other gay leaders across the country were equally critical. They described the bill, with its marital restriction, as a "cop-out," a "sell-out," and even disguised "discrimination." Only University of British Columbia law professor and veteran gay rights proponent Doug Sanders troubled to note that the legislation appeared to be "a compromise necessary to get it through the caucus," before going on to say, "She's giving us probably less than what the courts would give us."[49]

As for the Family Caucus, its most prominent member, MP John Reimer, issued a statement declaring, "I absolutely oppose the inclusion of sexual orientation." Reimer claimed that the CHRA was intended to protect only those of "unchangeable status," and that since "homosexuality is changeable," gays didn't qualify for CHRA protection. "Thousands of homosexual men and women have abandoned the homosexual lifestyle and changed," Reimer insisted.

This was the Conservatives' last legislative brush with sexual orientation law (as we'll detail below). Explicit protection for homosexuals in the Canadian Human Rights Act would be a long time in coming. On May 9, 1996, more than three years after Campbell's effort to secure passage of a sexual orientation clause, the Liberal government of Prime Minister Jean Chretien and his justice minister, Allan Rock, passed the long-delayed amendment by a vote of 153 to 76. It was opposed by 28 Liberals and all except one of Preston Manning's Reform Party legislative caucus. By then, almost the only Tory left in Parliament to vote for or against sexual orientation was Conservative leader Jean Charest, head of a two-member caucus. He voted in favour.[50]

On January 3, 1993, Campbell was called to Ottawa and informed by the prime minister that in a cabinet shuffle the next day he would name her to the dual post of Minister of Defense and Veterans' Affairs. The new Justice minister was Quebec MP Pierre Blais. Although Mulroney denied rumours that he was contemplating resignation, less than two months later, on February 24, 1993, he announced his departure, and speculation immediately focussed on Campbell as a potential leadership candidate at the June 1993 convention that the Tories called to select a new prime minister.

On June 25, 1993, Campbell defeated MP Jean Charest in the leadership contest and became Canada's first woman prime minister. In naming her cabinet, she retained Pierre Blais, who had been her leadership campaign co-chair, as Justice minister. Three months later, Prime Minister Campbell set October 25, 1993, as the date for the next federal election.

Between the January 1993 cabinet shuffle and the October 1993 election, Justice Minister Blais introduced and passed the child pornography law that became Section 163.1 of the Criminal Code. Blais, it was generally agreed in Ottawa circles, was no ideologue, but rather a pragmatic politician with an eye on party unity and the forthcoming election. While he, like most other parliamentarians, no doubt supported a child pornography law on its intrinsic merits, both his introduction of the kiddie porn bill as well as his decision to allow the CHRA amendments to die on the Order Paper have to be seen as primarily political moves aimed not only at positioning the Conservative Party for an impending election, but also at maintaining the loyalty of Family Caucus Conservatives and forestalling their defection to the rival Reform Party.

The Family Caucus had been grievously unhappy with the actions of the Department of Justice while Campbell had been in charge. It didn't like her abortion bill, it chafed under the new gun control legislation, it was offended by the feminist preamble to the revised rape shield law, it was unhappy with the department's handling of a series of court cases involving the extension of spousal rights and benefits to gays, and it positively detested the provision for the protection of gay rights in the CHRA. The presence of a new minister who, while not necessarily an ally of Family Caucus views, didn't share Campbell's activist agenda offered the ultra-conservative wing of the Conservative Party a last opportunity to secure some satisfaction before the present mandate expired.

Blais launched his first trial balloons on the kiddie porn issue in March 1993, telling a Toronto audience that he was "considering amendments to the [Criminal] Code to provide better protection to children against their exploitation through child pornography." In a radio interview in Hamilton, Ontario, the same month, the Justice minister admitted that the legislation he was pondering might not go as far as some people wanted. He may have been thinking of Saskatchewan NDP MP Chris Axworthy, who had put forward a private member's bill to outlaw child pornography. The government's plan, Blais conceded, wouldn't cover certain publications, such as the newsletter of the North American Man-Boy Love Association (NAMBLA). "So far we're not contemplating legislation on that, but I'm following it very closely," Blais said.[51]

So was the parliamentary Standing Committee on Justice, which held one of a series of public hearings on child pornography in Vancouver on January 20, 1993. It was there that Vancouver Police detective Noreen Waters (or Wolff, as she was then) brought up the subject of NAMBLA. The officer had previously been in contact with MP Tom Wappel, a "family values" Liberal and a member of the standing committee. She had informed Wappel about the *NAMBLA Bulletin* and was subsequently invited to testify at the justice committee hearings.[52]

The legal problem with the *Bulletin*, Waters explained, was that it wasn't obscene. Although it "advocated" sex between men and boys, she said, neither the photographs nor the articles it published were pornographic. Nonetheless, as she told the *Vancouver Province* a month before, "It's a textbook for pedophiles. It tells them how to seduce children and not get caught."

The standing committee held further hearings in Ottawa in

April and May 1993, inviting testimony from a series of expert witnesses, including academics, mental health professionals, law enforcement officers, and child advocates such as Rix Rogers, who had written the 1990 report for the federal Department of Health recommending child pornography legislation. Rogers was among those concerned about pornography where adults dress as children. On April 27, Justice Minister Blais appeared before the committee. Blais told the committee that he was preparing a "surgical intervention . . . addressing child pornography." When MP Tom Wappel asked him about the NAMBLA publication, Blais said that he didn't yet have a "straight answer," but was looking into it.

Both Detective Waters of Vancouver and Detective Robert Matthews of Toronto's Project P, an anti-pornography squad of the Ontario Provincial Police, were committee witnesses on May 10, 1993, in Ottawa. The Toronto officer urged the committee to define child pornography as more than just explicit sex and suggested that the definition include nude photos that showed children's genital areas. Perhaps the tenor of the discussions was best captured when the committee's most vocal member, Wappel, fervently declared, "I say that the sexual exploitation of children is so serious that the very existence of our society as we know it is threatened."

The next day in the House of Commons, MP Chris Axworthy's private member's bill on child pornography failed to get the unanimous consent necessary for it to be further considered, but MP Rob Nicholson, parliamentary secretary to the Justice minister, promised that the government would soon introduce legislation of its own and pleaded for patience.

The legislators didn't have long to wait. The following day, May 13, 1993, Blais rose in the House to table a child pornography bill. Its central feature was the one proposed by justice officials during

Kim Campbell's ministry: the criminalization of simple possession of child pornography, which was now a crime punishable by up to five years in prison. Blais described the move as the closing of a "terrible loophole" in the law. As well, maximum sentences for existing crimes, such as production and distribution of child pornography, were "dramatically increased" from two years to ten. The media described the bill as "tough legislation."[53]

The proposed law – again as had been urged during Campbell's tenure – focussed on visual materials, since "the major element of what is child pornography is visual," Blais argued. The definition of child pornography in this section of the law read, "'Child pornography' means a photographic, film, video or other visual representation, whether or not it was made by electronic or mechanical means." Although this definition closely resembles the original narrow focus on photographic or video materials, in fact it had been significantly expanded to include "other visual representation" – thus presumably including drawings, paintings, and computer simulations – a clause that would quickly prove to be relevant.

With Campbell gone, Blais was content to acquiesce to those of his justice officials who had been pressing for the most expansive definition of age available. The law said that child pornography was any visual representation "that shows a person who is or is depicted as being under the age of 18 and is engaged in or is depicted as engaged in explicit sexual activity." Blais opted not only for age 18 as a demarcation line, but also accepted the inclusion of adults who were "depicted as being under the age of 18." Thus the definition – which now included any visual representation and people who were not children – defeated the intention of earlier drafters that the law be strictly limited to capture only sexual representations whose creation required the criminal sexual use of children. Now child pornography could include visual products of the imagination (although the bill included a defence on grounds of "artistic merit") or representations not necessarily involving children. Still, the bill was narrowly enough conceived that Blais's officials could assure the minister that the legislation was consistent with the Charter of Rights, a certification of constitutionality required by law. What's more, the proposed law did not proscribe written materials and required that engagement in "explicit sexual activity" be present for a visual representation to be illegal.

However, as Campbell had been repeatedly cautioned during her attempt to craft such legislation, "control of the agenda" could easily be lost. It soon would be.

Several factors now came into play. The most urgent ones were timing and internal party politics. Parliament was scheduled to adjourn the following month, in mid-June, and it was likely that an election would intervene before its next sitting. If Blais intended not merely to table legislation as a symbolic gesture but to actually ensure its passage, the complicated process by which a bill becomes law – legislative hearings, clause-by-clause consideration, proposals for amendments, and all the rest – would have to be drastically telescoped. Doing so would mean that Blais would have to give up considerable leverage in terms of "controlling the agenda." He would have to agree to compromises, most likely in the form of amendments enlarging the scope of the law, which under normal circumstances the government might resist. The danger here was not from opponents of the legislation, but from right-wing partisans of it who would insist that the bill be expanded to cover more ground.

In fact, the immediate criticism offered by opposition parties was not opposition to the bill itself, but the charge that its introduction was simply a pre-election gambit. "This is showcase legislation in its worst form," complained Liberal justice critic

Russell MacLellan, who supported the bill but worried about whether it would receive sufficient public scrutiny. "They're bringing legislation forward to show people they're bringing it forward. If it doesn't pass, they'll blame the opposition," he charged.[54]

The second complicating factor for the legislation was the state of affairs in the Conservative Party. Even as Blais tabled his kiddie porn bill, the party leadership convention, in which Blais was the busy campaign co-chair for one of the leading candidates, was scarcely a month away. Presumably, passage of the legislation by the minister campaigning on behalf of Kim Campbell would improve his candidate's *bona fides* in the eyes of convention delegates closest to the views of the Family Caucus. A further irony of the situation is that the one person best positioned to offer advice on and criticism of the proposed child pornography bill, Kim Campbell, was effectively immobilized on this question by her own political ambitions. If she had any objections to the measure, she was in a double-bind, unable to alienate either her campaign co-chair or the Family Caucus.

The final hearings of the Standing Committee on Justice were held on June 15, 1993, a day before the summer adjournment of the Commons, and only hours before the House was scheduled to debate and pass the kiddie porn bill. The main witnesses were representatives of the arts and media – groups ranging from the ACTRA Performers Guild to the Canadian Broadcasting Corporation – who were primarily worried about artistic productions depicting teenage sexuality and child sexual abuse. Recent films such as *The Boys of St. Vincent*, a docudrama about child sexual abuse in orphanages, and current television programs like *Degrassi Junior High*, a teen coming-of-age series, might conceivably fall afoul of the new law, the arts representatives feared.

But it was clear that most of the committee's attention was on finishing the task at hand – producing an amended bill for passage that afternoon – rather than debating what seemed to them to be marginal artistic concerns. Not even the appearance of Allan Borovoy, representing the Toronto-based Canadian Civil Liberties Association, would delay the justice committee for long.

The objections of civil libertarians, both within and outside the political arena, had been curiously muted throughout the whole truncated, hasty process. Only one member of the committee, NDP justice critic Ian Waddell, a B.C. MP, had really raised the issue. In the course of declaring his party's support for child pornography legislation, Waddell nonetheless said that, as a civil libertarian, he was particularly worried about freedom of the press as well as the hastiness of the process. He cited former Justice minister Campbell's "inclusive justice" slogan. "Inclusive justice means that people from all sides come in and discuss the bill, and . . . then we will get the best bill possible," he said, presciently adding, "Then it will hold up in the courts and will not be thrown out as unconstitutional."

Once the witnesses were out of the way, the committee got down to clause-by-clause inspection of the legislation and the all-important matter of amendments. There were two crucial additions made to Blais's bill, both of which were accepted by the minister. The first amendment vastly expanded the range of visual materials that could be considered pornographic by adding a clause in the definition of child pornography that included any visual representation, "the dominant characteristic of which is the depiction, for a sexual purpose, of a sexual organ or the anal region of a person under the age of 18 years." Although there would eventually be considerable debate about what that ambiguously worded phrase actually meant, *prima facie* it suggested that any nude photo of anyone under eighteen might be illegal.

A second amendment completely undercut the notion of a law narrowly focussed on photographic visual materials involving children engaged in sex. An additional clause in the definition of child pornography now included "any written material or visual representation that advocates or counsels sexual activity with a person under the age of 18 years that would be an offence under this Act." For example, an essay calling for revision of the law prohibiting people under eighteen from engaging in anal intercourse could now conceivably be seen as "advocacy" or "counselling" that amounted to child pornography. Perhaps worse, written material that contained representations of children engaged in sex could be interpreted as constituting advocating or counselling.

The changes meant that not only had a new offence been created – simple possession of child pornography – but the definition of what that pornography might be had also been drastically expanded. For many in the House of Commons who debated the child pornography bill during its third and final reading that afternoon, such an expansion was precisely what they believed in and wanted. Family Caucus MP John Reimer was pleased to be the lead-off speaker.

Blais's parliamentary secretary, Rob Nicholson, rhetorically addressed NAMBLA, declaring, "This is one bad day for you because . . . we are zeroing in on publications like yours." Liberal Tom Wappel told the House how he had been alerted to NAMBLA by Detective Waters. The omission of written material was a serious flaw in the bill as it had been initially presented, but "I was instrumental in having that provision included."

Only Liberal MP George Rideout, a justice committee member, expressed some constitutional doubt. "My concern is that by adding the written word we may find ourselves vulnerable to a Charter challenge," he said. "I guess that in these circumstances one says . . . if it does not pass the test then we will try to correct it later on."

On June 15, 1993, the House of Commons passed the child pornography bill. A week or so later the bill received Senate approval, notwithstanding repeated objections by Liberal Senator Richard Stanbury that the bill would not stand up in court.

Two days after parliamentary passage of the kiddie porn law, Kim Campbell became prime minister of Canada, completing the political trajectory that the media had described as her "rise and rise." The child pornography law was officially proclaimed the law of the land by the time Campbell took her party to the polls for an October 25, 1993 federal election.

Although the Tories, during the final days of their administration, had brought in a law-and-order package, of which the child pornography law was a part, it would have little effect on the outcome, irrespective of whatever favourable impact it might have on party unity. At the end of a seemingly endless rise in the fortunes of Kim Campbell and her party, there wasn't merely a fall, but a catastrophic crash. In the 1993 election, Liberal leader Jean Chretien became prime minister with an overwhelming majority. Not only was Campbell defeated in her riding, but so were Conservatives across the country. The Reform Party and the Bloc Québecois became the leading opposition parties, and the Tories were reduced to a two-member caucus, facing possible extinction as a major Canadian political party.

A good many of the fears and warnings – especially the warning about "abusive enforcement tactics" – that had been voiced during the lengthy crafting of the kiddie porn law were borne out in the first major application of the law, less than half a year after its passage. In December 1993, a twenty-six-year-old Toronto artist, Eli Langer, exhibited drawings and paintings at Toronto's Mercer Union Gallery depicting children in sex acts with adults and other children. All of the images were drawn from the artist's imagination; no models were used. Ironically, even as lawyers at the annual meeting of the Canadian Bar Association were passing a resolution criticizing both the wording of the kiddie porn law and the speed with which it had been passed, Langer was charged under the new legislation with producing child pornography.

Langer's work had come to the attention of the police only when it was uneasily reviewed by *Globe and Mail* art critic Kate Taylor. Once the show was shut down by the police, Taylor voiced some second thoughts: "If I had not revealed the explicitness of the work, in all likelihood Langer would not have been charged – the show would have been seen only by people in the art community who could be counted on to bring some context to the work and usually have much broader standards of images they consider tolerable."[55]

The Langer affair occasioned considerable media meditation. *Globe and Mail* columnist Bronwyn Drainie, attacking her own paper's editorial urging that Langer's work should be exempt from censorship "simply because it is art" (an exemption provided by the kiddie porn law itself), argued that perhaps artists ought to be held responsible for how their "work may be used or abused." What if, imagined Drainie, an "unscrupulous" photo lab owner making transparencies of Langer's work – an ordinary part of the process of exhibiting works – produces and "under the counter sells a duplicate set of [transparencies] to one of the large pornography distribution firms in the U.S., who print thousands of postcards from Langer's images. When you come across one of Langer's drawings covered in greasy thumbprints and possibly other substances at the back of a porn shop in Philadelphia, is it still art?"[56]

It was exactly this sort of intellectual mock-agonizing that was meant to be avoided by those who had long argued for a law narrowly focussed on actual instances of sexual abuse of children and not the suppression of expression. As a further irony, it turned out that Langer's intention in visually retrieving painful childhood memories was to make an artistic statement against child sexual abuse.

Far removed from Drainie's "greasy-thumbed" handwringing, a February 26, 1994, *Globe* editorial headed "Bonfire of the inanities" sneered, "Well, Hosanna. Law enforcement authorities no longer want to throw . . . Eli Langer in jail as a pornographer . . . All they want to do is burn his pictures."

Having decided not to charge Langer or the owner of the gallery where his pictures were shown, the Crown nonetheless made an application to the Ontario courts to require Langer to forfeit his seized paintings and drawings.

"We have a better idea: burn the law," replied the *Globe* editorial. "Passed as an election gimmick last June . . . [the law] is a loosely drafted, ludicrously broad piece of legislation, and an unnecessary one at that. Were there any evidence that Canada was being engulfed by a wave of child pornography, the existing obscenity law would be more than tough enough to deal with it . . . Oh, and one other thing. The authorities should give Mr. Langer his pictures back."[57]

That's what the court thought, too. It held that "the depictions had artistic merit and did not pose a realistic risk of harm to children."[58] The court ordered that the paintings and sketches be returned to the artist. If many had anticipated that the first proto-challenge to the law would come from an artist – demonstrating that the fears of the arts community voiced at the previous summer's legislative hearings were well-founded – it was much harder to foresee that a more powerful constitutional challenge to the kiddie porn law would come from a self-declared pornographer. And very few people could have predicted what B.C. Supreme Court Justice Duncan Shaw would say to that challenge.

THREE

Judge Shaw Decides

One of the most striking icons of our culture is the blind-folded figure of the goddess Athena, holding up the scales of justice. Although that figure is sometimes regarded with irony or cynicism, she poses a question that goes to the core of our ideals.

Why, of all things, would we wish to value "blindness" in our justice? The answer, of course, is that the judicial blindness we desire – demand, really – is highly specific. If there is to be rule of law rather than persons, the court can have no "friends" or "enemies" before it; and if justice is to be equally done, courts must deliberate and decide the merits of cases without "fear or favour." In a way, truly wise judges must look closely in order to know precisely what not to see.

It would have been easy for Justice Duncan Shaw to have adopted the conventional view of Robin Sharpe. Even the elderly writer-photographer who appeared before the court to challenge the constitutionality of Canada's kiddie porn law in November 1998 understood that he was widely seen as a social pariah.[1] But that isn't the way the heretofore relatively obscure justice of the B.C. Supreme Court saw him.

Instead, when Shaw released his judgment on January 15, 1999, it quickly became apparent that the judge looked upon Sharpe as simply another citizen, "equal before and under the law." What's more, Shaw put aside predictable public perceptions, both reasonable and histrionic, that might serve as potential influences on his deliberative task and instead focussed his attention primarily on the legal arguments about Canada's constitution in relation to the country's child pornography statute. The result was a sober decision that nonetheless sparked an unprecedented uproar over a Canadian legal ruling.

The short version of what Justice Duncan Shaw decided in mid-January 1999 is that the section of the child pornography law that makes simple possession of kiddie porn a crime is unconstitutional because it violates constitutional guarantees of freedom of thought and speech. He therefore struck down the possession clause as "void" and ruled that the charges against Robin Sharpe of simple possession of kiddie porn were thereby dismissed (although the other charges against Sharpe remained, to be judged at a future trial). Understanding how Shaw arrived at that conclusion necessitates a detailed reading of his reasoning.[2]

"The accused Robin Sharpe challenges the constitutionality of child pornography provisions set out in Section 163.1 of the Criminal Code," Shaw began. "Mr. Sharpe contends that the impugned provisions violate the Canadian Charter of Rights and Freedoms . . . A *voir dire* has been held to hear the constitutional challenge. This is my ruling."

The justice then does a bit of scene-setting, listing the four charges against Sharpe and noting that the accused is challenging both Section 163.1's subsection (4), which "prohibits simple possession of child pornography," and subsection (1)(b), the part of the definition of child pornography that covers material which "counsels or advocates the commission of sexual offences against children." Justice Shaw then recites the text of the kiddie porn law (see Chapter One) and the parts of the Charter invoked by Sharpe, the most important of which is Section 2: "Everyone has the following fundamental freedoms: (a) freedom of conscience and religion; (b) freedom of thought, belief, opinion and expression, including freedom of the press and other media of communication . . ."

Having taken care of the preliminaries, Shaw proceeds directly to the question of simple possession, noting that the word "'possesses' is not limited; any purpose will suffice to make possession of child pornography a crime," in contrast to those sections of the law which prohibit possession of kiddie porn for purposes of publication, sale, or distribution. Justice Shaw's reasoning on the question of simple possession is divided into two parts: first, an examination of the evidence presented in court, which leads to a "finding of the facts"; and second, a "legal analysis" that involves both locating previous relevant court cases in order to establish a measure or test by which to judge the issue, and applying that measure to the present case.

Shaw first examines the evidence of the Crown's two expert witnesses, Vancouver Police Detective Noreen Waters and Dr. Peter Collins, a specialist in forensic psychiatry. It's important to observe that Sharpe was unable, due to lack of fiscal resources, to call expert witnesses on his own behalf. Such witnesses might refute Crown-obtained testimony, which would have possibly had some effect on the judge's "finding of facts."

Detective Waters' testimony is briefly summed up as claiming

1. that "with the Internet there has been a veritable explosion of the availability of child pornography,"
2. that the availability of simple possession charges has made it easier for police to obtain search warrants and "carry out searches which have assisted them in finding child molesters," and
3. that "children are abused when they are exploited in the production of filmed or videotaped pornography."

Shaw treats Dr. Collins' evidence at considerably greater length. Collins' views are the orthodox ones of the field he represents, and support for them can be found in numerous instances of similar testimony at various trials, commissions, and the legislative hearings that produced the 1993 child pornography law. "Dr. Collins offered several reasons why, in his view, child pornography is harmful to children," Shaw begins. The main ones are —

1. that child pornography is used as a tool to seduce children (a process known as "grooming"),
2. that kiddie porn incites some pedophiles to assault children,
3. that such material, even including the non-obscene matter of publications such as the NAMBLA *Bulletin*, creates and reinforces the "cognitive distortions" of pedophiles, and
4. "that children are abused in the making of pornography and that pornographic films or photographs are a record of their abuse."

As the main expert witness on the subject of "harm," Collins' testimony is afforded extended consideration by the judge. Shaw records that, in support of his views, Collins introduced two exhibits, both of them studies by other experts on the harm caused by child pornography. In one, a 1998 article by Dr. William Marshall, "The Use of Sexually Explicit Stimuli by Rapists, Child Molesters, and Non-Offenders," the "inciting" element of child pornography is addressed.[3] Dr. Marshall reports that about one-third of child molesters in the study claimed to have been occasionally incited to commit an offence by exposure to kiddie porn, although Justice Shaw underscores that the materials used in the study were "sexually explicit 'hard core' pornography." The second study introduced by Dr. Collins found that child molesters have greater exposure to pornography than rapists and use it more often than rapists "in association with criminal offences," as well as more often "to relieve impulses to commit offences." This second study, which used a wide range of pornographic materials, confirmed that "'mildly erotic stimuli' inhibited aggression while 'highly erotic stimuli' increased aggression."

Even at this early stage in Dr. Collins' presentation, it's possible to see why Justice Shaw will treat such testimony with caution. As with the causal relation between adult pornography and consequent attitudes and acts, which we discussed earlier in relation to the *R. v. Butler* case, the evidence here tends to be "soft," diffuse, and hardly conclusive.[4]

While a claim that actual children are abused in the making of photographic pornography is thoroughly uncontroversial (since it's almost tautologically true), claims based on the self-reporting of pedophiles in psychiatric treatment raise all sorts of methodological problems with respect to their scientific status, especially since the patients may consider it to be in their interests to report the use of pornography, both because they may think it's expected of them to do so, and to displace causal responsibility for their acts from themselves onto the porn. When Dr. Collins is faced with questions about such matters as the effects of pedophiles' use of pornography as a masturbatory aid, he is often forced to report that he simply doesn't know. Similarly, since there was no evidence presented that "cognitive distortions" – which Collins described as "erroneous beliefs by which pedophiles justify their aberrant behaviour" – caused any significant increase in the danger pedophiles pose to children, Shaw quickly decided that he would give "only minimal weight" to the "cognitive distortions" claim.

On the basis of the evidence he heard, Justice Shaw then made a "finding of fact." While findings of fact can be disputed, nonetheless, once made, they are treated as facts for the purpose of coming to a decision in a given case. Furthermore, since the facts are based on evidence heard only by the judge trying the case, these findings are seldom challenged by higher courts that hear appeals of an initial judgment (although, as we'll see, the testimony itself may be revisited by a subsequent court).

Justice Shaw found, first, that "sexually explicit pornography involving children poses a danger to children because of its use by pedophiles in the seduction process." Second, "Children are abused in the production of filmed or videotaped pornography." Third, fourth, and fifth: that while "highly erotic" pornography incites some pedophiles to commit offences, "highly erotic" pornography also "helps some pedophiles relieve pent-up sexual tension," and it's "not possible to say which of the two foregoing effects is the greater," but sixth, "'mildly erotic' pornography appears to inhibit aggression." Seventh and eighth, although pornography can be a factor in augmenting or reinforcing a pedophile's cognitive distortions, there is no evidence that demonstrates there's an increased risk of harm to children as a result of pornography possibly augmenting such distortions. Ninth, and finally, Justice Shaw found that "the dissemination of written material which counsels or advocates sexual offences against children poses some risk of harm to children."

The striking feature of these findings is how limited they are in terms of providing a conclusive argument about kiddie porn. The uncontroversial finding that children are abused in the production of photographic pornography was the basis upon which federal Justice department advisers made their initial recommendation for a narrowly conceived law that restricted itself to instances of sexual representations made possible only by the commission of crimes. Whether the law should or logically can be more extensive than that, is, as we've previously noted, a central issue in the kiddie porn law debate.

Two other claims that Justice Shaw accepts as facts are also important, namely, the finding that kiddie porn is used in a "grooming" process to commit offences against children, and that written material advocating sex with children poses "some" risk of harm. Though both of those findings are considerably weaker than the one about the direct harm caused to children used in pornographic productions, they had a significant bearing on Shaw's decision.

Justice Shaw then turns to the "legal analysis." Given that the Crown counsel concedes that subsection (4), the simple possession clause, violates the guarantee of freedom of expression set out in Section 2(b) of the Charter of Rights, but argues that the possession prohibition is "saved" by Section 1 of the Charter as being a "reasonable limit prescribed by law which is demonstrably justified in a free and democratic society," the judge can proceed directly to determining whether the simple possession offence can be justified under Section 1 of the Charter. This is a fairly standard approach to the issue and provides a bit of legal economy.

Shaw then looks at precedents. It turns out that there's only one previous case where the constitutionality of the kiddie porn law has been addressed, *R. v. Langer* (1995). In that case, which we discussed in the previous chapter, the judge, Justice McCombs, decided that artist Eli Langer's paintings and drawings had artistic merit – a defence provided for in the kiddie porn law – and didn't pose a realistic risk of harm to children. Therefore, he ordered that the artwork be returned to Langer and not "forfeited." But in making his decision, the Ontario judge also held that while the kiddie porn law violated the constitution, it was justified under Section 1.

To make that determination of justification, the Ontario court applied the "Oakes test" (named for *R. v. Oakes* [1986] in which this interpretive scheme was first established). This test of the validity of a law infringing a Charter right involves three inquiries:

1. Whether a rational connection exists between the limitation on individual rights and the government objective.
2. Whether the limitation only minimally impairs the Charter right.
3. Whether effects of the limitation so severely infringe the Charter right that the legislative objective is outweighed by the limitation.

People who are impatient with judicial deliberations generally, or with challenges to the constitutionality of the child pornography law specifically, tend to view devices like the Oakes test as legal nitpicking, semantic quibbling, or judicial obfuscation. Indeed, that's the way the Oakes test may appear on the face of it, until we consider the alternatives. How, in fact, do we determine whether something as significant as the denial of a citizen's fundamental right is justifiable in a democracy? Unlike the "community standard of tolerance" test, which we've argued is deeply flawed both in logical and empirical terms, the "Oakes test" is, at the minimum, a workable procedure for balancing the rights of individuals against the interests and laws of society. Once we recognize that rights must trump interests, but that no right is absolute, we can reconcile ourselves to the necessity of some version of the Oakes test as a way of dealing with the hard cases. It may not be ideal – what test could be? – but it does provide a measure that, applied to an accruing body of cases, strikes us as defensible jurisprudence.

Looking at the *Langer* decision, Justice Shaw notes that the Ontario trial judge found that the simple possession clause met the "rational connection" and "minimal impairment" parts of the Oakes test. "On the basis of the opinion evidence which I have accepted," said Justice McCombs, "private possession of child pornography poses a realistic risk of harm to children, by reinforcing cognitive distortions, fuelling fantasies, and its potential use in 'grooming' possible child victims. It is entirely reasonable and within the legitimate objectives of Parliament to criminalize private possession of child pornography." Although Justice Shaw allowed a more limited reading of opinion evidence facts, he was not especially worried about the "rational connection" or "minimal impairment" parts of the test.

He was much more concerned with "the final proportionality test . . . the weighing of the legislative objectives of s. 163.1 against the effects of the prohibitions." As Justice McCombs noted in *Langer*, "even if legislation otherwise meets section 1 criteria, a provision will not constitute a reasonable limitation if its effects are so deleterious that they outweigh the importance of its objectives." However, McCombs insisted that it was "appropriate to bear in mind the type of expression that has been limited," and he cited a precedent that found that not all expression should be treated "as equally crucial to those principles at the core of section 2(b)." From this, Justice McCombs ruled that "the expression inherent in the production of child pornography is not crucial to the principles which lie at the core of freedom of expression. There is no evidence to support the contention that the effects of the legislation are so deleterious that they outweigh the pressing and substantial objective of the legislation."

At this point, Justice Shaw steps in and makes his crucial jurisprudential move. He discovers another precedent-setting Supreme Court decision that sets out a slightly different interpretation of the "weighing of effects" part of the Oakes test. "On my reading of *Langer*, it is evident that the court did not deal with the 'weighing of effects' test formulated in *Dagenais v. Canadian Broadcasting Corporation* (1994)," says Shaw. "*Dagenais* was not cited, likely because it had only recently been decided and may not have been drawn to the court's attention." All of this literally "courtly" language is a polite way of Shaw saying that the Ontario court made a mistake, but the mistake was not entirely its fault.

Shaw then sets out the "weighing of effects" test, as articulated by Supreme Court of Canada Chief Justice Antonio Lamer in *Dagenais*. Lamer wrote: "While the third step of the Oakes proportionality test has often been expressed in terms of the proportionality of the objective to the deleterious effects, this court has recognized that in appropriate cases it is necessary to measure the actual salutary effects of impugned legislation against its deleterious effects, rather than merely considering proportionality of the objective itself." That is, rather than just measuring the effects of a law against the law's objective, Lamer was proposing to weigh the actual positive and negative effects of the legislation as they cashed out in reality.

Lamer then went on to say that considering this branch of the Oakes test "as being concerned solely with the balance between the objective and the deleterious effects of a measure rests on too narrow a conception of proportionality. I believe that even if an objective is of sufficient importance, the first two elements of the proportionality test are satisfied, and the deleterious effects are proportional to the objectives, it is still possible that, because of a lack of proportionality between the deleterious effects and the salutary effects, a measure will not be reasonable and demonstrably justified in a free and democratic society. I would, therefore, rephrase [this] part of the Oakes test as follows: there must be a proportionality between the deleterious effects of the measures which are responsible for limiting the rights or freedoms in question and the objective, and there must be a proportionality between the deleterious and the salutary effects of the measures."

Although this may look, to the innocent eye, like a very minor adjustment to the Oakes test, in judicial circles it's something closer to a sizeable jurisprudential tremor, if not an actual legal earthquake. What Lamer did, in *Dagenais*, is significantly raise the bar that must be met if the Oakes test is to be passed.

Justice Shaw declares that the *Dagenais* "weighing of effects" test is the appropriate one to apply to the question of the prohibition of simple possession of child pornography. "I will now enter upon the weighing process," he announces.

First, he weighs the salutary effects: "The prohibition combats practices and phenomena which, at least arguably, put children at risk. These include: the use by some pedophiles of sexually explicit images in the grooming process leading to sexual relations with children; the abuse of children in the making of pornography and the preservation of that abuse in photographs or films; the confirmation or augmentation of cognitive distortions of some pedophiles; the incitement of some pedophiles to commit offences against children; and the advocacy or counselling of the commission of sexual offences against children."

Shaw also notes some limitations of those salutary effects. "There is no evidence which demonstrates any significant increase of danger to children related to . . . cognitive distortions caused by pornography." Further, "there is no evidence that 'mildly erotic' images are used in the 'grooming process.'" As well, "only assumption supports the proposition that materials that advocate or counsel sexual crimes with children have the effect of increasing the occurrence of such crimes." This last observation will be important to subsequent debates about written pornographic materials, a significant element in the Sharpe case. Finally, Shaw finds "there is no evidence that the production of child pornography will be significantly reduced if simple possession is made a crime."

If Shaw is somewhat perfunctory in listing the salutary effects of the law, he is anything but that when he addresses the detrimental effects of the simple possession clause. His main focus is on the importance of free speech, thought, expression, and privacy.

"Freedom of expression plays an important role in this case," Shaw says. "The personal belongings of an individual are an expression of that person's essential self. His or her books, diaries, pictures, clothes and other personal things are intertwined with that person's beliefs, opinions, thoughts and conscience." He cites a 1988 Supreme Court case, *Ford v. Quebec*, which found that freedom of expression should be broadly interpreted because "it is also the means by which the individual expresses his or her personal identity and sense of individuality." In that case, and another one, *R. v. Keegstra* (1990), the court included "individual self-fulfilment and personal autonomy" within the concept of freedom of expression.

Shaw then observes that the proportionality tests for Section 1 of the Charter "include a consideration of the fundamental values that underlie" the Charter and not just those expressly set out in it. Citing a passage from *R. v. Oakes*, he affirms that those values and principles include "respect for the inherent dignity of the human person, commitment to social justice and equality, accommodation of a wide variety of beliefs," and many others. How much weight is to be given to particular values will depend upon the particular circumstances.

The B.C. Supreme Court justice then proffers a principle that he regards as especially important. "One significant value underlying the Charter is the individual's reasonable expectation of privacy," Shaw says, citing a precedent that declares "Society has come to realize that privacy is at the heart of liberty in a modern state" and that "the restraints imposed on government to pry into the lives of the citizens go to the essence of a democratic state." Shaw adds, "An important aspect of privacy is an individual's right of privacy in his or her own home." He then turns to a series of precedent-setting cases in which it was found that all sorts of private conversations and other expressions, no matter how seemingly offensive, are protected under the freedom of expression section of the Charter.

We understand the frustration of readers who see where this line of argument is leading and are appalled by what they regard as the overweening concern being devoted to people they find despicable and whose expressions strike them as noxious and worse. But perhaps that's one of the central points of the entire exercise of which Justice Shaw's decision is a small part, namely, that our legal concern is with what *any* citizen is allowed to think and say, and only coincidentally includes the rights of a particular and unpopular citizen, in this case, Robin Sharpe.

Having laid out his general line of argument, Shaw then specifies what he considers to be the "detrimental effects arising from the prohibition of simple possession of child pornography." First and foremost, he says, "the invasion of freedom of expression and personal privacy is profound." The prohibition, he says, "extends to all persons including those who make no harmful use of pornography," such as those who possess pornography out of "prurient interest" but without harmful intent, as well as those who use pornography "for very private purposes, such as relief from their affliction by masturbation."

The ban, he continues, includes "mildly erotic" pornography, such as nude photos, even though the available evidence suggests that such representations may have the effect of reducing sexual aggression against children. Equally, people who are not affected by material advocating sexual offences against children are nonetheless subject to criminal sanctions if it's in their possession. Finally, while people may possess magazines or newspapers that are mostly within the law, the fact that such publications "contain some material said to be pornographic" means that "purchasers of such publications will have to become their own censors."

Justice Shaw then comes to his conclusion in "weighing the effects": "In my opinion, the detrimental effects substantially outweigh the salutary effects; the intrusion into freedom of expression and the right of privacy is so profound that it is not outweighed by the limited beneficial effects of the prohibition." The simple possession prohibition, Shaw argues, "deals with a very intimate and private aspect of a person's life and, in my view, that fact should be given considerable weight. I find that the limited effectiveness of the prohibition is insufficient to warrant its highly invasive effects." Finally, Shaw notes that there are a great many other laws in place that he regards as sufficiently "powerful measures to tackle the problem of harm to children arising from pornography."

Thus, Justice Shaw rules: "I find that subsection (4) fails the 'weighing of effects' proportionality test formulated in *Dagenais* and is therefore not saved under section 1 of the Charter. As sub-section (4) is in violation of section 2(b) of the Charter and is not justified under section 1, subsection (4) must be and is declared void." The words may sound coldly legalistic with their repeated references to numbered sections of various laws, but under that jurisprudential formality there beats a heartfelt defence of individual rights to privacy and expression.

The rightness of Shaw's ruling is, naturally, a matter of debate. We are not the only ones who disagree with some of Justice Shaw's reasoning, but we also recognize the plausibility of that reasoning. His decision is neither irrational nor radical. In measuring whether a prohibition against simple possession of child pornography is warranted, Justice Shaw is making his judgment in light of what the law has defined as "child pornography" – a broad array of materials, visual and written, covering an extensive group of young people. Some of that material involves explicit sexual representations of actual people who are unarguably children, while other material captured by the law's definition represents neither explicit sex nor actual people. Whether Shaw might have ruled differently if the definition of child pornography had been significantly narrower is unknown; in any case, he was required to take the definition as enacted. But even within the legal requirements, in striking down the possession offence the judge had considerable room to manoeuvre in terms of which reasons to emphasize in making his decision.

Our own view is that Justice Shaw ought to have given more weight to those sexual representations whose creation requires, as a dedicated element, the commission of a sexual crime against children. Shaw recognizes "the abuse of children in the making of pornography and the preservation of that abuse in photographs or films," but doesn't underscore it when he considers which factors support a law against simple possession. We think he ought to because such abuse is absolutely distinct as a harm from speculations about the possible harm caused by such elusive notions as "cognitive distortions" or the uncertainties of the effects on "some" people of various forms of pornography. While the child pornography law we envisage is, of course, not the one that Justice Shaw was called upon to evaluate, it would have been possible for him to strike down the possession clause and recommend to Parliament that it could rewrite the clause, limiting the offence to possession of photographic representations in which actual children are abused.

With regard to whether the sexual representations resulting from crimes committed in the production of photographic kiddie porn using actual children are themselves harms, the stolen property analogy advanced by Justice Department advisers is relevant here. While it's apropos for Justice Shaw to argue that "the personal belongings of an individual are an expression of that person's essential self" and that "his or her books, diaries, pictures, clothes and other personal things are intertwined with that person's beliefs, opinions, thoughts and conscience," that doesn't mean that the possession of, say, a set of stolen automobile tires is thereby protected by such a principle.

What Shaw is referring to are "rightful" personal belongings. The sexual representations of what we can call "necessarily criminal" kiddie porn (as contrasted to kiddie porn that is solely a product of the imagination) are relevantly analogous to stolen property, even if those photographic representations have been produced by the possessor of the images. Without embarking upon a philosophic discussion of the senses in which one's own image can be regarded as "property," it's sufficient to note that like privacy generally, a very high value is accorded sexual privacy in our culture. A special horror attends the idea of one's most intimate characteristics and behaviour being exposed to the view of others without consent. And since meaningful consent is, by definition, not possible for young children, sexually explicit representations requiring the contrivance of a crime for their production are, in that sense, a "property" that has been wrongfully taken from them, and the exposure to others of those representations is a violation of a deeply held value, as well as a perpetuation of the original criminal act. Mere possession of such sexual representations is thus analogous to stolen property and should not be protected by notions of individual selfhood and rights of expression.

Justice Shaw's declaration that the simple possession clause of Section 163.1 is "void" was not the end of his decision. He had one other question to consider, namely, whether Sharpe was justified in his contention that the prohibition against materials advocating or counselling sexual activity with a person under eighteen, which would be an offence under the Criminal Code, was unconstitutional.

Having already declared one part of the law unconstitutional, Shaw made shorter work of this second question. Partly, that was because the law was now changed as a result of Shaw's own ruling. Therefore, he wasn't considering whether advocacy materials should be a simple possession offence, since simple possession offences were now void and those charges against Sharpe had been dismissed. Rather, he was judging whether advocacy materials should be an offence under the part of the law making it a crime to possess such materials "for the purpose of distribution or sale," charges that Sharpe also faced.

Here, Shaw simply ruled, "I agree with the Crown's contention that subsection (1)(b), at least in the context of subsection (3) [the clause that makes possession for the purpose of distribution or sale illegal], is justified under section 1 of the Charter." Shaw noted that he'd already reviewed all the tests in *Oakes* and *Dage-*

nais "and am of the view that the Crown must succeed on all of them." Adding, "I do not believe I need to go into the same detail as I did earlier in respect of subsection (4)," he nonetheless offered a couple of supporting considerations.

His central one was an unargued assertion that "the dissemination of materials that counsel or advocate sexual abuse of children must pose some risk to children. Possession for the purpose of sale or distribution of such material can hardly be justified on any level of reasoning." Further, prohibition of such material for purposes of sale or distribution "is far less invasive of an individual's freedom of expression and right of privacy than a total ban on possession."

As for Sharpe's concern "that the ban might interfere with advocacy by pedophiles to persuade Parliament to change the age of consent laws and other matters . . . I do not read subsection (1)(b) as outlawing that kind of advocacy." Shaw then considered various other sections of the Charter invoked by Sharpe as offering protection and quickly dismissed all of them. "In summary, I reject Mr. Sharpe's attack on the constitutionality of the definition of child pornography set out in subsection (1)(b) in the context of subsection (3) of section 163.1 [of the Criminal Code]." Sharpe's challenge to that section of the kiddie porn law was thereby dismissed.

Although this part of Justice Shaw's ruling excited little subsequent comment, his reasoning here is not only skimpy, but unsatisfactory. The main flaw in it is the failure to consider the extensive rights of advocacy protected by the freedom of expression doctrine. For example, say a political group advocates bank robbery as part of a strategy for overthrowing Canadian capitalism. While such advocacy poses some degree of risk to banks, if not to the entire structure of Canadian capitalism, it is protected by the Charter of Rights and Freedoms.

There are indeed limitations on freedom of expression, but general advocacy of crimes is not one of them. The principle limitation is on "incitement," where speech is likely to cause immediate acts that can't conceivably be prevented by further discussion because of the circumstances in which the inciting utterance is made. In such cases, as we noted earlier, citing Wendy Kaminer's remarks, speech is assimilated to acts. Similar to incitement are such things as "threats," where the threat isn't simply a matter of words, but is more properly regarded as an action. Although there has been considerable intellectual effort to treat various expressions as metaphorically similar to incitement and other action-like speech acts – Catherine MacKinnon has suggested that all offensive pornography be so regarded – for the most part it's been recognized that there are good reasons for keeping prohibitions of expression relatively narrowly defined.

There has been, in recent years, the implementation of novel expression restrictions, mostly in the form of laws prohibiting "hate speech" and other speech that is part of behaviour within various institutions, such as speech in schools and workplaces that is defined as "harassment." The discussion of the arguable foundations of such law is another and lengthy story, but it's sufficient to observe here that none of those prohibitions is particularly relevant to general advocacy of unpopular ideas or illegal acts.

A second flaw in Shaw's reasoning on "advocacy" materials is that it doesn't address the actual materials with which Sharpe is charged. Sharpe isn't charged with writing essays that advocate criminal acts, but with writing fiction that some readers say "amounts to" advocacy. In not addressing that problem, Shaw leaves open a range of murky interpretive claims that subject Sharpe to possible sanctions.

Justice Shaw's ruling on this part of the constitutional challenge is the weakest portion of his decision, not because it's necessarily wrong, but because it is so inadequately supported and because it fails to take any account of arguments of the sort we've offered.

Writing in the calm of his judicial chambers, Justice
Shaw could hardly have anticipated the full extent of the storm his decision in *R. v. Sharpe* would unleash.

On Friday, January 15, 1999, the day of its release, Shaw's decision striking down a section of the kiddie porn law instantly became the lead news item in broadcasts across the country. The next morning it was front-page news in the weekend editions of Canada's two national newspapers, as well as regional newspapers in Vancouver and almost everywhere else.

The reports in the mainstream press were seemingly sober and straightforward; this was a story that required no embellishment. The *Globe and Mail* headline read, "Child porn law is struck down by B.C. judge; Criminal Code ban on possession violates Charter of Rights, ruling says." The *National Post*'s front page announced, "Top B.C. court strikes down child porn law: Possession is legal." The *Post* ran a supplementary profile of Sharpe. It was much the same in the Vancouver press. "B.C. judge throws out child porn law," said the *Vancouver Sun*, which ran lengthy excerpts from Shaw's decision on its op-ed pages. The *Ottawa Citizen* and other urban newspapers published similar accounts.[5]

Despite the apparent restraint of sensationalism in the headlines, they were nonetheless profoundly misleading. The child porn law had in fact neither been "struck down" nor "thrown out." Only one part of the child pornography law had been declared unconstitutional; the rest of the law was completely in place, including the crucial definition of porn. The impression that the law had been struck down in its entirety afforded the opportunity for politicians opposed to the constitutional challenge to claim that the country was now without laws to protect children, that child pornographers were free to exploit children, and that we were in the midst of a moral and legal crisis requiring emergency measures. None of these claims was true.

Though the news reports mainly focussed on what Justice Shaw decided, quoting passages from his decision and providing background information on the case, the initial stories also included some of the immediate reactions to the judgment. The *Globe and Mail* reported that "police in B.C. said they are concerned about the decision. 'The consensus in the law enforcement community is that child pornography is a serious issue,' said RCMP Sergeant Russ Grabb. 'However, Charter rights are paramount in this country,'" he added, implying that perhaps they shouldn't be. Other law enforcement officials went further. "If this judgment is upheld in higher courts, I will simply retire," said Sergeant Keith Daniels, a child pornography specialist with the Ottawa police. "This absurd decision came from way out in left field."[6]

Shari Graydon, the executive director of Mediawatch, a Vancouver-based group monitoring depictions of women and girls in the media, said that allowing individuals to possess child pornography was tantamount to condoning the sexual exploitation of children. The *National Post* reported that Nicholas Bala, a law professor at Queen's University in Kingston, called for the reversal of Shaw's decision. "If it's not overturned, it's a very disturbing precedent," he said. "I don't think he gave enough weight to the harmful effects of child pornography, particularly the fact that some of this material is produced using children." Another law professor, Julius Grey, of Montreal's McGill University, cited the 1992 *R. v. Butler* decision and predicted that there was a strong chance that Shaw's decision would be overturned on appeal.

A spokesperson for federal Justice minister Anne McLellan said that the federal government hadn't yet had time to study the ruling, but pointed out that the decision to appeal it must come from the provincial attorney general, Ujjal Dosanjh. Pressure on Dosanjh to respond quickly came from Barry Penner, the B.C. Liberal Party's critic for justice. "I'm calling on the attorney general to make a swift appeal to protect children from sexual exploitation . . . I don't want to criticize the judge, but my primary concern is to protect children," Penner said.[7]

If the initial responses were the standard ones of concern about the appeal process and criticism by legal experts, by Monday morning the mob was in full throat.

"The bonehead should be removed from the bench," demanded CKNW radio talk-show host Peter Warren in what was described as "an emotional discussion of the issue with callers."[8] Warren wasn't the only "hotline radio" broadcaster to raise the temperature of the debate. The Lower Mainland area, where incendiary radio talk shows are a longstanding feature of popular culture, was filled with cries for action.

Nor was Justice Shaw the only target of outrage. In Robin Sharpe's neighbourhood, the controversial defendant was now the focus of a poster campaign, which featured a newspaper photo of Sharpe, included his address, and warned that he "proudly advocated sex with children." Newspaper clippings on the case were posted by the elevator in Sharpe's building, and Sharpe began to receive abusive and threatening phone calls.[9]

Members of the federal Reform Party led the political charge against the decision. Chuck Cadman, an MP from Surrey, B.C., and a Reform Party deputy justice critic, said he was disgusted by the ruling. "More and more, the rights of individuals to do whatever they want are being given supremacy over the common good of the nation." Another Reform MP, Reed Elley of Nanaimo, B.C., echoed Cadman's complaint. "This is one more example of social engineering where the courts make laws rather than Parliament," he charged. Various anti-crime organizations chimed in with similar claims.[10]

Adding to the sense that the community was suddenly at risk were news reports on Monday evening that a Surrey, B.C., provincial court magistrate had dismissed charges of possession of child pornography against an accused, saying he was bound by Justice Shaw's decision. Although the impression was given that the province was threatened by a horde of about-to-be-freed possessors of kiddie porn, in fact, in most of the pending cases the province would simply seek adjournments until the constitutional status of the law was settled.

By Tuesday morning, not only were the talk-show airwaves filled with angry expostulations, but the letters-to-the-editor columns of the local press were replete with outraged missives. "I am sickened by the ruling," declared one letter-writer, invoking the malevolent ghost of Ted Bundy, an executed American serial killer who had claimed he was incited by pornography. "Who cares about the rights and freedoms of perverts?" he asked. Another correspondent described the judicial system as "pathetic." Asked another, doesn't a child's right to grow up safe "outweigh some freak's right to play with himself?" Pleaded another, "Tell me it isn't true. Tell me that I'm not going to have to move myself and my family to another country."[11]

Some of what appeared to be a rising tide of public hysteria was stemmed by Attorney General Dosanjh's prompt announcement of an appeal of Shaw's decision. "Our position on the appeal is that the possession of child pornography provisions in the Criminal Code of Canada are constitutionally sound," he said, adding that the Crown would also seek to "expedite" the appeal, "as this case may have a significant impact on other cases before the courts." Until the appeal was heard, the Crown would ask for adjournments in the other cases, the attorney general promised.

The debate on the issue filled the columns of newspaper op-ed pages across the country for the rest of the week. At one end of the discussion was *Vancouver Province* columnist Susan Martinuk's essay "Justice Duncan Shaw: 'What planet is he on, anyway?'"[12] Calling Shaw's ruling "inane," deploring the judge's "ignorance," and citing the Ted Bundy serial murder case, the columnist charged Shaw with "succumbing to the growing judicial tendency to consider such cases in a vacuum that focuses solely on the rights of the individual, and excluded the detrimental consequences on the rest of society." Martinuk then borrowed the catchphrase of a fictional television journalist, Murphy Brown, to ask, "What planet is he on, anyway?"

Mediawatch executive director Shari Graydon, writing in the *Globe and Mail*, began with a riddle: "Question: When is child pornography acceptable in British Columbia? Answer: When you use it for your own pleasure in the privacy of your home. No," she continued, "this is not a joke, and there's no punchline to make you feel better."[13] Graydon, however, distinguished between pornography where adults "appear in the photographs of their own volition . . . deriving some personal or financial satisfaction from the act" – in which cases, the presence of such representations are tolerated "in a society that values freedom of expression" – and child pornography, where meaningful consent is not a possibility. "Either the decision should be overturned or the law should be rewritten, fast," she urged.

A *Vancouver Sun* editorial began to make some of the distinctions necessary to raise the debate above a level of visceral rhetoric. While acknowledging that "there are some court judgments with which we struggle, and this is one of them, we agree, reluctantly, with the judge's stress on privacy rights." But, argued the *Sun*, "the judge does not distinguish between the use of real and imaginary children in the making of smut. That is a striking mistake [and] here is where we would make [the] right to privacy subordinate to the safeguarding of children . . . In contrast, a collection of child pornography consisting of flights of fancy – cartoons, drawings, tales of fiction – and not based on real child models would not raise the same concerns about children's safety." The paper urged the appeal court to endorse part of Shaw's decision, "but remedy his error."[14]

An *Ottawa Citizen* editorial took a similar position. It noted that the paper would "normally applaud much of the court ruling, for Justice Duncan Shaw makes many sound observations about what harm pornography does and does not do in a free society . . . Yet, amazingly, Justice Shaw failed to focus on the central point that differentiates this free speech case from all others: the use – more accurately, the abuse – of children." Arguing that "child pornography manufactured without the use of a child . . . repugnant as [it is], ought not to be forbidden by law," the *Citizen* editorial stressed that "a child, however, is not a moral agent . . . The use of a child, therefore, can only be viewed as coercive, for the child cannot freely make the decision to participate."[15]

If the debate was becoming more temperate in some quarters, in the popular sector there were still demands for the judge's head. Such calls weren't merely metaphorical. On the weekend of January 23, 1999, the *Globe and Mail* reported that Justice Shaw had received a death threat, and Attorney General Dosanjh announced that he would order increased security for the B.C. Supreme Court justice.[16]

A spokesman for the court, former judge Lloyd McKenzie, confirmed that a threat was called in. "One of the secretaries received a threat on his head. I don't know the language of it, but that was the reaction she had to it." McKenzie added that in his forty years as a judge and lawyer he had never seen anything like the "battering" Judge Shaw was taking in letters to newspapers and phone-in shows. "People are phoning me and phoning a number of other people at the Law Courts, including the judge's secretary, just heaping invective on the judge."

Sharpe, whose case had sparked the outrage, and who had become the target of similar threats himself, told the press that he was saddened and shocked to learn of the death threat aimed at the judge in his case. "I don't know – what can you say? It's sad," Sharpe said. He added that media commentary had been "just an orgy of posturing. On a topic like this, your normal rules just do not apply – and by that I mean the normal reliance on reason and logic and assumptions that can be substantiated."[17]

Others also stepped in on behalf of Shaw. Said Warren Wilson, president of the Law Society of B.C., "No judge, nor anyone else involved in the justice system, should be subjected to such abuse." The Ottawa-based agency that handles complaints about federally appointed judges had also received an earful – as many as fifty calls of complaint a day – and was concerned. "It's most unfortunate," said Jeannie Thomas, executive director of the Canadian Judicial Council. "Imagine if you were a judge and you were personally criticized for a decision you made to the best of your ability based on your understanding of the law."[18]

Although one columnist had asked, "What planet is he on?" Shaw's friends and colleagues reported that the B.C. justice was a pretty down-to-earth guy. While Shaw, sixty-six, a married father of two children, was prevented by judicial custom and regulations from commenting on the controversy, some of his colleagues felt that the whirlwind of criticism had gone too far, and spoke up. "He's the kind of judge who looks at the law and the legal principles, and would say, based on that, that this law is unconstitutional," said criminal lawyer Glen Orris. "Nothing else would influence him, whether it was popular or otherwise."

Shaw, who had been raised in Vancouver and graduated from law school in 1958, had been a lawyer for thirty years at one of the city's biggest legal firms, Davis and Company, moving up to become a senior partner before being raised to the bench in 1987. "He's a very solid kind of by-the-book judge," said Ross Ellison, a senior partner at the firm and a friend of Shaw. "He decides cases only on what's in front of him, a very conscientious guy."

By the following week, the focus of the debate had shifted to the parliamentary front in Ottawa. Days before the House of Commons reconvened after its winter break, more than half of the governing Liberals' parliamentary caucus sent a letter to Prime Minister Jean Chretien, urging him to take immediate legal or parliamentary action to overrule Justice Shaw's decision. The letter, drafted by Liberal MP Albina Guarnieri and signed by some seventy of her colleagues, recommended "strong new child pornography legislation to be introduced as soon as the House resumes" and urged the prime minister to consider using the special constitutional clause that allows Parliament or provincial legislatures to pass laws that can override Canada's Charter of Rights and Freedoms. The Liberal backbench letter came as two Tory MPs announced that they planned to seek all-party approval for a motion reiterating support of the current anti-porn law.[19]

The next day, Justice Minister Anne McLellan attempted to slow the political juggernaut by instructing federal lawyers to begin preparing a rare application seeking permission from the Court of Appeal of British Columbia for Ottawa to take part in the case. The minister's press secretary pointed out that the federal government normally avoids intervening in appeals at the provincial level and does so only when "it is determined to be an issue of national importance." *R. v. Sharpe* was apparently such an issue.[20]

When Parliament resumed at the beginning of February 1999, McLellan stood her ground, rejecting opposition party demands for the government to immediately invoke the notwithstanding clause to overturn Shaw's decision. McClellan faced a barrage of angry questions from Reform, Tory, and independent MPs who accused the government of failing to take strong enough action. "This decision has given pedophiles the right to abuse children," charged John Reynolds, the Reform MP for West Vancouver, B.C.

Preston Manning, the Reform Party leader, said his party was calling for drastic federal intervention because it had "no confidence" that the courts would overturn Shaw's ruling. "The federal government should use the notwithstanding clause to make it crystal clear to the current courts and to the higher courts that the section of the Criminal Code is going to apply."

But McLellan replied that she was sticking to her plan. "This government took immediate action, and we have taken the extraordinary step of intervening at the B.C. Court of Appeal," she said. "Some amendments to the law may be required. But to preempt the appellate process is silly and wrong-headed."[21]

The following day, a Reform Party–sponsored opposition motion – supported by Conservatives, New Democrats, the Bloc Québecois, and even four Liberal MPs – demanding that the federal government immediately overturn Shaw's decision was narrowly defeated, 143 to 129. Reform's House leader, Randy White, said the government's refusal to quash Justice Shaw's decision established "an unprecedented criterion for the possession and production of child pornography. People are concerned that we condone something that is just immoral."

"The Reform party is wrong. They are also without courage," McLellan replied. "For it is in circumstances like the present that the tough thing to do is to show respect for and have faith in our legal system."[22]

Although there was sufficient political grandstanding to go around, in the main, McLellan was right. The federal government had never invoked the notwithstanding clause, since it was understood to be an instrument of last resort. The country was hardly faced with an emergency, despite the best efforts of political rhetoric to make it seem so. It was a long-recognized protocol of the "separation of powers" doctrine that once a process of appeal was underway in a case with constitutional implications, Parliament would await the completion of that process before acting. However sincere the protestations of the opposition parties, this appeared to be more an instance of the "politics of politics" than a case of legislative necessity.

This phase of the public fallout resulting from Justice Shaw's decision in the Robin Sharpe case – with its unprecedented invective, political and popular hyperbole, and even death threats – was finally brought to an end on February 5, 1999. That's when Allan McEachern, chief justice of the B.C. Appeal Court, held a hearing to set a date for the appeal in *R. v. Sharpe*. Robin Sharpe appeared before the court and asked the chief justice for more time to prepare for the appeal, citing failing health and the need to defend himself against the outstanding charges (which had been postponed to March 1, and would be further postponed).

McEachern wasn't having any of it. "I can save you some breath," he told Sharpe. "There are eighteen cases pending in B.C. courts. That alone is reason to expedite this appeal." He ruled that the Court of Appeal would hear arguments April 26 and 27, 1999, on the constitutional validity of the kiddie porn law possession clause.[23]

FOUR

An Appeal
to Reason

When the chief justice of the B.C. Court of Appeal set two days near the end of April 1999 to hear the appeal in *R. v. Sharpe*, he succeeded in providing speedy justice in response to public demands for it. However, in terms of "saving breath," McEachern in fact set the stage for a markedly increased expenditure of legal breath, much of which he would have to hear as a member – along with Justices Mary Southin and Anne Rowles – of the three-judge court that listened to the pleadings in the Sharpe case, and some of which he would have to expend himself in writing his opinion when the case was decided.

While the *voir dire* had gone publicly unnoticed until Justice Shaw's controversial decision in mid-January 1999, the impending B.C. Appeal Court case drew not only considerable media attention, but also a raft of organizations seeking to get in on the act as intervenors. First, however, Robin Sharpe, the respondent in the Crown's appeal, decided that he had reached the limit of his self-developed legal skills and acquired, through the Legal

Aid system, the services of two highly qualified lawyers, Richard Peck and Gil McKinnon. Peck, especially, had an enviable reputation as a Vancouver criminal lawyer and was widely regarded as a first-rate courtroom presenter. His presence also meant that the argument offered on Sharpe's behalf would significantly shift from Sharpe's rather pure libertarian position to a more nuanced stance on child pornography – a shift that found only grudging favour with his client.

While the Attorney General of Canada sought and received early intervenor status, naming lawyer Judith Bowers as its representative, a number of other groups also acquired standing, including a consortium of the Canadian Police Association and several national and international victims-of-crime groups. The Evangelical Fellowship of Canada and Focus on the Family Association had something to say, as did the B.C. Civil Liberties Association (BCCLA), which sent John McAlpine and Andrew Gay to argue its brief before the court. Before it was over, the crowded courtroom would be one of those proverbial scenes where "you can't tell the players without a scorecard."

Although the BCCLA's participation in the Sharpe case was somewhat belated in comparison to its usual early-warning sensitivity to civil liberties issues, its "factum" would have a significant impact on the court. As long-time associates of the BCCLA, and given that our own views are more or less identical to those in the BCCLA brief, this is the appropriate place – as the various participants in the case are lining up their arguments and the media editors are making their assignments to cover the hearings – to present a more detailed version of the civil libertarians' position. [1]

In laying out the issues on appeal, the BCCLA accepted the

generally agreed-upon interpretation of the main question, namely: Is the simple possession offence in the kiddie porn law, viewed in combination with the definition of "child pornography," a reasonable limit on the freedom of expression guaranteed in the Charter of Rights which can be justified in a free and democratic society? The BCCLA was prepared to argue that the answer was no.[2]

The BCCLA also immediately joined those who believe that there is no constitutional obstacle to criminalizing the simple possession of sexually explicit photographic representations "that are produced using children or youth in a manner that constitutes a sexual offence under constitutionally valid provisions of the Criminal Code." The making of such pictures, as many others had already pointed out, involves sexual exploitation, and their possession "represents a continuing, serious violation of the dignity of the children or youth employed in their production." This is the argument initially made by Justice department advisers attempting to craft a narrow child pornography law and is the one that we've supported throughout this account.

However, noted the BCCLA, the law that was eventually passed goes much further than that, proscribing "all sexual images of persons under age 18, including those that did not involve the commission of harm, criminal conduct, or even the use of a real child." The Crown attempts to defend this position, the BCCLA said, by claiming that such images "may induce criminally exploitative behaviour in pedophiles." And this is where the BCCLA sharply parted company from the Crown. "Against this line of argument, we respectfully submit that a free society cannot measure the allowable range of expressive freedom by reference to the appetites of the most deviant persons in our community. This has long been an accepted truth in connection with offences of production, distribution, publication and sale of expressive materials, and it should have even greater force in the context of an offence of mere possession."

If the BCCLA brief had gone no further than its contention that a free society shouldn't "measure the allowable range of freedom of expression by reference to the appetites of the most deviant persons," this passage would simply have been one of those occasions where the sense of what is logical and right attempts to overcome dreary reality. However, the additional claim that this is a long "accepted truth" was actually in error. As various other intervenors' briefs approvingly pointed out, ever since the 1992 *Butler* decision – where the Supreme Court of Canada reduced the strict standard of "distinct and assignable" harm to a much looser principle that recognized mere perception of harm – the notion that expressive materials might possibly induce criminal behaviour, and thus could be suppressed on those grounds, had a footing in Canadian jurisprudence.

Still, the argument that we shouldn't found a possession offence on the mere belief that expressive material may induce criminal behaviour in some few cases has considerable force. Some kiddie porn is inseparable from crimes committed against children and indeed constitutes evidence of those crimes, and the criminalization of such representations is not in any way dependent on how they affect viewers. Other representations simply do not have that character. Such "non-criminal" sexual representations shouldn't be judged, said the BCCLA, on how "some" people might be influenced by them. The familiar analogy here is that if we judged fictional films about bank robbery by whether or not they might inspire "copycat" crimes, we soon would be facing many blank screens. While some people might half-jokingly argue that that would be a social benefit, in reality such legally enforced policy would render notions of freedom of expression meaningless.

While the BCCLA agreed, along with most others, "that the prevention of the sexual violation or exploitation of children and youth is a state objective of pressing and substantial importance," Parliament had nonetheless, in its opinion, gone too far. If Parliament had limited the application of the simple possession clause "to pictures produced through the actual exploitation or assault of real children or youth, then its constitutional validity, in our submission, would not be in doubt." But in fact the definition of "child pornography" in the kiddie porn law extended well beyond that. "This overbreadth is particularly problematic in the context of a simple possession offence," said the BCCLA, using for the first time the legal term – "overbreadth" – that would soon be key to the Sharpe case.

The BCCLA made two more introductory points. First, the kiddie porn law's use of the "stigmatizing label" of child pornography to describe everything covered by the law "is unfortunate and potentially misleading." Much of what is captured by the law, said the BCCLA, simply isn't child pornography. Second, "the issue of age is significant. Under the Criminal Code, most sexual activity of youth aged 14 to 17 (including sexual activity with adults) is legal. This requires that the possession of child pornography be analyzed distinctly from the possession of youth pornography."

The BCCLA then dramatically pointed out that it was "not aware of another Canadian criminal law, either current or historical, that provides for a sentence of incarceration for the mere possession of expressive material."

In the civil libertarians' view, criminalizing simple possession of expressive materials that were not the product of a crime had profound effects: "It results in a violation of all section 2(b) freedoms at once: thought, belief, opinion and expression. Further, it necessarily entails a profound invasion of personal privacy. State efforts to coerce individuals into holding or abandoning thoughts, beliefs or opinions – no matter how evil or repugnant they may be if acted upon – are the hallmarks of a totalitarian society and antithetical to a free and democratic society." That's why, the BCCLA argued, simple possession offences involving expressive material should be upheld only in exceptional circumstances and only where the law was carefully tailored to capture material that was necessary to attaining an overriding state purpose.

The spectre of totalitarianism invoked by the BCCLA raised significant echoes in the courtroom, but is an image that remains debatable among the general public and conservative politicians. However, although the BCCLA didn't spell it out, its claim about totalitarianism is buttressed by the long historical experience of Western political and legal cultures attempting to govern persons by enforcing limits on their mental lives. That history goes back at least to the late Middle Ages, when ecclesiastical law was not satisfied by the mere outward show of religious conformity. There was a further and more strict requirement that one's inner life, one's most personal and private beliefs, had to conform to dogma, and vigorous steps were taken to "inquire" into such matters – notoriously, by the torturers of the Inquisition. Similarly, kings and queens quite logically believed that their reigns would be more secure if they enforced a civil orthodoxy with respect to seditious or treasonous writings.

In a sense, much of the historical democratic narrative is the story of the gradual recognition that the integrity of the spirit, conscience, and mind of the individual person has a worth that supercedes even the *raison d'etat* of monarchs or the revealed truth of papal authorities. The reason the BCCLA made so much of the constitutional fundamental freedoms of conscience, belief, and thought, as well as those of speech and expression, is because it can be fairly said that respect for the inherent dignity of persons lies at the very foundation of the democratic commitment to the essential equality of all citizens, no matter how different their claims to intelligence, energy, or courage. This belief, perhaps more than any other, defines the "Western" element of our civilization. We have spent, literally, centuries struggling to free the individual mind from the inquisitorial zeal of political and religious authority. Hence the extreme caution of civil libertarians in the face of any innovative prohibition of the mere possession of expressive materials.

Too often, the BCCLA brief implied, there is a willingness on the part of proponents of a "tough" law to jettison those freedoms in the name of a seemingly greater or immediate good. Irrespective of the motivations of such opponents – whether simply sincere or inspired by political considerations – the tendency to undervalue free speech, especially offensive speech, poses a danger to democracy. The main BCCLA proposal was that it is indeed possible to have a child pornography law that protects actual children while simultaneously preserving fundamental freedoms of expression, but only if all participants in the debate are willing to recognize the importance of fundamental freedoms in a democracy.

The BCCLA brief then described various specific ways in which the kiddie porn law was "overly broad." First, it captured "visual images of the sexuality of children and young persons that are purely the products of their creators' imaginations and involve no children or youth in their production"; second, the law overreached by proscribing sexual pictures of young people between fourteen and seventeen that are perfectly legal, even "pictures of one's own legal sexual activity"; and third, the law made illegal self-authored material that "advocates" illegal acts, even if that material has not been distributed to another person.

"These problems of overbreadth," argued the brief, "are acute when they form the basis of a charge of simple possession. When, for example, a person can be charged with an offence simply for possessing the products of his or her imagination, or a record of his or her legal sexual activity, the state is attempting to control thoughts or behaviour in a manner fundamentally inconsistent with an individual's dignity, privacy and constitutionally guaranteed section 2(b) freedoms." In sum, the civil libertarians recognized the importance of protecting children – and proposed a practical means of doing so through law, while preserving the fundamental structures of democratic society. But the way to protect children, the BCCLA argued, was not through the existing kiddie porn law.

The BCCLA filed its factum with the court on April 15, 1999, as did several other intervenors, the most prominent of whom was the federal government. Its thirty-three-page submission to the B.C. Court of Appeal, described by the press as "a vigorous defence of its law banning child pornography," argued that "possession of child pornography, whether visual or written, fuels the sexual fantasies of pedophiles and will lead some pedophiles to act upon their fantasies." As far as the government was concerned, "the fundamental and overriding importance of protecting children from all forms of sexual abuse far outweighs any possible benefit from permitting people to possess child pornography."[3]

Justice Minister Anne McLellan spoke up for the government's position, saying, "I think it's a very strong factum and it makes the federal government's views very clearly in terms of our belief that the law is constitutional." Predictably, that didn't satisfy her political opponents, who claimed that the government should be doing more than letting the case wind its way through the justice system. "It's definitely not enough," claimed the Reform Party crime critic, Jim Abbott, "because the meter is running on the number of people who stand with charges that have been set aside and the problem is . . . they're going to be dismissed as a result of taking too long."

On a Monday morning a little more than a week later, in a Vancouver courtroom filled with lawyers, media, observers, and respondent Robin Sharpe, proceedings got underway.[4] As attorney John Gordon, representing the province of British Columbia, began laying out the government's case for the kiddie porn law, anyone expecting a sedate, technical disquisition on abstruse points of law was in for a surprise.

Instead of sitting back to be guided through the government's argument, Justice Mary Southin quickly intervened, repeatedly interrupting Gordon's presentation with sharply pointed questions. Much would be made in the media subsequently of Southin's remarks, which tended to be portrayed as outrageous and quirky, but only because they were often taken out of the context of the animated back-and-forth conversation between the jurist and the Crown attorney. Southin was impatient with grandiloquent claims and wanted down-to-earth answers to specific concerns.

When Gordon cited Canada's international commitments to fight child pornography and exploitation of children, Southin pointed out that many of the subjects posed for sexually graphic pictures for profit. "Whether we like it or not, isn't it a fair assumption that they did it for money?" She added that some of the subjects appeared to be from impoverished countries and wondered aloud about Canadian concern for them. "What are we doing pontificating about street kids in Brazil?" she asked.

At that point Crown co-counsel Katherine Ker stepped in to

say that Canada had international obligations. Replied Southin sardonically, "We don't have international obligations to stop kids starving to death in the streets of Brazil, do we?" If the Crown wanted to talk about political obligations, Southin was willing to talk about political realities. Concepts like autonomy and integrity are often dictated by economic realities, she said, and people in impoverished conditions might have different views than those held by white, middle-class Canadians. "That's the trouble with these arguments," she said. "They all sound fine until you start looking at the real world."

When Gordon argued that possession of child porn needed to be illegal to help stamp out its production and distribution, Justice Southin questioned the effectiveness of such laws. "These sound like all the arguments that were advanced in the United States to support alcohol prohibition. And look at the results. It did not stop anything. It just made it worse."

Gordon allowed that criminalization could hardly be expected to be a hundred percent effective. "But you cannot throw up your hands," he replied, "and say, 'What's the point?'"

More than the broader political questions, what seemed to be on Southin's mind were doubts about the specifics of the law. She told Gordon that she was particularly troubled by the fact that Section 163.1 defined child pornography as material that depicted persons under the age of eighteen, despite the fact that the age of sexual consent was fourteen.

"At some point, are you going to explain how somebody between the ages of fourteen and eighteen is a child?" she asked the Crown counsel. "That's what troubles me about this legislation – its relationship to the age of consent." Southin asked if a seventeen-year-old boy who took sexual pictures of his sixteen-year-old girlfriend could be charged with possession of child pornography – and further, could the woman herself, if she cooperated, be charged as an accomplice? Gordon admitted that he didn't know the answer to that.

At one point, Southin referred to a recent and local beating death of a teenager by other teens. "They're not children in the sense that people use that word in ordinary speech," she remarked, hinting at the contradictory ways in which young people are viewed – as children when it comes to sex, but as adults when it comes to violence.

Southin pressed further, questioning Gordon on the fact that the law didn't distinguish between pornography using real children and material that was created out of a person's imagination. She noted that social views about subjects like pornography were, after all, subject to change. "We have to recognize that our views about these matters might change radically . . . over a very short period of time."

Gordon replied, "Is society going to evolve to the extent that material that promotes and encourages the sexual exploitation of children becomes acceptable? I submit not, because children, like homosexuals, deserve dignity, privacy, autonomy of body. Child pornography is antithetical to the rights of children."

Southin's remark about society's changing attitudes made some headlines and was subsequently widely cited. But it only appeared provocative when wrenched out of context. In talking about the difference between photographic pornography and merely imaginative material, she noted that D.H. Lawrence's *Lady Chatterley's Lover* had once been considered shockingly pornographic, but now it wasn't. Referring to Sharpe's writings, she went on, "It's all dreadful stuff, and besides that, badly written. I don't think *Lady Chatterley* is much of a book either. But I don't know how you draw the distinction. I don't have any problem with [the Crown's view] of the photographs . . . but I don't

know how that applies to the stuff he wrote. I don't see the connection. There are graphic books written about rape and all manner of things. But we don't ban them."

It is clear that Southin's remark about changing social attitudes
should be read as questioning the sweeping character of what was
defined as child pornography rather than a suggestion that actual
child pornography would one day become socially acceptable.

Though the exchanges between Justice Southin and the
Crown attorney were the most dramatic events of the day, the
court also heard other arguments. The lawyer representing the
Canadian Police Association, Tim Danson, argued that police
efforts to contain the spread of child pornography in Canada
would grind to a halt unless the courts overturned Justice Shaw's
ruling. "They will be placed in a legal straitjacket and the child
pornography industry will flourish," Danson argued, introducing an affidavit from Detective Robert Matthews, the Ontario
officer in charge of that province's child pornography unit.

The court also heard lawyer Gil McKinnon, on behalf of
respondent Sharpe, who charged that "the impugned legislation
is drafted so widely that it has the potential to catch or criminalize conduct the government is constitutionally not permitted to
catch. It catches conduct that cannot, by any stretch of the imagination, assist the government in its laudable objective of protecting children."

The next day, April 27, Sharpe's other lawyer, Richard Peck,
picked up where McKinnon left off. In what was described by
some of the media as a "significant retreat," both of Sharpe's legal
representatives made it clear that they were not urging that possession of sexually exploitative photographs of real children
under fourteen be removed from the Criminal Code, but rather
that the possession provision was too broad. Although Sharpe
was described as appearing "visibly agitated" as his lawyers

argued that some pornography should be banned, Peck's presentation of the respondent's position mirrored that of the civil libertarian intervenors.[5]

Peck hammered away at the invasiveness of the law. While
agreeing that parts of the law were warranted, he insisted that as
it stood, the kiddie porn law was so far reaching that it unnecessarily captured all kinds of material in a wide criminal net,
including material never meant to be seen by anyone other than
the person who made it. Citing several hypothetical examples, he
said it could criminalize a seventeen-year-old boy who took a
nude picture of himself that he never showed to anyone else, or
teenagers at a grad party who produced a video that depicted
sexual activity.

"This is censorship legislation," said Peck. "It impugns the
private possession of one's thoughts or imaginings that are committed to written or drawn form." Holding his thumb and index
finger less than a centimetre apart, he told the three appeal court
judges, "We're that far from an attempt at thought control." He
added, "I'm trying to show the profound value of privacy. What
we're doing here is trying to balance this fundamental value in
our society against this invasive statute. And in my view, it does-
n't balance in favour of the state."

After hearing all the other intervenors, the court wrapped up
its two-day hearing and retired to deliberate for the next few
weeks. Unlike Justice Shaw's *voir dire*, even while the appeal
court worked on a decision there was steady public commentary,
ranging from worried letters to the editor declaring "We all have
something to fear," to reports, especially in the *National Post*, of
scholarly debates about "judicial activism." "This case has
sharpened the debate over whether the courts are going too far,"
said Rainer Knopff, a political science professor at the University
of Calgary. Said his colleague Professor Ted Morton, "This case

focuses attention on who should have final responsibility for this policy decision, Parliament or the judges."[6]

National Post columnist Andrew Coyne chastised his own paper for promoting what he regarded as a specious debate about "judicial activism." The Sharpe case, he said, "is not about judicial activism, as this term is commonly understood." Noting that the catchphrase originated in the U.S., Coyne claimed that "Canadian critics have a much more radical agenda than their American counterparts. There, the case is confining judicial activism to what the constitution actually says. Here, it is judicial review itself, the very power of the courts to strike down laws as unconstitutional, that is under attack."

Coyne cited a recent editorial from his newspaper that insisted, "If the court fails to reassert the legality of the child pornography law, it will be furthering the [trend] towards judge-made law." And if Parliament didn't invoke the notwithstanding clause in the event the B.C. Court of Appeal upheld Justice Shaw's ruling, the *Post* editorial continued, it would have failed in its obligation "to show that Parliamentary sovereignty is still alive and well."

The *Post* columnist poured scorn on his *confreres*. "For the *National Post*, and for the ultraconservative legal theorists it has adopted and promoted," said Coyne, "the day the Charter of Rights and Freedoms became law, in the words of one, Canada 'surrendered any claim to democratic self-government.' In this definition, the courts are guilty of judicial activism any time they strike down any law . . . It doesn't matter how nutty the law, or how flagrantly it violates the Constitution . . ." Nor was it just so-called judicial activism that the paper opposed, Coyne claimed; worse, "the *Post* doesn't want to limit the Charter's reach: it wants to do away with it. Repeal being unlikely, it demands the next best thing, invocation of the notwithstanding clause – not occasionally, in extreme cases, but routinely, in every case . . . Parliament should do no such thing," he concluded.

While the internal debate raged at the *National Post*, other publications adopted both more sober and more silly postures. The *Vancouver Sun* published a lengthy and thoughtful discussion of the actual if "relatively narrow constitutional question," while at the other extreme, Ted Byfield, publisher of the right-wing *British Columbia Report*, authored a rather histrionic article titled, "Onward, the revolution: how media and government advanced the acceptance of pedophilia." Byfield waxed nostalgic for the bygone days of the mid-twentieth century, when "certainly there were male homosexuals, but their activity was considered a) disgusting or b) ludicrous, or c) both . . . Fast forward five decades," bemoaned Byfield, wondering, "what caused this dumbfounding change" in sexual morality?[7]

As for the man at the centre of the controversy, Robin Sharpe, he was once more before Justice Duncan Shaw. On June 27 he asked Shaw to again postpone his trial on outstanding child pornography charges; Shaw put it off until autumn.

If the Robin Sharpe case had been initially viewed as the unlikely legal manoeuvrings of a stereotypical "dirty old man" or, in the light of Justice Shaw's decision, as merely the eccentric ruling of a minor justice of a provincial supreme court, on June 30, 1999, it took on an entirely different dimension when the B.C. Court of Appeal, by a two to one vote, declared that the simple possession stricture, Section 163.1(4) of the Criminal Code, was "constitutionally overbroad," and that, "accordingly, the Crown's appeal fails."[8]

The main decision striking down the possession offence in the kiddie porn law was written by Madam Justice Mary Southin, with concurring reasons by Madam Justice Anne Rowles and a dissent by Chief Justice Allen McEachern. Southin's decision was strikingly vigorous and plain-spoken, though nonetheless learned in its minute attention to precedent and constitutional nuances.

After noting the charges against Sharpe and the *voir dire* in which Justice Shaw had struck down the possession offence because it wasn't a reasonable limitation of freedom of expression, Southin regretted that the present case didn't deal with all the issues. Since outstanding charges against Sharpe hadn't been heard, it was possible that further challenges would arise. She would have preferred "all issues of constitutionality" arising from Section 163.1 to be "addressed in one appeal."

However, be that as it may, Southin noted that Shaw's decision "generated a great deal of outrage in the media. I infer that many of those who gave vent to their outrage knew nothing whatever of the text of sec. 163.1. What, in their ignorance, they conjured up in their minds was the spectre of a judge giving judicial approval to sexual exploitation of the prepubescent . . . contrary to the will of Parliament," she said in sharp rebuke, making it clear that the court would not be daunted by outside pressures.

Southin then quickly turned to "the meaning of words." Again, she was strictly no-nonsense. "In this judgment, when I myself use the word 'child' . . . I mean those below the age of puberty. I define a 'child' as anyone under the age of 14 years." With that, Southin brushed away a good deal of obfuscation in the child pornography debate. She added, "When I use the term 'adolescent,' I mean anyone between 14 and 18. By 'adult,' I mean anyone over 18."

She then toured the relevant legislation, reciting the texts of the kiddie porn law, the obscenity law, and all the provisions in the Criminal Code concerning sexual activity with children and adolescents – including the section on anal sex, noting that it had been declared unconstitutional by an Ontario court [9] – as well as the pertinent sections of the Constitution. Next, there was a substantial summary of Justice Shaw's decision, and a lengthy review of the evidence that Shaw heard from Detective Waters and Dr. Collins.

Although her verbatim citations from the evidence occupy a good quarter of her judgment, Southin's remarks on it are noticeably sparse. After quoting a sizeable chunk of Detective Waters' testimony to the effect that the possession offence made it easier for the police to stop child pornography, Southin said, "This is an argument that possession laws are an essential element of a successful enforcement strategy against production and distribution." Citing an American judge as a precedent, Southin said, "The argument did not find favour with him and it finds little favour with me, nor is it at all clear that Parliament enacted subsection (4) for that purpose. I do not say that Parliament cannot enact legislation which infringes [freedom of expression] for the purposes of making easier the detection and prosecution of activity which is incontrovertibly criminal. That question is not before us. What I do say is that it ought not to do so unless there is compelling evidence, preferably by reference to actual events, that there is no other practical solution." Southin politely added, "By so commenting, I am not impugning the good faith of Detective Waters in her testimony on this aspect," but it was also clear that the justice was not setting much store by it.

Southin then reviewed Dr. Collins' claims that child pornography is dangerous because it reinforces cognitive distortions, fuels the sexual fantasies of those who possess it, and is used by pedophiles "in what has been called 'grooming children.'" With respect to cognitive distortions, Southin's only comment is in response to the witness's remark: "I don't believe that adults should have sexual relationships with either boys or girls." She replies, "If Dr. Collins had limited his evidence on [cognitive distortions] to children, I would have no difficulty with it. To believe that a child could not only not be harmed by premature sexual conduct, but also take pleasure in it, seems to me an absurdity, and, therefore, a 'cognitive distortion.' But to believe that sexual congress between an adolescent and an adult (who may only be 18) may be a good thing or, at least, is not an unmitigated evil, is not, in modern Canada, in which many adolescents, by their own choice, are not chaste, a 'cognitive distortion.' I may think it would be better if they were [chaste], but that is a matter of morality not reality."

Already it's clear that the direction of Southin's reasoning is to rein in claims that go beyond what's harmful to children, and to dismiss extraneous moral opinions. So, when she cites Dr. Collins on the question of "grooming," she doesn't dispute his claims about prepubescent children, but focusses her concern on "modern adolescents, [who] are in many parts of this country taught about sex in school. Some are no doubt eager to begin, and others not so eager. But they are not generally ignorant . . . [The] proposition Dr. Collins put forward as justification for the legislation encompasses not only the proverbial dirty old man approaching a 10 or 11-year-old, but also the 20-year-old bent on seducing a 17-year-old girl and using a copy of the *Kama Sutra* or any one of a number of salacious magazines for the purpose."

Southin listed the vast array of materials that had been put before the court – everything from the *Badgley* and *Fraser* reports (Canadian reports on sexual offences against children and pornography from the mid-1980s) to a range of recent international legislation. She then addressed the submissions by the various parties and intervenors in the case.

After briefly reprising the Crown's argument for upholding

the law, she ticked off the contributions of the federal government, the Canadian Police Association, and the international children's rights organizations as not being "significantly different . . . from what was said by counsel for the Crown." She observed that the respondent's lawyers did "not assert that Parliament could not craft on this subject a provision which would pass constitutional muster," but rather "they say simply that this section fails the proportionality test." It was the BCCLA argument that appeared to get most of Justice Southin's attention and agreement.

She cited the civil libertarians' factum extensively, quoting several of its passages, including its claim that "Provisions that make it an offence to create, distribute or simply to possess pictures that constitute a record of the actual sexual exploitation of a child or youth are a reasonable limit on freedom of expression." As well, she cited its objections to the "proscription of all sexual images of persons under 18" that may induce criminally exploitative behaviour, because a free society should not "measure the allowable range of expressive freedom by reference to the appetites of the most deviant persons in our community." Noting the BCCLA's claim that it was "not aware of another Canadian criminal law . . . that provides for a sentence of incarceration for the mere possession of expressive material," she quoted the entire argument centring on the notion that "state efforts to coerce individuals into holding or abandoning thoughts, beliefs or opinions – no matter how evil or repugnant they may be if acted upon – are the hallmarks of a totalitarian society." She also directly quoted the civil libertarians' whole account of the overbreadth of the possession offence, demurring only on the issue of whether the advocacy of sexual crimes clause prevented debate of such issues as the age of consent.

Southin reviewed the lower court's "findings of fact" and the legislative history of the kiddie porn law. Although she saw no need to agree or disagree with Justice Shaw's findings, she noted that most of the social science findings about harm appeared to be "more a matter of opinion than fact," and that social scientists and psychiatrists like Dr. Collins "are not men from Mars observing the world and recording what they see from a vantage point of pure detachment. Nor, for that matter, are judges," she added. The only one of Justice Shaw's findings that she underscored was his factual declaration that "children are abused in the production of filmed or videotaped pornography," because "I hold the opinion that it is morally wrong to use children, as I define that term, for sexual purposes, in which I include the production of erotica."[10]

Turning to Section 1 of the Charter, which might justify the kiddie porn law's infringement of constitutionally protected freedom of expression, she noted that although it contained "only 20 words," nonetheless they admitted of a wide range of interpretation. Focussing on whether the limit on freedom created by a possession offence could be justified, she returned to the BCCLA's claim that it was unaware of any other Canadian law that made "mere possession of expressive material" a crime punishable with a jail term.

In fact there was such a law, she pointed out, displaying the diligence of her research. It was an order-in-council passed during the First World War to prevent the "circulation of objectionable matter." The "objectionable matter" included a range of unfavourable statements questioning the government's motives for participating in the war, and the prohibition included having such matter in one's possession. But rather than citing this law as undercutting the BCCLA's claim, she instead used it to underscore such a statute's exceptional character. In the Second World War there were similar regulations, but "in even more fearful circumstances, simple possession of subversive materials was not made a crime . . . Other than the 1914 order in council, I know of no Canadian legislation except the section here in issue which has ever made the simple possession of any expressive material a crime. It is not a crime to possess expressive material which advocates genocide, it is not a crime to possess expressive material which is seditious, and it is not a crime to possess that which is obscene."

Having endorsed the point about the extreme rarity of such a law, Southin pressed on. "Since the great case of *Entick v. Carrington* (1765), a man's personal thoughts, opinions, expressions and beliefs as disclosed by his books and papers have been thought immune from intrusion," she said. "There is good reason for such freedom from intrusion being a profound constitutional value. This has been the century of the Gestapo and the KGB – of a state encouraging betrayal by children of their parents to the authorities, of smashing down doors and burning books, all in the name of some concept of the greater good. Even if the possession of material which advocates or counsels crime may lead to the inference that the possessor has bad thoughts and thence to the conclusion that he might or even will commit the crime thus advocated, it is not within our political ethic to make possession itself a crime. It is that notion which goes deep in our history which is at the root of the requirement that proof of treason requires proof of an overt act."

This is a remarkably resonant passage. It is a ringing endorsement of a conception of democracy seldom articulated in Canadian institutions. The conclusion towards which Southin was heading could not be plainer.

"I conclude, therefore, that legislation which makes simple possession of expressive materials a crime can never be a reasonable limit in a free and democratic society. Such legislation bears the hallmark of tyranny," Southin said. "In so concluding, I am not rejecting the concession of counsel that the protection of children from sexual exploitation is a pressing and substantial concern of our society. I am saying that some other way than making simple possession of this sort of material a crime ought to be found to attack it."

For all practical purposes, that constituted Justice Southin's rejection of the Crown's appeal, but there were still some legal issues to be settled, such as the tests of proportionality that might justify the kiddie porn law. After reviewing the relevant precedent cases – primarily *R. v. Keegstra* (1990) and *R. v. Butler* (1992) – Southin observed that this was a rather different case dealing with a rather different piece of statutory law than either the obscenity provision or the "hate speech" that previous courts had considered.

For one thing, subsection (1)(b), the clause that defined child pornography as including materials advocating or counselling a sexual crime, when put in the context of a possession offence, "has about it a most curious aspect. It makes possession of materials which advocate or counsel a certain form of criminal activity a crime, although [actually] counselling or advocating such activity is not itself a crime. It is as if the Criminal Code made it a crime to possess a book which counsels or advocates the overthrow by force or violence of the government, but did not make it a crime to advocate publicly the use of force or violence for such a purpose . . . For this reason alone, section 163.1, when analyzed, has about it an air of unreality."

From there, Justice Southin moved to her formal conclusions. "Whatever the objective of this statute was, I consider subsection (1)(b) in the context of subsection (4) fails the proportionality test . . . a legislative provision which makes criminal the possession of material which advocates certain behaviour when advocating that behaviour publicly is not itself a crime seems to me to lack all reason. That which is not 'reasonable' cannot be a 'reasonable limit.'"

If the advocacy part of the child pornography definition failed, what about the main part of the kiddie porn law's definition in relation to a possession offence? "As I read subsection (a), it does not, for instance, apply to books . . . but, as Mr. Peck pointed out, it would cover the case of an 18-year-old taking salacious photographs of his 17-year-old girlfriend," Southin said, adding, "The subsection would be less troubling if it were confined to persons under the age of 14 years."

Southin once more returned to the BCCLA claims of over-breadth and again quoted the passages presented by John McAlpine, the organization's lawyer, which argued that the main definition of child pornography in the law, "first, is overly broad by capturing the possession of visual images of the sexuality of children and young persons that are purely the products of their creators' imaginations and involve no children or youth in its production," and "second, [the definition] overreaches by including all pictures that record explicit acts involving youth or young adults who are or appear to be aged 14 to 17. Many sexual acts engaged in by persons who are or appear to be aged 14 to 17 are perfectly legal and are not defined as sexual exploitation by the Criminal Code. This overbreadth even extends to capture possession of pictures of one's own legal sexual activity."

Referring to the BCCLA counsel, Southin succinctly said, "I agree with him. Thus, as this legislation stands at present, it does not survive the proportionality test. For these reasons, which differ to some extent from those of [Justice Rowles], I would dismiss this appeal."

There was little ambiguity and considerable passion in Justice Southin's decision. In many ways, it went even beyond the lower court's ruling, definitively rejecting almost every aspect of the possession offence and firmly dismissing every counterargument defending it.

Madame Justice Anne Rowles' reasons for judgment concurred with Justice Southin's decision – thus producing a majority vote against the law – but differed in emphasis and tone. Justice Rowles' approach was not only more modulated, but more legally "traditional" in its careful step-by-step weighing of the proportionality of the law's virtues against its infringement of constitutional freedoms.

"The issue on this appeal is not whether Parliament was justified in enacting legislation to protect children," she began. "The contentious question is whether one of the provisions in the legislative scheme enacted for that purpose is unconstitutionally overbroad." Rowles turned immediately to judicial precedent on the concept of constitutional overbreadth. Her authority was Supreme Court of Canada Justice Cory, who explained in *R. v. Heywood* (1994), "Overbreadth analysis looks at the means chosen by the state in relation to its purpose. In considering whether a provision is overbroad, a court must ask the question: are those means necessary to achieve the State objective? If the State, in pursuing a legitimate objective, uses means which are broader than is necessary to accomplish that objective, the principles of fundamental justice will be violated because the individual's rights will have been limited for no reason. The effect of overbreadth is that in some applications the law is arbitrary or disproportionate."

Rowles reviewed the legislation, underlining the possession offence as the crux of the case, and citing the appropriate sections of the Charter of Rights to highlight the main legal question: "Accordingly, the arguments on the appeal focused on whether the violation [of the Charter] is justified under section 1."

She also reviewed the "Oakes test" and all the subsequent case law which refined it, citing *Vriend v. Alberta* (1998) as the most recent and relevant. This is familiar territory, but it's worth spelling out one more time: "A limitation to a constitutional guarantee will be sustained once two conditions are met. First, the objective of the legislation must be pressing and substantial. Second, the means chosen to attain this legislative end must be reasonable and demonstrably justifiable in a free and democratic society. In order to satisfy the second requirement, three criteria must be satisfied: (1) the rights violation must be rationally connected to the aim of the legislation; (2) the impugned provision must minimally impair the Charter guarantee; and (3) there must be a proportionality between the effect of the measure and its objective so that the attainment of the legislative goal is not outweighed by the abridgement of the right. In all section 1 cases, the burden of proof is with the government to show on a balance of probabilities that the violation is justifiable."

Having set out the terms, Rowles then proceeded to connect the dots. The first question about the pressing and substantial objective of the legislation was the easiest to answer. Almost everyone, including Rowles, agreed that it was. She felt it "important to reiterate that Parliament had a valid legislative objective in enacting [the kiddie porn law]," and then went slightly further, to indicate her agreement with the Crown that Parliament's valid objective extended "beyond the prevention of direct harm to children which results from their involvement in the production of child pornography."

In looking at whether the means chosen to attain the legislative objective were reasonable and demonstrably justified, Rowles took a more conservative view than Southin had, accepting the idea that expression can be further from or closer to the "core values" protected by the Charter. While agreeing that "child pornography does not lie close to the core of protected expression," she nonetheless repeated the caution of Supreme Court of Canada Justice Beverley McLachlin: "We must be careful not to allow the discussion of context to pre-empt the analysis itself. To allow the perceived low value of the expression to lower the bar of justification from the outset of the section 1 analysis is to run the risk that a judge's subjective conclusion that the expression at issue is of little worth may undermine the intellectual rigour of the *Oakes* test."

With that, Rowles turned to the crucial proportionality analysis, in turn examining the rational connection between the legislative objective and the law, the issue of minimal impairment of rights, and the "proportionality between the deleterious effects and the salutary effects" of the challenged law, the "weighing of effects" test that Justice Shaw had emphasized in his decision.

The law doesn't have to be "perfect," Rowles reminded everyone. Further, even though social science research about indirect harm to children may be "inconclusive," all that has to be established, she said, is a "reasoned apprehension of harm." In her view, therefore, the law passed the "rational connection" test. "The problem with [the possession offence], if there is one, must lie in its potential overreach."

Sharpe's lawyers, she observed, had conceded that the criminal law can and should prohibit simple possession of kiddie porn using actual children, but claimed that the possession offence was overbroad and therefore caused more than "minimal impairment" of fundamental rights. Rowles then returned to overbreadth as a topic, again citing precedents, but now going further to establish that it was valid for a court to use hypothetical examples, such as the ones raised by Sharpe's lawyer, Richard Peck, to test the law. "The problem of overbreadth, like that of vagueness," she said, "is of particular importance where a statutory provision is found to violate freedom of expression because of the chilling effect such a law could have . . . Reasonable hypothetical examples serve to illustrate the unintended reach and potential effect of such a provision."

Rowles now homed in on the possession offence because the "respondent's overbreadth argument is directed solely to s. 163.1(4)." She added, "This point cannot be over-emphasized," and cited the BCCLA's claim that it was unaware of any other Canadian law that made mere possession of expression materials a crime. She also cited all the previous cases which pointed out that Parliament was concerned not to intrude on the privacy of individuals.

"The impugned law makes private possession of expressive material a criminal offence," Rowles declared unequivocally. "Making it an offence to possess expressive material when that material may have been created without abusing children and may never be published, distributed or sold, constitutes an extreme invasion of the values of liberty, autonomy and privacy" protected by the Constitution. Since the possession offence can make it a crime to record one's own thoughts or to create works of one's imagination, it "profoundly violates freedom of expression." It was gradually becoming clear that, in Rowles' view, the law would have trouble passing the "minimal impairment" test.

In almost microscopic fashion, Rowles looked at all the possible aspects of overbreadth, agreeing with Sharpe's lawyers that the possession offence captured "materials which cannot be said to pose any danger to children," that it extended to works "which do not involve the participation of any actual child," and that the inclusion of written material was "particularly troublesome." Even taking into account a notion of indirect harm, said Rowles, "given the lack of social science evidence regarding the effects of works of the imagination, a court should be reluctant to draw [the] inference" that such materials cause harm. Worse, the possession offence "applies with equal force to the very persons it is purportedly designed to protect," namely, people under eighteen.

At this point, Rowles raised some hypothetical examples to show that "the difficulties with the impugned legislation are the product of the interaction and combination of these various aspects of overbreadth, and the full extent of the difficulties is not apparent until this interaction is considered." Among her examples: a sexual drawing of someone under eighteen which is never shown to anyone; a crude drawing of a breast of someone under eighteen; a married couple between fourteen and seventeen who recorded their own lawful sexual activity and never showed it to anyone; "a narcissistic 17 year old youth . . . if he simply took an erotic nude photograph of himself and kept it in his private possession"; even "a diary entry," never shown to anyone, which advocated sexual offences with a person under eighteen. All of those would be criminally liable.

And such examples, declared Justice Rowles, "illustrate the degree to which section 163.1(4) is truly only one step removed from criminalizing simply having objectionable thoughts. The Charter should never, or perhaps only where the most pressing need is demonstrated, permit the state to regulate an individual's private recorded thoughts, no matter how objectionable those thoughts may be." She cited the now familiar BCCLA fear of the spectre of totalitarianism and concluded, "The impugned legislation cannot be shown to minimally impair freedom of expression."

While that was enough to reject the Crown's appeal, Rowles added that it was also her view that, "in addition to failing at the minimal impairment stage, the impugned legislation would also fail for want of proportionality between its salutary and deleterious effects." As Justice Shaw had done earlier, Rowles cited the

Supreme Court of Canada's reformulation of the last stage of the proportionality test in the *Dagenais v. CBC* case, and like Justice Shaw, she concluded that the detrimental effects on freedom of expression and personal privacy were simply too great to justify the law. The possession offence, she formally concluded, "does not meet the proportionality test under the section 1 Charter analysis, and is constitutionally overbroad. Accordingly, the Crown's appeal fails." Admittedly, much of Justice Rowles' analysis is quite technical and fine-grained, but it's important because it anticipates exactly the sort of considerations that the Supreme Court of Canada would likely have to make when the Sharpe case reached its chambers.

The dissenting judgment in the two to one vote was provided by Chief Justice McEachern. He promised, given that the "case has attracted wide public interest, . . . to explain my decision in the plainest possible language," and noted that since it had been conceded by the lawyers for the respondent that "possession of some kinds of child pornography should be unlawful," that the case was now a somewhat different one from that decided by Justice Shaw. Its focus was the question of overbreadth.

Like his colleagues, McEachern reviewed the law, the evidence presented, and Justice Shaw's decision, especially his weighing of beneficial and detrimental effects of the possession offence. He disagreed with Shaw on two points: first, in recognizing as a fact that "children are abused in the production of filmed or videotaped pornography," the trial judge didn't give enough attention to the prospect that a possession offence helps reduce the market for child pornography, and thus aids in protecting children from the abuse of making such pornography; second, and related, in recognizing that children are harmed in the production of kiddie porn, the trial judge didn't give sufficient weight to the abuse done to children in such productions. "In my judgment, the inadequate weight given to these factors in the judge's analysis constitutes legal error that is sufficiently serious to permit us to undertake our own independent assessment of these competing factors," McEachern decided.

The chief justice then turned to the various parts of the proportionality test. As did his colleagues, he concluded that the legislation was "rationally connected" to the objectives aimed at, even though there had been substantial last-minute amendments to the law. "I am not prepared to second-guess Parliament on either the scope of the definition it chose . . . or on the prohibition of simple possession," he said.

Where McEachern disagreed not only with Justice Shaw, but also with his Appeal Court colleagues was on the questions of "minimal interference" and the "weighing of effects." For the chief justice, the fact that the simple possession of expressive materials in this instance could lead to "cognitive distortions," or "get accidentally passed around," constituted a sufficient danger of harm to children. As for the substantial impairment of rights that the other judges saw, McEachern doubted that they greatly mattered. "The fact that some anomalies may arise is not fatal," he said. "In this case they are very remote and likely to arise very infrequently." That is, rights might be more than minimally impaired on rare occasions, but that was acceptable "considering the infinite varieties of child pornography, the many different ways it can be created and used, and the harm Parliament believes it causes to children." Thus, the possession offence, in his view, met the minimal impairment test.

Finally, and this is perhaps the prime legal point of interest in his dissent, Justice McEachern asserted, "There is, in my view, a distinction between private thoughts and thoughts recorded, which Parliament has recognized." He duly noted the importance of the protection of "the privacy of our citizens" and admitted "that the definition we are considering could criminalize some conduct that does not present a serious risk of harm to children."

But again, he thought such instances would be "very rare" and that the material involved was "so far removed from the core values of the Charter" that "the general right of our citizens to the privacy of their lives is threatened hardly at all by this definition." Parliament, said McEachern, "has considered it necessary . . . to require that anyone who imagines or muses about sex with children refrain from recording or possessing such material lest it get into the wrong hands and cause harm to children." Thus, the benefits of the possession offence, in his view, outweighed the detriment caused to "extremely few persons." McEachern ruled that he would allow the appeal, "set aside the acquittals, and direct that the trial [of Sharpe] proceed on all" the original charges.

McEachern's dissent did not attract a great deal of attention in the wake of the Appeal Court's majority decision that found the kiddie porn law constitutionally flawed. However, it's important to understand his argument, since it's one that appeals to a significant segment of the general public and to a great many politicians. McEachern is saying, yes, free expression is generally important in a democracy, but not so important when it comes to something that might harm children, such as kiddie porn. He's also saying, yes, you have the right to think what you want, but you don't necessarily have the right to write down what you want, especially in the case of certain material such as child pornography.

Of course, that's not good enough for civil libertarians, and it wasn't good enough for his colleagues on the Appeal Court bench. There's a temptation to accuse McEachern of not really respecting freedom of speech at all – especially in the light of much recent history where violating the prohibition on recording one's thoughts has proven fatal – but that overstates it. What there is, is a difference of opinion about how important freedom of expression is in all instances. For Justice McEachern, there are occasions when it's simply not that important; for Justices Southin and Rowles, there are no occasions when the sanctity of a citizen's thinking, beliefs, and expression should be breached by the state.

While dissenting opinions don't have any formal significance in the ruling of a given court, such dissent justifies a higher court's acceptance of a further appeal, and the dissenting opinion of a lower court judge is not only read by the higher court, but may find itself transformed into the majority opinion of that higher court.

On Canada Day 1999, the country was greeted with news of the B.C. Court of Appeal's decision declaring part of the kiddie porn law unconstitutional. If the first decision in favour of Robin Sharpe provoked immediate roars of outrage, the second decision against the kiddie porn law yielded a more diffuse, even puzzled, response. "Am I the only one who has that nightmarish feeling of sitting in a vast lecture hall, completely unprepared for the exam and buck naked?" asked one bewildered columnist, gazing at the questions raised by the Appeal Court decision.

If most everyone had initially thought – perhaps without much considered thought – that *R. v. Sharpe* was an obvious and easily decided case, it was now clear that two levels of the Canadian judiciary had decided otherwise. Was it possible that there was indeed something seriously wrong with the child pornography law Parliament had passed?

The *Globe and Mail* reported that the B.C. Court of Appeal had, according to legal experts, "struck down a poorly crafted law."

The expert cited by the newspaper was law professor Bruce Ryder of York University's Osgoode Hall law school – one of the principal authors of the B.C. Civil Liberties Association's brief – who said that the appeal court ruling recognized an "unprecedented feature" of the kiddie porn law, namely, that it made it an offence to possess material that is an expression of one's own thoughts. "That is close to thought control, it's the hallmark of a totalitarian society, not a free and democratic society," Ryder said.

"One of the most frustrating aspects of the whole debate," Ryder noted, "is that no one disagrees, pornographic pictures involving children in production are evil and ought to be suppressed. But [the kiddie porn law] goes far beyond that. The flaw in the legislation is so obvious to anyone who takes the time to read it. The law was drafted carelessly and in haste, and is too broad to accomplish its objective."[11]

Outside the courtroom, Sharpe's lawyer, Richard Peck, told reporters, "The problem with this legislation was that it was overly broad. This case is about my rights, your rights, our collective rights."

Along with the reports of the decision and the comments of various participants came B.C. Attorney General Dosanjh's announcement, within an hour of the ruling, that he would appeal the judgment to the Supreme Court of Canada. "I think it's important that the ultimate arbiter of these kinds of issues . . . speak on this very important issue," he said. In Ottawa, a disappointed Justice minister, Anne McLellan, in announcing that the federal government would join B.C. in vigorously arguing the case at the Supreme Court, said, "One thing is absolutely clear for us as a government: we believe the protection of children in this country is a paramount value."

However, the parliamentary opposition wanted the government to go much further. The Reform Party called on Prime Minister Jean Chretien to bring MPs back to Ottawa from their summer break to hold an emergency session of Parliament to overrule the court decision. Reform leader Preston Manning sounded the alarm. "I believe that parents and grandparents across the country are appalled by the decision . . . which in effect puts the demands of adults to possess child pornography ahead of the protection of children," he said. He also had harsh words for Justice Minister McLellan. "She faithfully insisted that if you let the B.C. Appeal Court do its work, that it would put the protection of children from pornography ahead of any other demand. Now she has been proven dead wrong. We don't think you can wait for a further appeal now." Manning was seconded by B.C. Reform MP John Reynolds. "When Parliament disagrees with the courts, it's their right to use the [notwithstanding clause], and I think right now it's their duty. For all intents and purposes, the court has given license to pedophiles," he said.

The government also had the option of introducing new legislation that could pass constitutional muster. But that would contravene the long-standing and sensible convention that once a law is under scrutiny by the judiciary, Parliament ought to wait until the courts have finished their business. Both Chretien and McLellan attempted to offer reassurances. "The government of British Columbia will appeal to the Supreme Court," said the prime minister. "We'll have to let due process take place." Added McLellan, "There are those out there who will choose to alarm people unnecessarily, but let me be absolutely clear that the laws in this country in relation to production, distribution [and] importation [of child pornography] continue to be in full force."[12]

Among those unmollified by the government's reassurance was the Canadian Family Action Association. Its national affairs director, Peter Stock, demanded that Justice Southin be fired. "Canadians from coast to coast are outraged at this court's decision."

As had occurred during the reaction to Justice Shaw's decision, the legal community stepped in to defend Justice Southin, a 1952 University of British Columbia law school graduate, who had been a member of the appeal court since 1988. "She is considered here to be a respected, hard-working judge who has what I would call a scholarly approach to the law," said Tom Woods, editor of *The Advocate*, a Vancouver law review. "She has a very direct manner, and a very direct way of expressing herself. She is not known to back down." Another Vancouver lawyer, David Roberts, who had known Southin for over four decades, said in defence of her decision in the Sharpe case, "I think that this decision shows a fair amount of intellectual integrity because she certainly would not take kindly to child pornography. She would abhor it. But she had the courage to decide what she perceives as right, in light of the Charter [of Rights], whether she likes it or not."[13]

Media commentary on the decision was prompt and intense. In a front-page opinion piece, *National Post* reporter Mark Hume said, "In a less sensitive age, Robin Sharpe would have been called a dirty old man, and sent to jail. Today, thanks to the courts of British Columbia, he is a crusader for human rights." Hume sounded like he would have preferred "a less sensitive age." He recited the various hypothetical examples of who might be captured by the law, which the court had invoked, and argued that the court "drew on examples that seemed absurd when compared to the realities of child molestation." Those examples were not what parliamentarians had been thinking about, he insisted. "What parliamentarians were thinking about were children. They were thinking about little kids who are sexually abused," Hume dramatically claimed, although obviously without benefit of the inside story of how the law had been crafted. He granted that the law might "not be perfect," but added, "In her judgment, Judge Southin says judges aren't from Mars. Sometimes, you have to wonder."[14]

The *Vancouver Province* had a less charged view of the matter. It recalled Justice Duncan Shaw. "Not long ago, Canadians ganged up on the then low-profile judge . . . Turns out, Shaw was right." The tabloid paper cited Justice Southin's view, quoted from the BCCLA brief, that "such a blanket law 'bears the hallmarks of tyranny,'" and stated its agreement with Southin and the BCCLA. It also offered some practical advice to MPs: "Ottawa legislators need to get back to the drawing board and write it right: ban material that directly supports the exploitation of kids in the porn industry, such as photos, videos, anything that uses real children, and leave the make-believe, distasteful as it is, alone."

The *Province*'s civic counterpart, the *Vancouver Sun*, was considerably more cautious. "Child pornography is repugnant and it is intolerable that the Criminal Code section concerning possession of child pornography is in confusion," wrote its editorialist, citing Justice McEachern's dissent as the only court opinion worth quoting. Its bottom line, however, was no different than what the BCCLA urged: "We believe that possession of photographs, videotapes and depictions of sexual abuse of real children must be a crime."[15]

Perhaps the most thoughtful of all the editorials was the one in the *Ottawa Citizen*, crisply headed "Too sweeping." "British Columbia's court of appeal has gone a long way towards explaining what's wrong with Canada's child pornography laws," began the *Citizen*. "If hysteria-mongers don't drown it out with ridiculous scenarios of pedophiles running amok, the court's views on possession of kiddie porn may prompt some badly needed debate on free expression." The newspaper didn't think that the judges got it exactly right, "but they have identified flaws in the Criminal Code that go beyond the highly charged issue of child pornography." The *Citizen* urged, "What the law should say was best summed up by the civil liberties association: 'Provisions that make it an offence to create, distribute or simply to possess pictures that constitute a record of the actual sexual exploitation of a child or a youth are a reasonable limit on freedom of expression.' That is what the Criminal Code should say. If the court gets the justice minister any closer to clarifying this point, then it has strengthened both children's rights and free expression."[16]

The public debate, which was voluminous, expectedly had its extremes of rhetoric, but intelligent editorializing and commentary generally outweighed name-calling in the pages of most of the country's mainstream publications. As George Jonas summed up the discussion, "one needn't approve of the sexual tastes" of pedophiles "to acknowledge that the current law on child pornography is noxious and dumb. This is why the B.C. Court of Appeal found it unconstitutional . . . To their credit, the media have begun to see this. The *Toronto Star*'s Richard Gwyn wrote that the law is 'disgracefully badly drafted.' The *National Post*'s Jonathan Kay convincingly outlined why the law isn't only one step removed from Orwellian thought control, but actually amounts to thought control."

Those who didn't see it that way, Jonas argued, were legislators on both the liberal and conservative sides of the spectrum. They "know full well it's thought control; they just don't give a damn. There have always been people who couldn't understand why George Orwell was going on so about the thought police. They've viewed Big Brother's ability to control 'wrongthink' as quite admirable. There are people who cherish the thought police, provided it only restricts ideas or tastes of which they disapprove. They include right-wingers and left-wingers." All of this was unnecessary, Jonas pointed out, since "the law could be remedied by restricting it to the possession of pornographic photos or videos prepared with the involvement of children under 14."[17]

The same day as Jonas's article appeared, Crown counsel Geoffrey Gaul, spokesman for the B.C. Attorney General's ministry, announced, "The Crown filed its notice of appeal in the Supreme Court of Canada." Not everybody was happy about that. The vice-president of the conservative REAL Women of Canada group, Gwen Landolt, didn't think much of the highest court in the land. "Basically, the Supreme Court will go whichever way the wind is shifting," she said. "Our whole social agenda is in the hands of ideologues who even outguess themselves at times." But BCCLA president Craig Jones welcomed the chance for the issue to be settled. "We think parliament should enact a new law that is constitutional," said Jones. "We are glad that it's going up to the Supreme Court of Canada because it's obviously a question of national concern and the court needs to speak out on it."[18]

In early autumn, the Supreme Court of Canada set January 18, 2000 – a winter day in the new millennium – as the date it would hear the final appeal in *R. v. Sharpe*.

FIVE

At the Supreme Court of Canada

If the wheels of justice in the Robin Sharpe case would grind with magisterial slowness at the Supreme Court of Canada – partly, as we'll see, due to significant personnel changes within the court – the media and politicians continued spinning their wheels at the usual speed during the latter half of 1999.

The Supreme Court's announcement that it would hear *R. v. Sharpe* in January 2000, rather than "fast-tracking" the case onto its fall agenda, spurred the Reform Party into renewed action, which in turn put additional political pressure on federal Justice minister Anne McLellan. Instead of reading the court's normal scheduling procedures as a sign that the uncertain constitutional status of one section of the child pornography law didn't presage a national emergency, some politicians found it an occasion to whip up public sentiment.

"Our children are at risk," declared Alberta Reform MP Ken Epp upon learning of the Supreme Court's schedule. Noting that it often takes six months or more for a Supreme Court ruling,

Epp said that West Coast porn purveyors would have a lengthy open season during the wait for a final decision on the constitutionality of the kiddie porn law. The Justice minister's failure to take decisive action to protect children was immoral, the MP charged. "Anne's asleep at the switch . . . The gates are open," said Epp. "I have four grandkids. When I think of anyone using any one of them as a sexual toy, either in pictures or reality, I am very, very upset. I think the Liberals, and particularly the justice minister, are acting in an extremely immoral fashion by not doing anything about this."[1]

If Epp's comments represented the more inflammatory extreme of political rhetoric, McLellan was also hearing criticism from her own caucus. In mid-October 1999, just as the autumn parliamentary session was getting underway with a throne speech that included promises of a "children's agenda," Liberal MPs Paul Steckle and Dan McTeague urged the government caucus to use the notwithstanding clause to outlaw possession of kiddie porn.

"This is an issue that goes right to the heart and soul of people in this country," said Steckle. "I think it should have been a companion to what we did for families on the child issue," he said, referring to throne speech measures to combat child poverty in Canada. "You can't have a children's agenda without being able to make sure there are safeguards in place to ensure children are not molested by economic deprivation or the kind of deprivation perpetrated by individuals who are trying to manipulate laws to their own advantage." Other Liberals disagreed. B.C. MP Lou Sekora said the government would be wrong to use the notwithstanding clause, despite the uproar. "The decision has to come down from the Supreme Court. I think that's the best way to do it, have the decision made forever and a day," Sekora said.[2]

The next day, Justice Minister McLellan refused to budge in the face of questions in the House and a dramatic display at the doors of Parliament. Alberta Reform MP Eric Lowther, the party's family issues critic, and Darrel Reid, the former chief of staff of Reform leader Preston Manning and now president of Focus on the Family, a Christian "family values" lobby group, appeared for a photo opportunity in front of Parliament, along with a cart full of petitions signed by 150,000 Canadians urging the government to overturn the two court rulings on child pornography.

Inside the House, Lowther tabled the petitions. "If this isn't cause to step up to the notwithstanding clause, I don't know what is," he later told reporters. Citing other court cases on hold because of the unsettled status of the law, Lowther said, "Canadians are outraged by this government's unwillingness to uphold the law against child pornography. How many more concerned Canadians will it take for this government to protect our kids?" he asked the Justice minister.

McLellan replied that the Reform MPs were exaggerating the effect of the B.C. case. "Let me say that our friends on the other side are scaremongers," the Justice minister charged. "What they suggest is that there are no pornography laws in force in this country. In fact, it is against the law in this country to produce child pornography, to distribute it, to sell it, and to import it . . . Police investigations continue. Charges are being laid."

But outside the Commons, lobbyist Reid and MP Lowther, as one reporter put it, unwittingly provided support for "McLellan's contention that Canadians are being led to believe there are no laws against child pornography."

Said Reid, "You members of the media, you're pretty hard-bitten, you're dealing with a lot of cynical issues here. I come from British Columbia where child pornography is now legal. I'm concerned for my kids. If legislators will not protect our children, who will?" When one reporter reminded Reid that production, distribution, sale, and importation weren't affected by the Sharpe rulings, the Focus on the Family president retorted, "I don't think it's very easy to draw a distinction between possessing child pornography and the production of child pornography. I don't think the 12-year-old children used for these purposes draw any distinction."[3]

It was not only federal politicians who contributed to the sound and fury. Less than a week after the debate in Parliament, the province of Manitoba announced it would exercise the automatic right available to provinces to intervene whenever the Supreme Court is asked to consider constitutional issues.

Before it was over, B.C. and the federal government would be joined by provincial representatives from Ontario, Quebec, Nova Scotia, New Brunswick, Alberta, and Manitoba as intervenors in the case. "As a government," said Ontario attorney general Jim Flaherty, "we have a responsibility to do everything we can to protect society's most vulnerable members, that is, our children, from the harm of sexual exploitation." Flaherty's decision to intervene – the first time Ontario had done so in more than a decade – was backed by the province's premier, Mike Harris. "We support the law that gives the police the tools they need to arrest and to prosecute those who exploit children through pornography. In the interests of children we believe it is important that we defend this law," he said.[4]

Meanwhile, back in Vancouver, Robin Sharpe was the focus of a local literary dustup. Whatever responsibility he bore for being in the legal spotlight, this minor *contretemps* was created through no fault of his own. Sharpe merely accepted an invitation to participate in a panel discussion on September 30, 1999, sponsored by the Small Press Action Network, a non-profit group supporting independent publishers. As part of its three-day festival "Generous Margins," the group was hosting a panel titled "Sex,

Drugs and the Law: Pushing the Boundaries," to be held at the downtown Vancouver campus of Simon Fraser University.

In short order, the usual suspects were under fire, along with the man charged with child pornography offences. The university was required to defend its decision to provide space for the panel discussion. "The space was provided by the university because the university supports the reasoned discussion of issues of concern to responsible citizens," said a Simon Fraser spokeswoman, who added that "it should not be taken that the university endorses the controversial nature of the presenters or their material." The organizer of the festival assured all and sundry that "we're not taking these emotions lightly that people have," and said he was beefing up security for the event.

B.C. Reform MP Randy White announced that he was wary about the "soapbox" the panel would provide Sharpe. Naming a notorious convicted murderer, White said, "I guess I don't see much difference in this and asking Paul Bernardo to come out of prison and talk about what makes a sick, sexually molesting psycho." In an effort to display fair-mindedness, the Reform House Opposition leader added, "I'm trying to balance myself between complete distaste for this person and the right of the public to debate these issues." The *National Post* was up in arms, as well. "The seminar, held rent-free at British Columbia's Simon Fraser University, was sponsored by a fringe group that receives thousands of dollars from the Canada Council — that is, from taxpayers," fumed the paper's editorial. "It is one thing for Ottawa's Liberals to countenance pedophiles by permitting this dangerous court decision to stand . . . but it is another thing to actively fund and promote Sharpe, by paying for a platform for his views."[5]

All of this would barely merit mention but for the extreme level of vitriol. Even MP White's remarks, which otherwise might be dismissed as political rhetoric, were extraordinary in their vituperation. The *Post*'s editorial, inaccurately and sensationally headlined "Pedophile gets a grant," bordered on irresponsibility. Disguised as a protest against misappropriation of public funds, it was not hard to read in it a demand that Sharpe be silenced.

Behind the theatrical scenes of petitions and polemics, there was a more serious and interesting discussion of the issues taking place through the last months of 1999 as the various parties and intervenors submitted their briefs to the Supreme Court. Even with all the interventions – some fifteen in addition to the briefs of the appellant and respondent in the case – the January 2000 hearings at the Supreme Court of Canada promised to be somewhat anti-climactic, given that the main arguments had already been heard. However, it is interesting to examine the way in which arguments were subtly refashioned and emphasized in light of the decisions of the lower-level courts.

The appellant's brief of the B.C. government, for example, filed at the beginning of October 1999, urged the court to take account of the will of the public and politicians. "The court must be mindful of the concerns of the community as a whole expressed by our legislators," said the B.C. government's sixty-page submission. John Gordon, the Crown attorney arguing the case, warned that it was not the role of the courts to overturn the will of Parliament. "I'm not suggesting that the courts take a hands-off stance because of the public clamour," Gordon said. "I'm suggesting that it's a parliamentary function to make social policy and criminal law decisions in areas such as this."[6]

The B.C. Civil Liberties Association filed its intervenor's brief at the end of the year, on December 30, 1999. Given that it presented the most comprehensive argument against the child porn law that the Supreme Court heard – and that it covered ground similar to that canvassed by Sharpe's lawyers and the Canadian

Civil Liberties Association in their submissions to the court – it's worth examining the latest refinements in the BCCLA's thinking.

Notwithstanding the overwrought claims of Reform politicians and various "pro-family" and anti-crime organizations that opponents of the law were advocating a child-endangering pornographic free-for-all, the moderate civil libertarians began their argument by accepting the idea that "the Charter poses no constitutional obstacle to the criminalization of the possession of photographs, films, [or] videos that involve the sexual exploitation of children or youth in their production. The making of such pictures involves the commission of a criminal offence, and their possession and distribution represents a continuing, serious violation of the dignity of the children or youth employed in their production."[7] The BCCLA fully recognized that the prevention of exploitation of children was a state objective of "pressing and substantial importance." Thus, "a possession offence limited to pictures involving harm in their production would constitute a minimal and proportional impairment of [free speech] and privacy rights." If Parliament had written such a law, there wouldn't be an argument about constitutional validity, the brief asserted.

However, the definition of child pornography in the law "extends well beyond pictures produced through the actual exploitation of children or youth," the association said. Further, such "overbreadth is particularly problematic in the context of a simple possession offence." The civil libertarians rejected the Crown's worry that possession of the images of the legal, consensual activity of youth aged fourteen to seventeen "may induce criminally exploitative behaviour in pedophiles. Against this line of argument, we respectfully submit it is a basic tenet of our political and legal traditions that an offence of simple possession of expressive material cannot be justified only on the basis of apprehended future harm."

The issue of harm had become especially problematic since the *Butler* decision of 1992, when the Supreme Court affirmed that mere perception of harm was now sufficient in law (though in *Butler* the court was referring to distribution and sale of obscene materials, not to simple possession). The BCCLA once more pointed out that "state efforts to coerce individuals into holding or abandoning thoughts, beliefs or opinions . . . are the hallmarks of a totalitarian society." Because of the profound violation of free speech and personal privacy entailed by a possession offence, such a law, argued the BCCLA, "should only be upheld in extraordinary circumstances where the law in question is restricted to preventing direct harm."

The civil libertarians reiterated that they were "not aware of another Canadian criminal law . . . that provides for a sentence of incarceration for the mere possession of expressive material." The problem was "the breadth of the definition of 'child pornography' when coupled with the extraordinary nature of a possession offence."

The law was overbroad in three specific respects. First, it captured the possession of sexual representations "that are purely the product of their creators' imaginations and involve no children or youth in their production." Second, it captured the possession of pictures that recorded completely legal sexual activities of persons aged fourteen to seventeen. Third, the law potentially criminalized young people it purportedly was protecting.

The BCCLA also underscored what it called "the unprecedented nature of the violation" of free speech rights. Although the Criminal Code contains a number of provisions that target expressive activity, "none of them contains a simple possession offence . . . a reflection of the weight accorded to the values of privacy and freedom of thought" in the tradition of democratic societies. The brief cited the observation of Justice Southin of the B.C. Court of Appeal that "unpublished writings cannot constitute the crime of treason." Rather, treasonous ideas have to manifest themselves in treasonous acts before they constitute an offence. "Similarly, the recording of seditious thoughts is not a crime," said the brief. "Likewise, defamatory libel requires publication to a person other than the person defamed . . . The possession of racist or hateful ideas is not a crime, nor is expressing them in private conversation. Possessing materials advocating genocide is not an offence . . . Finally, the simple possession of obscene material is not a crime."

In sum, "the inevitable and serious violations of privacy rights and fundamental freedoms authorized by a possession offence outweigh the speculative risks of future harm. To deprive persons of their physical liberty for recording their 'bad thoughts' on the grounds that their recorded thoughts may pose a risk of future harm to others bears . . . 'the hallmark of tyranny.'"

There was, however, one extraordinary circumstance that civil libertarians were prepared to recognize. "Where 'direct harm' has been caused to children and youth in the production of sexual imagery, and the traditional offences of production, distribution and sale have proven ineffective in combatting the harm in production, then Parliament has an extraordinary rationale that can justify a possession offence."

The BCCLA brief offered this moderate proposal for protecting children and preserving free speech, one that gingerly navigated between the lower court decisions to completely overturn the possession clause, and the demand of right-wing political forces that the possession clause be left absolutely intact. It would be difficult for those who wanted a black-and-white simple solution to a complicated problem to grasp its careful distinctions about harm and the boundaries of free speech, but if any institution might appreciate such distinctions, it would have to be the highest court in the land.

Not only was the Sharpe case a potential landmark in free speech jurisprudence; it also promised to be a weathervane indicating the direction that the Supreme Court would take in coming years. A few days before the hearing on Canada's child pornography law, Justice Beverley McLachlin, a ten-year veteran of the high court, was sworn in at Rideau Hall in Ottawa, the home of Governor-General Adrienne Clarkson, as the first woman chief justice of the Supreme Court of Canada, succeeding retiring chief justice Antonio Lamer.

In an interview before her swearing in, the fifty-six-year-old McLachlin told the press that public pressure would not colour decision-making on the legality of the child pornography possession law.[8] "We will decide the case the way we decide all our cases, in accordance with our understanding of the law," she vowed. However, she wasn't naive about the realities of jurisprudence. "I think it is increasingly acknowledged that judges have to be aware how their decisions are going to play out in the real world. Of course, we're aware that the decision will have a practical effect on society," she said, "but we don't necessarily wake up in the morning and say there's going to be a negative headline if we decide this way, so we won't decide that way. We don't look to what is going to play well in the headlines tomorrow. That is definitely not part of our decision-making process. Our concern is to come up with the right decision."

The day before the opening of the Sharpe case, a ceremony marking McLachlin's elevation to chief justice was held in the Supreme Court, at which fellow justices, law society officials, and the Justice minister offered tributes. McLachlin reminisced about her childhood as a Pincher Creek, Alberta, farmgirl, and for the first time placed emphasis on her gender, recalling that there were no women judges and few women lawyers when she was growing up in Alberta and British Columbia. She also got a laugh when she revealed her discovery of a sub-genre of chief justice jokes on the theme of the powerlessness that the robes of office concealed.

The official photograph taken that day of the new McLachlin-led court displayed the nine justices in their red-and-ermine-trimmed robes. The reconfiguration of the court, in addition to the elevation of McLachlin, included several recent appointments, the most prominent of which were Louise Arbour, former chief prosecutor at the international war crimes tribunal, and former Quebec justice Louis LeBel. The ascension of McLachlin and the others marked one of the court's periodic generational successions, and the Sharpe case would be its first major test.

On Tuesday, January 18, 2000, while a group of fifty or so demonstrators stood outside the Supreme Court on the snow-covered Ottawa sidewalks and waved placards urging the court to uphold the child pornography law, some two dozen lawyers and the sixty-six-year-old defendant, Robin Sharpe, trooped into the crowded courtroom.

As the lawyers and justices waded into the arguments, *National Post* columnist Christie Blatchford was struck by the sight of two men, sitting side by side in the front row of the public gallery, "who have come to represent for many Canadians the very forces of good and evil." They were Detective Inspector Bob Matthews, the longtime head of the Ontario Provincial Police child pornography unit, who actively pushed for the legislation being argued before the bench, and Robin Sharpe. The journalist saw them both as being very much in character. The policeman, with his "silver-flecked hair," was "beautifully mannered and impeccably attired in a fine navy suit and crisp white shirt . . . Det.-Insp. Matthews could play himself in the movie," she observed, "so whistle-clean and wholesome-handsome is he." As for Sharpe, "he, too, looked and acted every inch his part: he arrived late; dressed shabbily in a brown leather jacket, blue shirt, too short black jeans and camel-coloured vest with a hole in it; he alternately rolled his eyes in disdain, fell asleep, and for a time actually picked his nose in court."[9]

But beyond the fashion reviews, bits of human-interest colour, and invidious comparisons, once the lawyers began presenting alternate visions of what was at stake, observers like Blatchford shrewdly noted that one of the issues – advanced by Canadian Police Association lawyer Tim Danson, among others – was the question of law enforcement convenience versus freedom of expression. Danson argued that without the law, the police would be lost. The possession clause gave police the necessary "foot in the door" that might lead them to more serious crimes, he said. Like the judges, who challenged many assertions of the various lawyers, Blatchford asked, "But since when are laws driven by their usefulness to police? And is a bad law rendered good merely because cops like it?"

The two-day hearing of the case offered a wide array of similar claims and counterarguments. "This legislation is thought control," said Sharpe's lawyer, Richard Peck, citing George Orwell's futuristic novel, *Nineteen Eighty-Four*. "We are there," he declared. When challenged during his presentation by Justice Charles Gonthier, Peck replied that a democratic society must permit citizens a "zone of privacy" where their thoughts and creations are protected. "The minute the state infringes that zone by telling me what I can and cannot write to myself – that I cannot possess a photograph of myself or a drawing I have made –

then that zone, that bubble, has been burst . . . I defy the state to do that," said Peck.[10]

The press noted that the argument presented by Sharpe's lawyers put counsel and client somewhat at odds. While lawyers Peck and McKinnon argued that the definition of child pornography was far too broad, they were willing to make a distinction that appeared to differ significantly from Sharpe's views on the matter. Peck and McKinnon proposed distinguishing between so-called Category A and Category B materials. They defined Category A materials as sexual representations involving real children under the age of fourteen, whereas Category B materials included fictional and other writing, such as their client's stories, or photos of legal sexual activity between teenagers. The latter category, they argued, should be seen as legally unobjectionable. It was unnecessary to ban the possession of such materials to protect children, Peck and McKinnon insisted. However, Category A materials, conceded the lawyers, "may give rise to a sufficient degree of harm to be criminalized." When Sharpe was asked about his lawyers' distinction, he tersely replied, "That, I feel, was unnecessary."[11]

In contrast to the emphasis on the law's overbreadth, proponents of the possession clause, such as federal Department of Justice lawyer Cheryl Tobias, defended the law as a vital tool in "diminishing the market" for child pornography. The right to free expression for pedophiles, Tobias said, "is dwarfed by the interest of children in our society. In my submission, we ought not sacrifice children on the altar of the Charter."

In the course of the presentations, each of the nine justices weighed into the fray. Justice Ian Binnie observed that, as the law stood, even a book such as Vladimir Nabokov's *Lolita* could be seen as advocating sex with children. "It seems like a difficult line to draw," he mused. Justice John Major appeared skeptical about legislation that criminalized what he described as "trivial breaches" which don't involve real children. Chief Justice McLachlin had concerns, too. What about a girl's diary in which she expressed private delight at her first sexual experience? Could that run afoul of the possession law? Though various lawyers assured the justices that no prosecutor would take such a case to court, McLachlin appeared unimpressed. "Assuming the legislation is overly broad, can it really be saved by saying, 'Trust us to use it wisely?'" she asked.

If Binnie and McLachlin expressed doubts about the scope of the law, other justices had doubts about the bounds of freedom of expression. When civil liberties lawyers claimed that the possession law amounted to tyranny, Justice Gonthier pointedly asked, "So, you take the position that the freedom to record thoughts is an absolute freedom that cannot be restricted, whatever the harm it causes to society?" Added Justice Claire L'Heureux-Dube, "You are relying on the Americans, but as you know, on freedom of expression, we have been diverging from the Americans."

At the end of the two-day hearing, the participants emerged into the bracing air of an Ottawa winter and filed past a protester's sign mounted in a snowbank that declared, with dubious spelling, "We look upon are [sic] childrens [sic] with pure love."

At the conclusion of the pleadings, Chief Justice McLachlin convened all of the justices in closed chambers to take a preliminary sounding of their views in the Sharpe case. Tradition provides that each justice gives his or her opinion in turn, starting with the most junior and moving around the table to the most senior. A straw poll is taken, and the chief justice appoints a single justice to begin the work of crafting a majority decision or, as would happen here, takes on the task herself.

From the point of view of the public, however, what happened next was mystifying. The legendary slow-grinding wheels of justice appeared to come to a complete standstill over the next year. The Supreme Court heard other cases of course, the most important of which, relative to the Sharpe case, was the long-delayed Little Sister's appeal, in which the Vancouver gay and lesbian bookstore asked the high court to overturn the law that allowed Canada Customs to exercise prior restraint on expression materials.

Court watchers speculated that the Sharpe decision would come down in early fall 2000, as soon as the court resumed sitting after the summer break. But to the puzzlement of the media and those involved, it didn't. While the court was lengthily deliberating on whether to strike down, uphold, or change the child pornography law, the country was going through a few changes of its own.

The attorney general of B.C., Ujjal Dosanjh, whose department brought the Sharpe case to the court, became premier of the West Coast province when NDP premier Glen Clark was forced to step down amidst allegations of influence peddling. The Reform Party of Canada, which had demanded that court decisions in the Sharpe case be overturned by Parliament, underwent a transformation into the Canadian Alliance Party, with a new leader, Stockwell Day, a former Alberta provincial politician. Coincidentally, Day was also indirectly involved in a child pornography case. The previous year, while serving as treasurer of the Alberta government, Day had written a letter to a Red Deer, Alberta, newspaper, attacking a lawyer defending a client accused of child pornography possession; the lawyer had sued Day for libel, and the case was wending its way through in- and out-of-court negotiations. In the fall, Prime Minister Jean Chretien sent the country to the polls as he sought a third term in office. Observers speculated that the Supreme Court decided to withhold the

Sharpe decision during the six-week campaign, not wanting to be seen as in any way interfering with the electoral process. But even after Chretien and his Liberal Party secured a third term with a solid majority victory in late-November 2000, there was still no decision.

There were occasional hints, however. Court watchers looked for clues in earlier free speech case decisions written by the new chief justice. They noted that in 1993, McLachlin had written the four to three majority decision that found the law used to prosecute Ernst Zundel, a notorious Holocaust denier, was unconstitutional. And in 1990 she had written a significant dissenting opinion in another hate-speech case, in which she argued that the law against hate propaganda was so broad that it could have a "chilling effect" on legitimate speech. As University of British Columbia law professor Joel Bakan summed up her record, "She has been very consistent in upholding the individual's right to free speech."[12]

A far more substantial indicator appeared in mid-December 2000, when the court released its verdict in the Little Sister's case. In the December 15 ruling on *Little Sister's v. Canada*, the court decided that the bookstore's appeal "should be allowed in part." Specifically, the court overturned a provision of the Customs Act that put the onus on the importer to prove expressive materials were not obscene. "An importer has a Charter right to receive expressive material unless the state can justify its denial," said the court.[13] Henceforth, it would be up to Customs to show that an imported book, magazine, or video was obscene. That was enough for the decision to be characterized by the media as a victory for the gay and lesbian bookstore. "A new standard for obscenity," said a *Vancouver Sun* front-page headline, adding, "Supreme Court toughens rules under which Canada Customs can seize material." The heading of a related story declared, "After 15 years, a victory at last for Little Sister's bookstore."[14]

It was true that the court had harsh words for Customs, chastising the agency for "excessive and unnecessary prejudice" against the beleaguered bookstore during its fifteen-year legal battle, and the court indeed provided some practical relief to Little Sister's by reversing a section of the Customs Act. But if the court partially allowed the bookstore's appeal, it was the smallest part of the appeal. The main thrust of the bookstore's bid – to overturn the law that made censorship at the border possible – was rejected. Further, Justice Ian Binnie's majority decision also rejected most of the arguments about obscenity that underpinned Little Sister's efforts to dismantle the censorship regime.

Although much of Binnie's ruling was necessarily taken up with the mechanisms and minutiae of the Customs Act and its operational regulations, the intellectual heart of his reasons for judgment reaffirmed the definition of obscenity established in the 1992 *Butler* ruling. Little Sister's hadn't raised a formal constitutional challenge to the obscenity law, but Binnie recognized that much of its argument focussed on the landmark *Butler* ruling that set out the legal test for determining obscenity. He noted that the criticisms made of *Butler* were:

1. "the community standard of tolerance is majoritarian and suppresses minority speech, including homosexual expression,"
2. the test of determining whether a sexual representation was degrading or dehumanizing was open to homophobic prejudice, and
3. the harm-based approach that the court adopted was merely morality in disguise.

If the Little Sister's case offered the opportunity for the new court to revisit a decision that had been widely criticized in legal circles, it quickly became clear that the McLachlin court was not planning to define itself by offering a broader interpretation of freedom of expression.

The Supreme Court unanimously rejected all criticisms of the *Butler* decision. "It may serve repeating that the national community standard relates to harm not taste," Binnie insisted, ". . . harm that rises to the level of being incompatible with the proper functioning of Canadian society." Similarly, the court dismissed the criticism that "a harm-based test effectively rests on [a] discredited moral foundation." Binnie reiterated the court's position, saying, "The community standard of tolerance is based on the reasonable apprehension of harm, not on morality . . . We have no evidence that the courts are not able to apply the *Butler* test." One could hear the carver's mallet tapping away, inscribing the obscenity law in judicial stone.

One final hint of at least some of the new Supreme Court's thinking appeared in a rare, outspoken interview that Justice Michel Bastarache, a 1997 appointee to the court, gave to a legal journal in mid-January 2000. The court, said Bastarache, sometimes goes "too far" in Charter of Rights rulings. "It's important for the court to be in step with the general public." Bastarache called for a more "deferential" approach to Parliament when the Court assessed whether laws complied with the Charter. "I don't think that we have a mandate to sort of define a whole social policy for Canada. What is possible in a free and democratic society has to be interpreted in terms also of the role of Parliament in determining policy for the country," said Bastarache.[15]

On January 26, 2001, slightly more than a year after it

heard the Sharpe case, the Supreme Court of Canada unanimously ruled that the possession section of the child pornography law of Canada was constitutional. The two lower court decisions were thus overturned, the appeal by the governments of
British Columbia and Canada was allowed, and Robin Sharpe was
ordered to stand trial on the original charges laid against him.

The nation's media, in lead broadcast items and front-page
headlines, duly reported that the "high court upholds child porn
ban." While sub-headlines noted that the court, in a six to three
majority decision, had written two "narrow exceptions" into the
existing law, the court's main decision dramatically and conclu-
sively ended the two-year-old public debate on child pornography legislation. As the *Globe and Mail* put it: "Top court rules
9-0: child porn law stays."

However, the text of Chief Justice McLachlin's decision for the
majority was rather more subtle than the blunt political impact
conveyed by a unanimous ruling upholding the child pornography law. Equally, the minority decision, recognizing no imper-
fections in the law, cast an ominous shadow on future free speech
cases. As has been true of so many facets of this complex legal
and social story, there's both more and less than meets the eye in
the Supreme Court decision on child pornography.

"Is Canada's law banning the possession of child pornography
constitutional or, conversely, does it unjustifiably intrude on the
constitutional right of Canadians to free expression?" asked
Chief Justice McLachlin at the beginning of the court's sixty-
nine-page ruling.[16] She promptly answered that question, offering a summary of her decision: "I conclude that the law is
constitutional, except for two peripheral applications relating to
expressive material privately created and kept by the accused
. . ."; further, the two exceptions "can be read into the legisla-

tion." That is, by virtue of the Supreme Court decision itself, it would now be the case that the "exceptions" would become part of the official interpretation of the statute, obviating any need for Parliament to amend the legislation. Other than the two "peripheral" exceptions, the law "strikes a constitutional balance between freedom of expression and prevention of harm to children," said McLachlin. "As a consequence, I would uphold the law and remit Mr. Sharpe for trial on all charges."

The chief justice now turned to the reasons for coming to that conclusion. As is customary, McLachlin recited the various constitutional and statutory laws relevant to the case and offered a brief summary of the lower court decisions. Recalling the heat taken by Judge Duncan Shaw for his initial decision at the B.C. Supreme Court level, McLachlin pointedly noted that Shaw "courageously ruled that [the possession clause] is unconstitutional." The chief justice's use of "courageously" was a clear signal of support for the trial court judge and a warning against intemperate responses to judicial findings.

Expressions of solidarity aside, McLachlin briskly launched into her legal critique of Justice Shaw's decision. She noted that while the Supreme Court in *Butler* "did not require conclusive proof that obscene materials cause harm, Justice Shaw apparently required such proof and found little scientific evidence linking the possession of child pornography to these risks. As a result, he considered the salutary effects of the law to be limited" and outweighed by the deleterious effects of the law's profound "invasion of freedom of expression and personal privacy." The suggestion here is that if Shaw had properly interpreted *Butler* as requiring not hard evidence of harm, but only reasonable "apprehension" of harm, he might have ruled otherwise than he did. The fact that the Supreme Court had reaffirmed the *Butler* ruling only ten days earlier in the *Little Sister's* judgment gave added significance to McLachlin's early reference to the landmark obscenity decision.

In summarizing the B.C. Court of Appeal's judgment upholding Shaw's ruling that the possession section was unconstitutional, McLachlin simply noted that the decision revealed "four distinctive arguments." First, "at the far end of the spectrum" was Justice Southin's argument "that prohibition of private possession of child pornography can never constitute a justifiable infringement on free expression." Second was the position of the trial judge that the limited benefits of the law didn't outweigh its negative effects, an argument that Southin accepted as an alternative to her primary view. The third argument was the one put forward by Justice Rowles that the law was unjustifiably overbroad. Finally, there was the dissenting opinion of Justice McEachern that, with respect to the issue of overbreadth, the law's infringement on freedom of expression was justified. It was now left to the Supreme Court of Canada to decide which of those arguments, if any, ought to be upheld.

McLachlin's lengthy analysis begins by examining the values at stake in *R. v. Sharpe*. The chief justice acknowledged that the fundamental right of freedom of expression "makes possible our liberty, our creativity, and our democracy. It does this by protecting not only 'good' and popular expression, but also unpopular or even offensive expression." The reason for doing so is the conviction that "the best route to truth, individual flourishing and peaceful coexistence in a heterogeneous society . . . lies in the free flow of images and ideas."

However, "freedom of expression is not absolute," said McLachlin, in a phrase that would be picked up by the media and frequently cited as the sum of the decision. "Overarching considerations, like . . . the prevention of harm that threatens vulnerable members of our society may justify prohibitions on some kinds of expression in some circumstances." Nonetheless, McLachlin rejected any claims that the possession section "does not raise free expression concerns . . . The right to possess expressive material is integrally related to the development of thought, belief, opinion and expression" and thus "falls within the continuum of rights protected" by the freedom of expression section of the Charter of Rights. Furthermore, "the private nature of the proscribed material may heighten the seriousness of a limit on free expression." But the privacy issue, cautioned McLachlin, "cuts two ways." While it raises the question of freedom of thought, "at the same time, the clandestine nature of incitement, attitudinal change, grooming and seduction associated with child pornography contributes to the harm it may cause children."

The latter consideration, said McLachlin, "brings us to the countervailing interest at stake in this appeal: society's interest in protecting children from the evils associated with the possession of child pornography." The links between possession of child pornography and harm to children, she conceded, "are arguably more attenuated than are the links between the manufacture and distribution of child pornography and harm to children. However, possession of child pornography contributes to the market for child pornography . . . [and] may facilitate the seduction and grooming of victims."

Having set out what was at stake in *R. v. Sharpe*, McLachlin now turned her attention to the claim of overbreadth made by critics of the possession section. We can't really understand the extent to which freedom of expression rights are infringed by the law, she argued, without examining the scope of the possession section. "Until we know what the law catches, we cannot say whether it catches too much . . . So we must begin by asking what [the possession section] truly catches as distinguished from some of the broader interpretations alleged by [Sharpe] and some of the intervenors in support." Here, McLachlin offers her first hint that the overbreadth claims of the law's critics are perhaps exaggerated.

While Parliament's main purpose in passing the kiddie porn law, McLachlin observed, was to protect children, "Parliament did not cast its net over all material that might conceivably pose any risk to children or produce any negative attitudinal changes." Not only did Parliament "set its targets principally on clear forms" of child pornography, it also provided qualifications and defences that further limited the scope of the law.

McLachlin now zoomed in on the disputed passages of the law, examining Section 163.1 of the Criminal Code on an almost word-for-word basis. She reminded readers that "a visual representation can constitute child pornography in three ways." First, "by showing a person who is, or is depicted as being, under the age of 18 years and is engaged in, or is depicted as engaged in, explicit sexual activity." Second, a visual representation can be child pornography "by having, as its dominant characteristic, the depiction, for a sexual purpose, of a sexual organ or the anal region of a person under the age of 18 years." Finally, a picture can be child pornography "by advocating or counselling sexual activity with a person under the age of 18 years that would be an offence under the Criminal Code." Written material, she noted, can constitute kiddie porn in only the last of these ways.

Since "the ambit of these provisions depends on the meaning of the terms used," McLachlin now offered her judicial interpretation of each of the important terms. It must be remembered that a Supreme Court judgment interpreting the meaning of the words and definitions of a law has the special characteristic of itself becoming the official interpretation of those words and definitions. So whatever McLachlin, writing for the majority of the court, says that "person" or "explicit sexual activity" or any other term means is henceforth, for all practical purposes, the legal meaning of the term. All judges trying subsequent cases must turn to the Supreme Court's interpretation and base their rulings upon it. The creative aspect of such interpretation will become immediately obvious.

McLachlin's analysis of the word "person" provides a clear example. A visual representation, she noted, must show, depict, advocate, or counsel sexual activity with a "person" in order to constitute child pornography. According to McLachlin, "Two issues arise here: (1) does 'person' apply only to actual, as opposed to imaginary persons; and (2) does it include the person who possesses the material?"

The first question is important, McLachlin points out, "because it governs whether the prohibition on possession is confined to representations of actual persons, or whether it extends to drawings from the imagination, cartoons, or computer-generated composites. The available evidence suggests that explicit sexual materials can be harmful whether or not they depict actual children ... I conclude that 'person' in s. 163.1 includes both actual and imaginary human beings."

Although what McLachlin has decided here will become more explicit in the overall judgment upholding the possession section, already she has dismissed the civil libertarian argument that the definition of child pornography ought to be confined to sexual representations of actual children, and has accepted a broadened definition of kiddie porn that includes all visual representations on the grounds that "explicit sexual materials can be harmful whether or not they depict actual children."

However, McLachlin recognizes that such an interpretation poses a dilemma. "This definition of child pornography catches depictions of imaginary human beings privately created and kept by the creator. Thus, the prohibition extends to visual expressions of thought and imagination, even in the exceedingly private realm of solitary creation and enjoyment." That, "combined with the unlikelihood of its causing harm to children, creates problems for the law's constitutionality," she admits, laying the groundwork for an eventual exception to be written into the law.

With respect to the second issue raised by the term "person," McLachlin asks, "Does the definition of 'child pornography' catch 'auto-depictions' – for example, sexually explicit photographs a person has taken of him or herself alone?" Given that Parliament hasn't limited the definition of person, "I conclude that Parliament intended to catch such auto-depictions, even where the person making the depiction, although under 18, does not appear to be a child, and intends to keep the depiction entirely in his or her own possession." This also, she says, "creates constitutional problems," a recognition that again lays the grounds for an amendment to the law.

Finally, with respect to the meaning of "person," McLachlin touches on the long-vexing controversy that "the legislation defines children to include all those under the age of 18." That, too, is a problem because "this age limit extends the reach of the law to material beyond the ordinary conception of child pornography. For example, it raises the possibility that teenagers, perhaps even married teenagers, could be charged and imprisoned for taking and keeping photos or videos of themselves engaged in lawful sexual acts, even if those materials were intended exclusively for their own personal use." Such a possibility again raises "particularly troubling constitutional concerns," says McLachlin, as she concludes this particular section.

This analysis of "person" illustrates the method used by the court in its judgment, one that not only legally "reads" Parliament's intentions in creating a definition of child pornography, but that also validates portions of the definition, while question-ing other parts of it on constitutional grounds. That is, to use a term from linguistic philosophy, McLachlin's words have a "per-formative" function and not merely a descriptive one. Their utterance has the function of establishing the meaning of the law.

The important issue – a political as well as legal one – is whether the problems that McLachlin has already flagged are significant enough to invalidate the possession section of the child porn law, or if they're minor or "peripheral" enough that the law can be upheld with a bit of tinkering. As we already know, McLachlin's ruling is an argument in favour of the latter interpretation. Yes, there are problems with the law, she says, nodding to the critics, but the difficulties are not as great as the critics claim and can be easily enough remedied without requir-ing Parliament to rewrite the law.

McLachlin then considers, in turn, the terms "depicted," "explicit sexual activity," "dominant characteristic," "sexual purpose," and "advocates or counsels." She is "working" the law, first deciding what a term means, and then deciding whether the meaning causes constitutional difficulties by being overly broad. For example, in looking at "explicit sexual activ-ity," she says that "Parliament intended to draw the line at the extreme end of the spectrum" of sexual activity, namely, "only depictions of sexual intercourse and other non-trivial sexual acts." Thus, "the law does not catch possession of visual material depicting only casual sexual contact, like touching, kissing or hugging, since these are not depictions of nudity or intimate sexual activity. Certainly, a photo of teenagers kissing at summer camp will not be caught." Similarly, when examining the terms "dominant characteristic" and "sexual purpose," she says, "Fam-ily photos of naked children, viewed objectively, generally do not have as their 'dominant characteristic' the depiction of a sex-

ual organ or anal region 'for a sexual purpose.'" Snapshots of a
child in the bath will not be caught. In such remarks, McLachlin
is not so much offering reassurance to those worried by the possible reach of the law, but ruling out critics' claims of overbreadth by instructing future trial judges that it is not the intent
of the law to reach so far.

McLachlin has several things to say about written or visual
material that "advocates or counsels" sexual activity with a person under eighteen that would be a Criminal Code offence, an
issue that had raised alarm among various artistic and political
groups. As she tended to do throughout the judgment, here
again McLachlin hastens to put the most reasonable face on the
law. Thus, "works aimed at description and exploration of various aspects of life that incidentally touch on illegal acts with
children are unlikely to be caught," she says. "While Nabokov's
Lolita, Boccaccio's *Decameron*, and Plato's *Symposium* portray or
discuss sexual activities with children, on an objective view
they cannot be said to advocate or counsel such conduct in the
sense of actively inducing or encouraging it."

Similar reassurance is offered to political advocates. The section would not "catch political advocacy for lowering the age of
consent because such advocacy would not promote the commission of an offence but the amendment of the law." McLachlin
notes that it must "be remembered that it is only the advocating
or counselling of sexual activity with a person under the age of
18 *that would be an offence under the Criminal Code* that is captured by this part of the definition of child pornography."[17]
Thus, among many available examples, "advocating the consensual sexual touching of a 16-year-old is not an offence . . . and
therefore would not be caught by this part of the child pornography definition."

However reasonable McLachlin's reading of the advocacy section of the law, she still worried "that the provision is broad enough to capture written works created by the author, solely for his or her eyes," such as "a teenager's favourable diary account of a sexual encounter." Although such possibilities might be remote, nonetheless this and similar examples rendered the "advocacy" definition constitutionally problematic, in the chief justice's view.

McLachlin now looks at another limitation on the scope of the law, namely, defences that an accused can make to charges of possessing child pornography, particularly the defence of "artistic merit." Although her remarks about artistic merit do not require writing an exception to the law, they are another example of the court engaged in crafting the law through defining it. In this instance, McLachlin broadened the artistic merit defence, narrowing the scope of the law.

First, she offers a reminder of what the court has already said about art in the *Butler* decision: "Artistic expression rests at the heart of freedom of expression values and any doubt in this regard must be resolved in favour of freedom of expression." Adds McLachlin, "Simply put, the defence must be construed broadly."

McLachlin then looks at three questions in relation to the artistic merit defence:

1. What does artistic merit mean?
2. Do artistic works have to conform to the "community standards" test?
3. What is the procedure for considering the defence?

Does "artistic merit" refer to the quality of the art? No, says McLachlin. "A person who produces art of any kind is protected, however crude or immature the result of the effort in the eyes of the objective beholder. This interpretation seems more consistent with what Parliament intended . . . I conclude that 'artistic merit' should be interpreted as including any expression that may reasonably be viewed as art. Simply put, artists, so long as they are producing art, should not fear prosecution under [the child pornography law]."

Equally important in defining the artistic merit defence are McLachlin's remarks on whether art has to meet the "community standards" test as defined in *Butler*. The test was invoked by the judge in the case of artist Eli Langer. Again, McLachlin broadens the interpretation, saying, "I am not persuaded that we should read a community standards qualification into the defence. To do so would involve reading in a qualification that Parliament has not stated." So even though works of art might pose risks of harm to children, McLachlin declares that they can be protected by the artistic merit defence. Further, in terms of the procedures for invoking the defence, "the accused raises the defence by pointing to facts capable of supporting it, at which point the Crown must disprove the defence beyond a reasonable doubt."

All of this, obviously, could be directly relevant to Sharpe once the Supreme Court remitted him to stand trial on the original charges. Where the Crown suggested that Sharpe's stories amounted to a violation of the proscription against advocating or counselling illegal sexual acts with children, Sharpe might now plausibly claim that his fictions are protected by the artistic merit defence. Sharpe's standing as a recognized writer in his community, plus the fact that his stories are conventional to the extent of having characters, plots, and denouements would appear to meet the requirements newly enunciated by McLachlin. And should Sharpe succeed in an artistic merit defence with respect to possession, presumably he would also be exempt from charges of intent to distribute, since one has the right to disseminate art. Although that doesn't cover all of Shape's legal problems, it may address a significant portion of them. More important, McLachlin's definition of the defence provides us with another example of how a legal decision can substantially affect a law without formally altering it.

McLachlin now sums up her reading of what material is and isn't caught by the possession section of the law. On the whole, she says, "Parliament has attempted to meet the dual concerns of protecting children and protecting free expression." Nonetheless, "problems remain." The law, even in the "reasonable" interpretation McLachlin has offered, still "may catch some material that particularly engages the value of self-fulfilment and poses little or no risk of harm to children." That material falls into two classes.

First, there are "self-created, privately held expressive materials," such as "private journals, diaries, writings, drawings and other works of the imagination, created by oneself exclusively for oneself," all of which may "trigger" the possession offence. This is particularly disturbing, says McLachlin, because the law "reaches into a realm of exceedingly private expression" and because "the risk of harm arising from the private creation and possession of such materials . . . is low." The second class of materials is "privately created visual recordings of lawful sexual activity . . ." Like the materials in the first category, says McLachlin, such recordings pose little risk of harm to children. Further, "because the law reaches depictions of persons who are or appear to be under 18, the person or persons depicted [in such material] may not even appear to be children." In sum, then, the examples cited by McLachlin "suggest that s. 163.1(4), at the margins of its application, prohibits deeply private forms of expression, in pursuit of materials that may pose no more than a nominal risk of harm to children." While McLachlin clearly recognizes a constitutional problem, it's equally important to note her use of the word "margins," suggesting that the magnitude of the problem is such that it might be easily remedied.

From here, McLachlin proceeds to the standard legal analysis of the "Oakes test" to examine whether the infringement on freedom of expression by the child pornography law can be justified under Section 1 of the Charter of Rights and Freedoms. She first dismisses B.C. Appeal Court Justice Southin's argument that, as a matter of principle, a prohibition on possession of expressive materials can never be justified. The very existence of Section 1 of the Charter, which provides for a lawful overriding of constitutional rights, argues against such a notion, McLachlin rules, and then immediately moves on to the familiar Section 1 analysis.

McLachlin immediately recognizes that the required "pressing and substantial" legislative objective of the child pornography law is present. The more difficult parts of the analysis concern the law's "rational connection" to Parliament's goal, the issue of whether the infringement of the constitutional right of free expression constitutes only "minimal impairment" of the right, and, finally, whether the law is "proportional" in the sense that its merits outweigh its defects. It is here that McLachlin will firm up the problems of constitutionality and overbreadth that she has already identified, thus setting the stage for a modest remedy to the defects of the legislation.

In considering whether possession of child pornography, as opposed to its manufacture, distribution, or use, causes harm to children, McLachlin identifies "a question pivotal to this appeal: what standard of proof must the Crown achieve in demonstrating harm – scientific proof based on concrete evidence or a reasoned apprehension of harm?" Justice Shaw, the trial judge, "insisted on scientific proof based on concrete evidence." McLachlin now makes a crucial overruling. "With respect, this sets the bar too high," she says. "In *Butler* . . . this Court rejected the need for concrete evidence and held that a 'reasoned appre-hension of harm' sufficed. A similar standard must be employed in this case."

Once the "reasoned apprehension of harm" standard is reaf-firmed, McLachlin is able to say, "While the scientific evidence is not strong, I am satisfied that the evidence in this case sup-ports the existence of a connection here . . . I conclude that the social science evidence adduced in this case, buttressed by expe-rience and common sense, amply meets the requirement of a rational connection between the purpose of the law and the means adopted to effect this purpose. Possession of child pornography increases the risk of child abuse."

Given that the law passes the "rational connection" test, McLachlin asks, "Does the law impair the right of free expression only minimally?" Sharpe's lawyers had argued that the possession section "fails the minimal impairment test because the legal defin-ition of child pornography includes material posing no reasoned risk of harm to children." However, replies McLachlin, "properly interpreted, the law catches much less material unrelated to harm to children than Mr. Sharpe suggests." What's more, "many of the other hypothetical examples relied on in the [lower] courts as sug-gesting overbreadth . . . disappear entirely on a proper construc-tion of the statutory definition of child pornography" – namely, the "construction" provided by McLachlin herself.

Nonetheless, "the fact remains," McLachlin observed, "that the law may also capture the possession of material that one would not normally think of as 'child pornography.'" Once more she specified "(1) written materials or visual representations cre-ated and held by the accused alone, exclusively for personal use; and (2) visual recordings, created by or depicting the accused, that do not depict unlawful sexual activity and are held exclu-sively for private use." The fact that "the government's argument

on this point is, in effect, that it is necessary to prohibit possession of a large amount of harmless expressive material in order to
combat the small risk" that some material in this class may cause
harm to children, said McLachlin, "suggests that the law may be
overbroad."

But before making a definitive decision on overbreadth,
McLachlin embarked upon the final branch of the proportionality inquiry, deciding "whether the benefits the law may achieve
in preventing harm to children outweigh the detrimental effects
of the law on the right of free expression." Although McLachlin
concluded that "in the vast majority of the law's applications" it
was "proportionate and constitutional," she continued to be
troubled by "peripheral" applications of the law that posed "the
most significant problems at this final stage of the proportionality analysis."

First, she once again cited "the law's application to self-created
works of the imagination, written or visual, intended solely for
private use by the creator." Here, McLachlin underscored her
concern that the "intensely private" nature of such materials,
however offensive, "deeply implicates" freedom of expression
rights. "Personal journals and writings, drawings and other
forms of visual expression may well be of importance to self-fulfilment. Indeed, for young people grappling with issues of sexual identity and self-awareness, private expression of a sexual
nature may be crucial to personal growth and sexual maturation.
The fact that many might not favour such forms of expression
does not lessen the need to insist on strict justification for their
prohibition."

McLachlin pushed the point further. "The restriction imposed
by s. 163.1(4) regulates expression where it borders on thought,"
she said. "Indeed, it is a fine line that separates a state attempt to
control the private possession of self-created expressive materi-

als from a state attempt to control thought or opinion . . . To ban the possession of our private musings thus falls perilously close to criminalizing the mere articulation of thought." Although she thought the danger only applied to "peripheral applications" of the law, nonetheless this passage appeared to be a nod towards the arguments of the lower courts, civil liberties intervenors, and Sharpe's own lawyers.

The same concern, she said, arose in relation to sexual self-depictions. Such self-recordings, she suggested, "may be of significance to adolescent self-fulfilment . . . and identity." Similar considerations applied where "lawful sexual acts are documented in a visual recording, such as photographs or a videotape, and held privately by the participants." In any case, "the cost of [prohibiting] such materials . . . outweighs any tenuous benefit it might confer in preventing harm to children."

Summing up the proportionality tests, McLachlin concluded that the possession section of the child pornography law was constitutional, except for the two categories she had carved out. "The inclusion of these peripheral materials in the law's prohibition trenches heavily on freedom of expression . . . To this extent, the law cannot be considered proportionate in its effects and the infringement of [freedom of expression] contemplated by the legislation is not demonstrably justifiable under Section 1 [of the Charter]."

Having ruled that the possession law was not fully constitutional, McLachlin now considered possible "remedies." The court could "strike out the entire law," as the lower courts had done. "The difficulty with this remedy is that it nullifies a law that is valid in most of its applications," she argued. Other alternatives included finding the law valid and ignoring its excesses, or providing for a constitutional exemption in actual cases where unconstitutional applications arise. McLachlin rejected all of those remedies because, she wrote, "in my view the appropriate remedy in this case is to read into the law an exclusion of the problematic applications" of the child pornography statute.

McLachlin again spelled out the exceptions for "self-created expressive material" and "private recordings of lawful sexual activity," and then considered "the question of whether reading in this exception is the appropriate remedy for the overbreadth of s. 163.1(4)." She argued that "carving out those applications by incorporating the proposed exceptions will not undermine the force of the law; rather, it will preserve the force of the statute while also recognizing the purposes of the Charter." Furthermore, "since the problematic applications lie on the periphery of the material targeted by Parliament, carving them out will not create an exception-riddled provision bearing little resemblance to the provision envisioned by Parliament." The exceptions, in other words, "will not subvert Parliament's object," whereas striking down the statute would "assuredly undermine" Parliamentary intentions.

The final paragraphs of McLachlin's majority decision reiterated for a last time her overall view of the disputed passage. "The British Columbia Courts found the law constitutionally wanting and struck it down in its entirety," she said. "I, too, find it to be constitutionally imperfect. However, the defects lie at the periphery of the law's application. In my view, the appropriate remedy is to uphold the law in its broad application, while holding that it must not be applied to two categories of material . . . self-created, privately held expressive materials and private recordings that do not depict unlawful sexual activity." Thus, McLachlin's literal bottom line: "I would therefore allow the appeal and remit the respondent for trial on all charges."

If the six-member majority decision was disappointing to the respondent, given the narrowness of its recognition of constitutional defects, the three-member minority opinion of Justices L'Heureux-Dube, Gonthier, and Bastarache was disturbing not only to Sharpe, but to civil libertarian intervenors and everyone else concerned with the protection of fundamental speech freedoms. Notwithstanding the minimal incursions made on one section of the child pornography law, the dissenters were adamant that the majority had gone too far.

The dissenting justices emphasized the importance of "society's protection of its vulnerable members," particularly children, and argued that "the constitutional protection of a form of expression that undermines our fundamental values must be carefully scrutinized." In the end, said the minority, "we cannot agree with Chief Justice McLachlin that the scope of the prohibition against the possession of child pornography is overbroad, and must conclude that the legislation is justified under section 1 [of the Charter] in its entirety."

Although it's not necessary to reprise the minority judgment in detail, some of its points are worth repeating since they provide both a reflection of much popular opinion, as well as an echo of some its excesses. L'Heureux-Dube, Gonthier, and Bastarache consistently focus their attention on what they regard as the harms caused by the mere possession of any and all of the materials captured by the child pornography law, including the exceptions carved out by the majority.

"The very existence of child pornography . . . is inherently harmful to children and to society," proclaimed the minority, extensively citing a series of parliamentary and other commissioned reports as evidence of the dangers of child pornography. The dissenters also cited the 1992 *Butler* decision as the judicial moment when "the Court broadened the traditional individualistic notion of harm, and recognized that all members of society suffer when harmful attitudes are reinforced," thus grounding the case for the state's intervention in matters of thought and belief. And since, according to the minority, "the possession of child pornography has no social value" and "only a tenuous connection to the value of self-fulfilment underlying the right to free expression ... it warrants only attenuated protection. Hence, increased deference should be accorded to Parliament's decision to prohibit it." Not only did the minority repeatedly urge deference to Parliament; it also, citing *Butler* again, reasserted the right of Parliament "to make moral judgments in criminalizing certain forms of conduct."

The minority reviewed in detail the expert testimony in the trial, fully accepting the claims of Crown witnesses that there were multiple harms caused by mere possession of child pornography. Such possession, the minority found, "contributed to the cognitive distortions of pedophiles," fuelled their fantasies, and was used in "grooming" children to commit sexual acts. Furthermore, the ability of police to lay simple possession charges was a helpful part of an "integrated law enforcement scheme which protects children."

Most significantly, the minority sharply disagreed with the exceptions read into the law by the majority. "We see no evidence to support the notion that sexually explicit videos of teenagers 'reinforce healthy sexual relationships and self-actualization,' as suggested by Chief Justice McLachlin, rather than being harmful self-indulgence supporting unhealthy attitudes towards oneself and others," the minority found. The dissenters conceded that "adolescents between the ages of 14 and 17 may legally engage in sexual activity," but "the creation of a permanent record of such activity has consequences which children of that age may not have sufficient maturity to understand." In their perhaps most extreme remark, the dissenters insisted, "Moreover, there is no valid reason to presume that teenage authors of sexually explicit videos cannot themselves be pedophiles." The minority was clearly appalled by the notion that youths might record their own lawful sexual activities, reflecting a depth of unease about youth sexuality found in the general public, or at least the "social conservative" segment of the general population. "The Court should defer to Parliament's decision to restrict teenagers' freedom in this area," the three dissenting justices concluded.

The minority also "firmly disagreed" with the chief justice's protection for self-created, privately held expressive materials. "The harm which Parliament sought to prevent . . . extends beyond the harm which flows from the use of children in pornography," the dissenters argued. "Parliament also sought to prevent the harm which flows from the very existence of images and words which degrade and dehumanize children and to send the message that children are not appropriate sexual partners." Rebutting the view that "the inclusion of material that is only a record of the author's private thoughts (and not shown to anyone) came very close to criminalizing objectionable thought," the minority wrote, "In our view, the inclusion of written materials in the offence of possession does not amount to thought control." In sum, Justices L'Heureux-Dube, Gonthier, and Bastarache found the possession clause to be entirely constitutional and not in need of the sort of remedy fashioned by the majority.

The Supreme Court of Canada's notice on Thursday, January 25, 2001, that it would issue its decision in *R. v. Sharpe* the following day sent the media machinery scurrying into motion. CBC Newsworld set up for a live broadcast from the foyer of the Supreme Court that commenced at noon Friday, with reporters and in-studio legal experts clutching unread copies of the

Court's ruling. Interested parties were rounded up for instant reactions, while Osgoode Hall law professor Bruce Ryder, who had appeared in court on behalf of the B.C. Civil Liberties Association, offered running commentary. Other experts posted around the country scanned the headnotes of the judgment in an effort to lend a semblance of coherence to the daylong bout of punditry.

Although the media was positioned for political pyrotechnics should the judgment enrage any or all of the contending parties, once everyone figured out the rough outline of what the court had decided, the reactions quickly dampened expectations of fireworks. Indeed, the loudest sound to be heard in response to the decision was the large sigh of relief heaved by federal Justice minister Anne McLellan. "The Supreme Court has spoken. They have upheld the law. The exceptions are extremely narrow," said McClellan, "Obviously, the Supreme Court was well aware of the fact that one has to balance the rights of freedom of expression against Parliament's right, and all of us as parents and children in this society, to be free from the pernicious harm of child pornography. I think the court struck the appropriate balance in its judgment."[18]

Not only was the Justice minister spared the odious chore of having to rewrite the statute, but she could also claim vindication for her decision to stay the course with the judicial process and not panic in the face of demands for precipitous parliamentary action to overturn court decisions. However, in anticipation of a negative decision from the court, McLellan had instructed Justice ministry officials to draft legislation that could pass constitutional muster and that she could introduce immediately, in a bid to stifle the inevitable cries to overturn the court decision. The draft not only rejigged the statute to satisfy possible court objections, but it also contained new "tougher" measures to deal with Internet child pornography. The Supreme Court decision, to the relief of the government, obviated the need for the hasty introduction of a new law; the additional measures could be transferred to a general Criminal Code omnibus bill addressing various issues that the minister subsequently introduced in March 2001. For the moment, however, McLellan could stand pat on the upheld legislation.[19]

Official opposition leader Stockwell Day, of the Canadian Alliance, also greeted the decision favourably. "I think parents can take some relief," he said, adding that the decision sent out a strong message to child pornographers that "Canada is not a place where they're going to be at home." Although he pledged to look at the exceptions to ensure there were no loopholes, he allowed that he didn't see the need to use the constitutional notwithstanding clause in order to overturn the exceptions that Chief Justice McLachlin had written into the law.

Perhaps the most important clue to what the decision meant in practical terms could be found at the press conference Detective Inspector Bob Matthews of the Ontario Provincial Police held in Toronto. "I have to say that I really appreciate the Supreme Court for the decision they handed down," enthused the head of the province's kiddie porn squad. "The Supreme Court has given us the ability to continue investigating the way we always have . . . When I look back at investigations we've done, in no way would this have tied our hands at all." The head of the Canadian Police Association, Grant Obst, backed up Matthews, saying that the status quo for policing child pornography had been preserved. "We were getting prepared for them to strike the section down, and we didn't know what we would do then," Obst admitted. Earl Moulton, a chief superintendent at B.C.'s RCMP headquarters, seconded Obst. The ruling, he said, "returns a very effective tool to the policing community."

Child welfare advocates also seemed satisfied. "Canadian parents can sleep more soundly tonight knowing that a large chunk of the loophole on child pornography has now been closed," said Darrel Reid, a spokesman for Focus on the Family. However, Brian Clemenger, the even more conservative spokesman for the Evangelical Fellowship of Canada, was still worried. "If you see the law as being a wall against the intrusion of child pornographers, they've opened a crack in the wall," he said. "The question is: Does that crack become bigger?"

If the politicians, police, and proponents of family values were pleased, interestingly, civil libertarians appeared to share some of their satisfaction. "The court has rescued the law by shearing off the most problematic areas and saving the rest," said law professor Bruce Ryder. He called the decision "a real achievement." BCCLA President Craig Jones said, "It's almost overwhelmingly a positive decision. I know some people are saying it's giving too much to the civil libertarians, but I can't see a scenario in which a child is actually abused and still not captured by the law as it stands." Some civil libertarian commentators, however, were more cautious. "They had an extremely hot potato in their hands, and they shrank from what the civil liberties association preferred they did with this law," said a BCCLA official, "but they have improved it materially" by striking down the "most obnoxious parts" of the legislation. Whether the civil libertarians were as satisfied as they sounded, or whether they merely decided that it was important to know when to claim victory in a losing cause was not entirely clear.

About the only person who disagreed with the Supreme Court's decision was the man at the centre of the controversy,

Robin Sharpe. Barricaded behind the closed green door of the rented room in Vancouver's downtown eastside, where he had recently been forced to move from his former apartment because of the attendant publicity and financial hardship, Sharpe refused to appear before the cameramen who prowled the hall of his rooming house. "I don't think I'll dare go out of my room for a while yet," Sharpe said in telephone interviews. "For the next little while, I have concerns for my personal safety." That didn't stop photographers and television cameramen from banging at the door, or the telephone from ringing, while voice-mail messages piled up. In his most widely reported remark, Sharpe asked CBC Newsworld anchor Don Newman, "If God didn't mean children to have sex, then why does puberty happen so early? Did God goof?" It was a query hardly calculated to win public favour.

Most of the post-decision commentary by the media reflected public approval of the decision. The *National Post* editorialized in a now familiar vein. "Until yesterday, child pornography enjoyed two years of de facto legal protection in Canada. It is a scandal," the paper harrumphed, not entirely accurately. "The B.C. courts did something very foolish. Instead of scissoring out those sections of the hastily drafted law that offended the principle of free speech . . . the courts struck down the law in its entirety." That wasn't entirely true either, since all of the law had remained in force, except for the possession section. "It didn't have to be this way. As we argued from the outset, the courts overstretched by striking down the whole law . . . Yesterday's welcome Supreme Court decision agreed with this reasoning," declared the paper. The *Vancouver Sun* offered slightly more moderate views, calling the decision "a sound compromise." Said the paper: "Effectively, the Supreme Court ruling affirms that it's not illegal to have a sick mind, but that those who do are not allowed to inflict their perversions on others . . . The charges against Mr. Sharpe can now go to trial. The sooner, the better."

The *Globe and Mail's* justice reporter, Kirk Makin, offered a lengthy analysis under the heading "Activist days long gone for deferential court." Said Makin, "The once-bold Supreme Court of Canada is turning into a cautious court of deference . . . The court was careful to do as little damage as possible to the child pornography law, fine-tuning it while stopping short of striking it down and throwing it back to Parliament."

Indeed, the only mainstream voice in the country offering something of a dissent to the chorus of praise was that heard in the editorial columns of the *Globe and Mail*. Although the *Globe's* editorial was headlined "Bringing proportion to the child-porn law," most of the editorial was critical of McLachlin's decision. "The judges were not arguing over whether child pornography was a bad thing. All agree it is ugly and offensive," said the paper's editorial. "What the judges debated was whether the law's definition of child pornography is too broad, and how far society may legally go in cracking down on child porn. To that end, the Supreme Court struck down part of the law, but left most of it intact." The editorial praised McLachlin for doing "the country a service," but also chided her for being "too cautious in her remedy."

On the vexed issue of whether "reasoned apprehension of harm" rather than scientific evidence was sufficient, it observed that "the court walked a muddy road here . . . Judge McLachlin concluded it was not for the court to second-guess Parliament." Similarly, the paper worried about the notion that the law was in part justified because "criminalizing possession helps police reduce the distribution and production of child porn. It's a slippery argument, suggesting it's fine to create a thief to catch a thief." The editorial approved the court's refusal to "accept the law's more indefensible violations of free expression. Rather than strike the law down, it struck down two parts." But perhaps that wasn't enough. "We suggest the majority should have gone further. The criminalization of material that 'advocates or counsels' illegal sexual activity with someone under 18 crosses the line from the protection of children to the suppression of offensive arguments . . . any [attempt] to criminalize speech should have to scale a much higher hurdle that this law sets."

University of Toronto law professor Brenda Cossman, writing in the gay and lesbian newspaper *Xtra West*, was also critical of the outcome. However, "given the hysteria over the constitutional challenge to Canada's child pornography law, it is impressive that the court was prepared to address the most egregious parts of the law," she said. The exceptions created by Chief Justice McLachlin were "a stunning example of just how broad the definition of child pornography is." Given the pressure on the court by its conservative critics, "there was reason to doubt whether the court would dare venture into the terrain of kiddie porn, and actually suggest that Parliament had not done such a good job with the legislation." Though Cossman commended the court for "daring to do so," she also noted "there's still a lot of bad stuff remaining." Summing up a series of particular concerns about the law's remaining overbreadth, Cossman concluded, "This law still tramples on the very civil liberties that are crucial to [gay and lesbian] survival. And we should be worried, very worried, that this may be the best that we can hope for from the current court."

Perhaps the most notable aspect of public reaction to the ruling was how short-lived it was. Within forty-eight hours, the debate was over. Whatever else one might say about the Supreme Court decision, its political impact was indisputable. While the court's "deference" to Parliament was widely noted, it could be as easily argued that the court wasn't deferential at all. It had rolled up the sleeves of its ermine-trimmed judicial robes and done the work it judged Parliament incapable of performing, rather discreetly elbowing the legislature out of the way. In any case, this was an instance where the judiciary had the unequivocal final word.

If the decision was admittedly politically shrewd – both on behalf of the Supreme Court and Parliament – what should be said about its legal acuity and its overall wisdom?

First, we must admit that the Supreme Court's ruling, although perhaps not as reasonable as Chief Justice McLachlin made it out to be, is certainly plausible. Even critics of the decision, such as us, recognize that the court's reading of the impugned possession section is well within the range of what any dispassionate observer might conclude. It is hardly a radical judgment, but neither is it a judgment insensitive to the issues of free expression, as we believe the court's minority opinion to be.

The place to begin our summation is not with the possession section but with the definition of child pornography upon which the entire statute is based. Even after the court's decision, the law continues to say that child pornography is any visual representation that shows a person under eighteen (or depicted as under eighteen) engaged in explicit sexual activity or portrayed in such a way that the dominant characteristic of the representation is the display of a sexual organ or the anal region for a sexual purpose, and any written or visual material that advocates or counsels sexual activity with a person under eighteen that would be a crime under the Criminal Code.

There's something deeply anomalous about a law that criminalizes the representation of a non-criminal act. Since two sixteen-year-olds are legally free to engage in sexual acts, why should it be a crime to represent those acts? There's something fundamentally illogical about the conceptualization of the definition of child pornography. If the law merely criminalized possession, distribution, and sale of the representations of sexual abuse of children under fourteen and criminal sexual acts involving youth between the ages of fourteen and seventeen inclusive – that is, acts whose representation recorded a sexual crime against children and youth – it would remove the anomaly. But even with the new exceptions, the present law continues to trouble common sense. The two sixteen-year-olds can engage in sex, and they can now record their activity. But if they show the photographic representations they've made of themselves to their friends at school the next day, they're guilty of distributing kiddie porn, and their friends are guilty of possessing it. It's not clear why that should be the case.

Defining child pornography as sexual representations of people under eighteen is at the centre of the problem. As various judges considering the case have noted, the definition captures material that doesn't look like child pornography or accord with our notion of what kiddie porn is. The only judge who directly dealt with the problem of age was B.C. Appeal Court Justice Southin who, in looking at "the meaning of words," explicitly declared, "When I myself use the word 'child' . . . I mean those below the age of puberty . . . I define a 'child' as anyone under the age of 14 years." Correspondingly, "adolescents" are people between 14 and 18, and "adults" are people over 18.

At various places in her decision, Southin demonstrates the implications of her common-sense definition of "children," as applied to the question of child pornography. The clearest instance of this is when she's reviewing the expert testimony of Dr. Collins on the matter of cognitive distortions. Southin remarks, "If Dr. Collins had limited his evidence on this point to children, I would have no difficulty with it. To believe that a child could not only not be harmed by premature sexual conduct, but also take pleasure in it, seems to me an absurdity, and, therefore, a 'cognitive distortion.' But to believe that sexual congress between an adolescent and an adult (who may only be 18) may be a good thing or, at least, is not an unmitigated evil, is not, in modern Canada in which many adolescents, by their own choice, are not chaste, a 'cognitive distortion.' I may think it would be better if they were, but that is a matter of morality not reality."

Indeed, the only way to make sense of the insistence on retaining an under-eighteen definition of "child" is to speculate that what's at play here is the importation of a particular moral view into what ought to be a matter of judging harm. That is, the conflation of a widely shared concern about child pornography with moral disapproval of aspects of youth sexuality generates an overbreadth in the law that isn't remedied by the Supreme Court's majority decision. The tone of suppressed rage in the court's minority opinion is evident. The dissenting justices speak derisively of youthful sexual self-recordings as "self-indulgences"; they foresee the immaturity of adolescent judgment in recording legal sexual activities and invoke the possibility that teens themselves may be pedophiles, all in justification of a restriction of "teenagers' freedom in this area." It seems plain enough that such claims, however well-intentioned, are about morality and reflect conflicted adult views about youth sexuality in a culture that at once salaciously displays such sexuality while seeking to renounce it in the name of protecting children. But since the law emphatically claims to be not about morality, but about the prevention of harm to children, such reasoning, however reflective of societal confusion, seems disconnected from the legislative aims.

There are a number of other problems with the child pornography law as it stands after the Supreme Court decision. They are wide-ranging, and include a variety of matters, most of which we will only briefly address.

The question of the need for scientific evidence of harm in relation to offences, especially a possession offence, is badly resolved by the court's reaffirmation of the *Butler* decision. There, the notion of harm was broadened so that the mere perception that a sexual representation can cause bad attitudes, which may lead to bad acts, is considered a "reasoned apprehension of harm" and is now treated as legally sufficient. One may call such apprehension "reasoned," but the reasonableness of such a definition of harm is arguable at best.

Similarly, although B.C. Appeal Court Justice Southin pointed out the anomaly of making possession of material advocating or counselling illegal sexual activity with children a crime when such advocacy itself isn't a crime, the Supreme Court ignored the contradiction and let the possession offence stand, excepting only self-authored material. That is, if a person is in possession of material advocating sexual crimes against children written by someone else, they are guilty of possessing child pornography, even though what they possess isn't child pornography in the usual sense, but only a thought that most people find offensive.

When we began our consideration of the child pornography law, we took – and still hold – the view that there isn't a constitutional obstacle to criminalizing possession of sexual representations in which actual children under fourteen are sexually abused. But given the political and social reality that a possession offence can't be confined to representations that are criminal abuses of actual children, we need to reconsider the question of the profound invasion of privacy involved when the possession of materials not involving real children is criminalized. The new exception to the law permits the retention of self-authored materials, but a wide range of other-authored materials puts the possessor at legal jeopardy. Is the capture of materials that several courts have declared comes perilously close to outright thought control justified if it allows the law to capture some genuinely objectionable material in the name of protecting children? We are reminded that representations of children are, after all, not children, however repulsive the actions to which the representations and their production testify. It's not an argument we accept, but it's one which we must in some sense respect. At the end of the exercise, we find ourselves more dubious about the benefits of a unique possession offence in Canadian criminal law than we were at the outset when earnest government advisers wrote innocent memos urging a "narrowly focussed" provision against child pornography.

Perhaps the main thing that gets lost in the Supreme Court decision is the recognition that the lower courts got something fundamentally right when they identified the deep danger of trenching upon free speech, even in a good cause. The Supreme Court justices, in *R. v. Sharpe*, nodded to that insight, but in the end they overrode it.

However, it's appropriate to take a step back from the decision itself and reflect on some of the broader issues raised by this case. After all, it cannot be sensibly said that the child porn possession law, as finally edited and augmented by the chief justice of the Supreme Court of Canada, poses a spectacular threat of widening state censorship. Very, very few Canadians are even faintly interested in sexually graphic representations of children. And it is reasonable to hope that policing authorities will not be anxious to push the margins of the statute where issues of artistic merit come into play, or where the maturity of the models makes the "appearance of age" evidence a matter of guessing. In any case, the civil rights sky is not about to fall.

Still, we find it hard to rejoice in the national consensus that the issue is now dead, or comfort ourselves that a sensible compromise has been struck. For, as social critic John Ralston Saul puts it, the two persistent illusions about freedom of speech are that a) we have it, and b) it is a luxury.[20]

Canadians do not have a surfeit of freedom of expression in the wake of the *Sharpe* judgment. This case stands at the end of a line of decisions that have ratcheted up the obstacles to a successful challenge to state censorship. From such cases as *Keegstra* and *Butler*, decided at the beginning of the 1990s, to the *Little Sister's* decision of 2000, the burden on the Crown to prove that the infringement of an expression right is rationally connected to the prevention of real and substantial harm has grown lighter and lighter. With the *Sharpe* decision in hand, it may be fairly said that the approach of the courts is that whenever Parliament censors offensive speech, it must be presumed to have done so rationally. The only thing that can disturb that default presumption is a demonstration that the connection is irrational to the point of absurdity. And since showing that a connection is not absurd is absurdly easy, the real burden has shifted to the party seeking a constitutional remedy. This has effected a transformation of the *Oakes* test from one in which the Crown must take up the burden of demonstrating a rational connection when there is a Charter breach, to what is effectively a reverse onus situation.

Join this to the result in *R. v. Sharpe*, which left in place the overbroad definition of a child, and also left in place the prohibition of the possession of non-self-authored texts, and there is not a lot for free speech enthusiasts to celebrate. It may be argued that all we have lost is the civil liberties "luxury" of expression protections for pedophiles, and surely that cannot be assessed a grievous loss.

We persist in disagreement. What is weakened, if not positively lost, is the foundational democratic idea of the integrity of the mind of the citizen. This is not a luxury, but the necessary linch-pin of any coherent account of democratic government. Of course, there was mention of the democratic importance of freedom of expression in all of the cases we have been discussing. But these gestures amount to little more than a respectful nod to the democratic idea, an idea that should stand at the centre of any adjudication of the expression rights.

As a concept, democracy is not particularly complicated, but as a commitment it makes considerable demands upon us. The core idea is that all persons are of equal worth and dignity. Further, that self-governing people, as the ultimate source of political authority and legitimacy, can never delegate the constitutive element of their sovereignty, which is the deliberative work of free minds.

There are two principal corollaries of the "deliberative democracy" idea. The first, and more familiar one, is that a sovereign citizenry may not permit any subordinate branch of their government to exercise a censoring authority over the content of their forum deliberations. Political speech – where "political" is given the correct liberal interpretation as any matter of public concern – is practically inviolate.[21]

The second corollary of the democratic ideal is, however, less commonly considered. This is the value of the inviolable integrity of the inner workings of the mind of the individual citizen. Conscience, religion, thought, belief, opinion – these freedoms of spirit and imagination are listed and protected before expression in democratic constitutional instruments because state inquiry into them, and interference with them, has always involved the most profound violations of democratic principle while yielding only the most speculative public benefits.

We emphasize democratic principle, as contrasted to privacy, not because privacy is not violated – it is – or because privacy is not a value of great importance – it is – but because it is often only privacy and expression rights that are placed in the balance against the public interests sought through censorship.

There is an argument against this view that is relevant to the matters we have been discussing. Sexual representations cannot be compared to discussions of the best form of government or the wisest course for public policy. It seems ludicrous to claim that when we happen upon some pornographic image, we have stumbled into the presence of the deliberating citizenry.

The response to this argument is that while a democratic people demands an absolute freedom where the discussion of political matters is concerned – not a luxury, but a democratic necessity – they also demand an absolute freedom where issues of conscience, belief, opinion, and uncommunicated thought are concerned. These freedoms of spirit and imagination may not be compromised without compromising the vision of human worth, dignity, and equality that animates the commitment to democracy. Again, not a luxury.

If there was a proverbial "dog that did not bark" – or did not bark often enough or loudly enough – in the pornography story, from *Butler* to *Sharpe*, it is the democratic idea. Part of the reason for this may lie in certain features of a national character that distinguishes us from the United States. Where the Americans have an allegedly "absolutist" constitutional First Amendment protecting speech, the Canadian Charter of Rights and Freedoms, while declaring thought and expression a fundamental freedom, also provides a constitutional clause that can limit fundamental freedoms, including those of speech. Unsurprisingly, this limitation is reflected in the practices of our judiciary and hence requires the sort of close scrutiny we've sought to provide here. Our very constitutional instruments seem to argue a willingness to trim the sails of democratic freedom in favour of fostering a distinctively Canadian civility.

This is not evil, of course, but it is a disposition that melds two errors, one ancient, and the other a relative novelty. The old mistake lies in the conviction that tolerance, respect, and mutual understanding can be enhanced through censorship. The new mistake is the belief that fundamental social change can be achieved simply by changing the language in which change is described and understood. So if thoughts that offend orthodox sexual morality can successfully resist censorship when described as immoral, there is a temptation to redescribe them as attacks on equality and thus justify silencing them.

In writing this book, we have not been motivated by a burning desire to make our country safe for child pornography. Far from it. Rather, we have sought to participate in a discussion that seeks to find the appropriate balance between upholding the social interest of protecting children, while at the same time preserving the democratic freedom of free speech. It is because of this that the constitutional cases on the question of the child pornography law ought to be a matter of interest to all Canadians.

NOTES

One: The Making of a 'Pervert'

1. The quoted material in this and subsequent paragraphs relating to Sharpe's arrest is taken from Robin Sharpe, *R. v. Sharpe: A Personal Account*, Dec. 1999 (unpublished).

The complete title of Sharpe's seized volume of stories is *Sam Paloc's Boyabuse: Flogging, Fun and Fortitude – A Collection of Kiddiekink Classics*. Sharpe used "Sam Paloc" as a *nom de plume*; it's derived from the word for a tamarind fruit (*sampaloc*) in the Tagalog language, spoken in the Philippine Islands. The title, or parts of it, was cited in almost every newspaper account of subsequent judicial proceedings relating to Sharpe, presumably not simply for purposes of information, but to suggest a moral implication about the gravity of the alleged offence.

2. Criminal Code of Canada, Section 163.1, *Martin's Annual Criminal Code* (Canada Law Book, 1999). In the Canadian system of justice there are three types of criminal offence: indictable, summary conviction, and "hybrid." The child pornography law is a "hybrid" offence, which means that the Crown can elect to proceed either by way of indictment or by summary conviction, depending on how serious it estimates the given offence to be, and this procedural option is reflected in sub-paragraphs (2), (3), and (4) of Section 163.1. In the case of indictable offences, the accused has the right to have the trial conducted before a judge and jury; in summary conviction proceedings, the case is heard by a judge alone.

3. Criminal Code of Canada, s. 159. However, the Ontario Court of Appeal declared Section 159 unconstitutional in *R. v. M.(C.)* (1995) on the ground that it infringed the "equal protection under the law" provision (Section 15 (1) of the *Charter of Rights and Freedoms*). The Crown did not appeal that decision.

Subsequently, the federal government appeared to announce its intention to establish a uniform age of consent for all sexual acts, thus eliminating the discriminatory gap created by the separate and higher age of consent for anal sex, which had effectively allowed heterosexuals to engage in sex at a younger age than homosexuals. See "Age of consent to change for gays," *Vancouver Sun*, April 10, 2000. However, a Justice Department spokesperson subsequently denied that the government was contemplating anything other than simply raising the age of consent. See Tom Yeung, "Anal consent not on agenda," *XtraWest*, May 4, 2000.

4. Since Sharpe is still charged with offences against Section 163.1 as we write this, we won't speculate on the evidentiary character of the material seized by the police. For example, with respect to the photographs referred to above, we'll leave aside discussion of whether the people represented are under eighteen, whether they're "engaged in explicit sexual activity," or whether body parts are depicted "for a sexual purpose," etc. For the most part, we'll confine ourselves to examining the constitutional validity of the law, referring only to evidentiary materials when they're constitutionally relevant.

We haven't examined the evidentiary exhibits presented in court since they aren't strictly material to our argument; however, in November 1999 a Vancouver gay newspaper, *XtraWest*, sought and obtained a court order from the B.C. Court of Appeal allowing the newspaper access to the court exhibits. An account of the application for access, which was unsuccessfully opposed by the B.C. government, and the subsequent examination of materials is contained in Garth Barriere's, "A youth's right to sex – and Polaroid pics," *XtraWest*, January 13, 2000.

5. Attention to media treatment of both Sharpe as a criminal defendant and the constitutional court cases arising from the charges against him is germane to our analysis. This is because the media play such an important role in affecting public attitudes towards child pornography legislation and relevant related issues (in this case, the issue of homosexuality), which in turn helps to shape an even broader public forum that includes institutions of government, the judiciary, and civil society.

In what follows, we shouldn't be misunderstood as making the simplistic claim that the media, in some conspiratorial fashion, "manufactures" public attitudes. Rather, we're pointing to a complex dynamic by which public mentalities develop, a process in which the media plays an indispensable role in reflecting, rebroadcasting (often at a higher decibel level), and reinforcing a developing mentality that is shaped reciprocally through the activity of many institutions and individuals.

To take a simple relevant example, if a newspaper consistently displays stories about alleged child pornographers with front-page prominence, we take it (and we assume the newspaper's readers take it) as, in addition to information, a public alert to a danger confronting the community, and we assume that readers take that alert into account. By contrast, the display of the same information in a less prominent location would be a sign that while the newspaper regards the material as newsworthy, it doesn't necessarily regard it as more than that. This is one way the media contributes to the construction of a public mentality. Indeed, the role of the contemporary media is so inextricable from debate in the public forum that it's always a fair question to ask about any issue, What is the media's role in this story?

6. *Vancouver Province*, May 14, 1993, and June 24, 1993.

7. *Vancouver Province*, January 19, 1999.

8. Tom Yeung, "Bennest gets suspended sentence," *Xtra West*, October 16, 1997. We aren't commenting on Bennest's guilt or innocence with respect to particular charges, and we're aware that charges are often dropped or stayed in the course of "plea bargaining," not necessarily because acts haven't occurred, but because it's convenient to the legal process not to pursue those charges in order to achieve a certain outcome. Our concern is limited to the magnitude of the media representation of the accused in relation to what turns out to be a relatively minor outcome.

9. Gareth Kirkby, "A message to Ujjal," *Xtra West*, October 16, 1997.

10. Gareth Kirkby, "Lessons from the Bennest case," *Xtra West*, February 19, 1998.

11. *Ibid.* The coverage of the Bennest case was not an isolated or atypical example. Shortly after the passage of the federal child pornography law, in 1993, there was a sensational case in London, Ontario, that led to the arrests of several dozen gay men. Although the case was initially billed and widely publicized as one of child pornography, it turned out that the overwhelming majority of arrests were in connection with youth prostitution, itself a disputed issue (given that those involved are all above the age of consent), and one at some distance from crimes of sexual representation of children under the age of consent. Again, the conflation of such issues was a matter of central concern for homosexual organizations such as the Homophile Association of London, Ontario and the Coalition for Lesbian and Gay Rights in Ontario. See Eleanor Brown, "How to cope . . .," *Xtra West*, October 1, 1998, and Tom Yeung, "Beware witchhunt," *Xtra West*, October 30, 1997.

Closer to Vancouver, there was the notorious and long-running case of the "Chicken Book," based on the allegation by a Los Angeles police officer that an American immigrant residing in Canada had produced an address book that contained the names of prominent public figures, including Canadians, all of whom were connected to a "kiddie porn and child prostitution ring." Although the address book was in the possession of the police for a number of years, and the Vancouver press speculated about its alleged contents, ultimately the rumours of a criminal conspiracy were revealed to be the invention of the Los Angeles police officer, and no charges were laid. The officer involved was convicted, in an unrelated case, of armed robbery and rape. See Daniel Gawthrop, "Sexual McCarthyism," *XtraWest*, December 10, 1998.

12. Peter Wilson, "Kiddie porn laws make freedom of speech a tough sell," *Vancouver Sun*, July 7, 1993.

13. In what follows we're making use of Ian Hacking's *The Social Construction of What?* (Harvard, 1999), especially Chapter 5, "Kind-Making: The Case of Child Abuse," and Wendy Kaminer's *Sleeping with Extra-Terrestrials: The Rise of Irrationalism and Perils of Piety* (Pantheon, 1999), especially Chapter 6, "The Therapeutic Assault on Reason and Rights." Our discussion of social construction analysis in relation to various topics taken up in this book is merely schematic. The questions raised about how we develop interpretations of the world and the relationship between such "world-making" and political outcomes (such as the child pornography law) and public mentalities are important philosophical issues, even apart from the debate about legal philosophy in which we engage here, but for the purposes of this text we can do no more than point to those larger questions.

14. One of the standard works providing a history of the development of the category of "child" is Philippe Aries, *Centuries of Childhood: A Social History of Family Life* (Knopf, 1962).

15. Hacking, *Social Construction*, p. 156. As of this writing, there is a discussion among Canadian attorneys general of a proposal to raise the legal age of consent in Canada from the current age of fourteen to possibly age sixteen. Whether or not that occurs does not substantially affect the argument we'll be making about sexual representation in relation to age of consent.

16. These practices are famously discussed in Plato, *The Symposium* (tr. Walter Hamilton, Penguin, 1951), and commented on by Michel Foucault in *The Use of Pleasure* (Penguin, 1984).

17. See, for example, Gilbert Herdt, *Guardians of the Flute* (University of Chicago, 1994). In many contemporary cultures, both Western and non-Western, such relations occur in the form of prostitution, which raises additional and often controversial questions.

18. See David Halperin, *One Hundred Years of Homosexuality* (Routledge, 1989).

19. See Andrew Sullivan, *Virtually Normal: An Argument about Homosexuality* (Vintage, 1996). Our remarks on homosexuality are meant to sketch in the broadest outlines of a complex issue. We are concerned with

the impact that views on homosexuality have on the legislation and case at hand, but our argument is neither germane to homosexuality as such, nor dependent on particular sexual preferences, except with respect to certain narrow issues, which we will flag as they occur in the course of the text. Though homosexuality is more than tangentially relevant to our main themes, the argument we're presenting about child pornography legislation and freedom of expression applies equally to heterosexual and homosexual expression.

20. A particular Canadian aspect of the perceived extent of child abuse was linked to a series of revelations in the 1980s of extensive patterns of child abuse that had occurred at church-operated orphanages and residential schools. Although the events referred to had occurred, in many cases, as much as thirty or forty years earlier, their discovery intensified contemporary consciousness of the problem.

21. Hacking, *Social Construction*, p. 133.

22. *Ibid.*, p. 137.

23. *Ibid.*, p. 144.

24. Kaminer, *Sleeping*, p. 190.

25. Hacking, *Social Construction*, p. 126.

26. Kaminer, *Sleeping*, p. 193.

27. *Ibid.*, p. 192.

28. *Ibid.*, p. 215. Kaminer is not alone in her criticisms. Social psychologist Carol Tavris writes in a similar vein, "The subject of childhood sexual abuse was highjacked. In America, it became a vehicle for American puritanism, religious fundamentalism, sexual hysteria, ignorance about children's sexuality, the vested interests of therapists, and a fast track to advancement for ambitious prospectors. Feminists had exposed each of these cultural forces when women were the victims of them. When women became the promulgators of puritanism and sexual hysteria, and when their own vested interests were at stake, many feminists found this reversal hard to take." (Carol Tavris, "Lest we forget," *Times Literary Supplement*, March 17, 2000.)

An example of the excesses of child abuse ideology was revealed in a discussion on CBC Radio where it was reported that film-processing firms in Canada routinely engage in surveillance of pictures of nude babies or children that reveal "genital areas." Just to be safe, and for fear that they may themselves be subject to prosecution if they do not act, the photo processors notify local police. The police, the Crown, and various child welfare agencies are quickly brought onto the scene. Apparently, though no statistics were provided, scores of such cases have occurred. Although charges are often dropped after it turns out that the photos are quite innocent, the amount of misery inflicted on families is significant. (Michael Enright, *This Morning*, CBC Radio, April 17, 2000.)

29. Kaminer, *Sleeping*, p. 216.

30. Hugh Brody, *The People's Land: Whites and the Eastern Arctic* (Penguin, 1975), pp. 7-13.

31. There's no need for us to recapitulate the lengthy exchanges that took place – although much of the testimony has an intrinsic interest – since the relevant parts will be considered and judged in the legal decisions that we'll examine in due course. We're naturally disposed to provide a blow-by-blow account of the development of the case as it unfolded in the courtroom, but we've decided to restrain ourselves here, both in order to keep our text to a manageable length and to accommodate readers who want the main outlines of the issues at stake, but don't necessarily share our interest in the details.

We'll provide one brief example of the sort of thing that's of interest to more avid observers of the case. At one point in the *voir dire*, Sharpe was cross-examining Detective Waters. Waters had claimed, plausibly enough, that the availability of child pornography had increased dramatically with the introduction of Internet technology in recent years. Sharpe then, quite relevantly, asked Waters if the magnitude of increase in the availability of child pornography through the Internet was matched by a corresponding increase in the number of child sexual assaults. Waters replied that she didn't know.

The importance of a tiny testimony-based exchange like this – which we could multiply almost at will from the proceedings – is obvious. If it's claimed that one of the principle justifications for the law is that child pornography is a contributory factor in causing harm to children, then obviously the increased availability of a contributory cause can reasonably be expected to produce more harm to children. If it turns out that there's a lot more child pornography available, but not a lot more harm caused to children, then the theorized link between child pornography and harm is called into question. Waters' inability to provide information about increased actual harm – and she is, after all, a person who's accredited as an expert in the field and would be expected to have such information at hand – in itself becomes evidence undercutting the alleged connection between child pornography and harm.

In a particularly sensationalistic *Newsweek* magazine "special report" on the exponential increase in the availability of kiddie porn through the Internet, the writers ask, "But how many consumers of pornography actually cross the line to soliciting and abusing children?" They then concede, "Overall, the evidence on child molestation in the United States is mixed: after a surge in the early '90s, the total number of substantiated cases of sexual abuse known to child-protection authorities declined by 31 per cent between 1992 and 1998," the very period in which the increase of child pornography on the Internet was at its height. (Rob Nordland and Jeffrey Bartholet, "The Web's Dark Secret," *Newsweek*, March 19, 2001.)

This is only one of many possible examples – and not necessarily a critical one – that occur in the record as the participants try to determine the issues in this case. The claims of the experts with respect to harm to children will turn out not to be conclusive in determining the outcome of the deliberations. Indeed, the inconclusiveness of expert claims will be a significant factor in judges' determinations of how much weight to give to constitutional claims.

Two: The Making of the Kiddie Porn Law

1. We should note that we're friends and colleagues of former Justice minister and former prime minister Kim Campbell, though neither of us are associated with any of the political organizations or parties that she's represented.

John Dixon worked for the Department of Justice when Campbell was minister. Stan Persky and Campbell worked together as "friendly rival" B.C. political correspondents on Peter Gzowski's *Morningside* radio program in the 1980s. In addition, Campbell served as an honorary board member of the non-partisan B.C. Civil Liberties Association, where we were also members of the board, and she's been a guest lecturer in college classes we've taught.

In this chapter, in addition to our own and other sources, we make use, naturally, of Campbell's well-written and informative political memoirs, *Time and Chance* (Seal Books, 1996). Curiously, however, Campbell makes no mention whatsoever of child pornography legislation in her account, and we've had to rely on internal documents and memos produced within the Department of Justice, principally those of adviser John Dixon.

One of this book's authors has also been a participant in the events described here, which naturally poses a slight technical problem for our narration. Although any solution is bound to be arbitrary, we've chosen to represent John Dixon in the third person, as an actor in the story, and to rely primarily on written materials he produced during the period under review to minimize the vagaries of memory.

2. In addition to Campbell's memoirs, for details on her political career see also Pete McMartin, "Candid Kim," *Vancouver Sun*, February 24, 1990; Graham Fraser, "The woman behind the robe," *Globe and Mail*, December 12, 1992.

3. For the text of the Morgentaler decision, see Shelagh Day and Stan Persky (editors), *The Supreme Court of Canada Decision on Abortion* (New Star, 1988).

4. There is, of course, a larger story to be told about the legislative agenda and political problems of the second Mulroney administration that is beyond the scope of this text except as it specifically impinges on the

activities of the Justice ministry. However, it may be useful to remind readers of the status of the "Quebec question" as of 1990, when Campbell took office.

An earlier attempt to achieve Quebec's explicit approval of the 1982 Constitution Act – an agreement between the federal government and the provinces dubbed the "Meech Lake Accord" that was reached during the first term of Mulroney's tenure – had failed in various provincial legislatures. Mulroney was already working on a second effort by 1991 – what became known as the "Charlottetown Accord" – which would deploy considerable government resources in the following year, 1992, when a national referendum on the constitutional proposal was held and again failed to secure passage.

It's helpful to distinguish between national political objectives and the "politics of politics," especially those political concerns internal to the Conservative Party, since those are germane to the subject of this book. So while the attempt to secure a constitutional accord with the province of Quebec may well have been motivated by a notion of the "good of the country" (as well as the desire to achieve re-election), such efforts were also pragmatically intended to undercut and forestall the possibility of a referendum in Quebec authorizing the province's nationalistic government to seek some form of independence from Canada (an earlier referendum on that question had failed in 1980).

The effort to secure national unity through a constitutional agreement also would have an impact on the internal tensions of the governing party. There were two significant threats, as we've noted. The right-wing Family Caucus of the party was drawn towards a nascent populist organization, the Reform party, led by Preston Manning (this party would later transform itself into the Canadian Alliance). The ideology of the Family Caucus was in many ways indistinguishable from that of Manning's party, and the Family Caucus was often referred to in government circles as the Reform-party-in-waiting. A similar threat was posed by Conservative MPs from Quebec, a group retrospectively referred to as the Bloc-Quebecois-in-waiting. As it happened, the leader of that group, Lucien Bouchard, and several of his associates formally defected from the government caucus in May 1990 and subsequently sat in the House of Commons as the Bloc Quebecois. By contrast, a mass defection to the Reform party did not occur until the 1993 federal election.

5. Cited in Graham Fraser, "Woman behind the robe."

6. We'll do no more than briefly refer to the general debate about pornography, except where it impinges on the thinking and actions of the Justice department in the context of child pornography legislation. We will, however, subsequently examine in some detail an important Supreme Court of Canada decision – R. v. Butler (1992) – about pornography that has direct relevance to the development of the kiddie porn law.

There is, for interested readers, a rich literature available on the general pornography question. Works that we've found useful are primarily those written by feminists and include: Catherine MacKinnon, *Only Words* (Harvard, 1993); Judith Butler, *Excitable Speech* (Routledge, 1997); Drucilla Cornell, *The Imaginary Domain* (Routledge, 1995); Lynn Hunt (ed.), *The Invention of Pornography: Obscenity and the Origins of Modernity, 1500-1800* (Zone, 1993); Varda Burstyn (ed.), *Women Against Censorship* (Douglas and McIntyre, 1985); Walter Kendrick, *The Secret Museum: Pornography in Modern Culture* (University of California, 1996); and James Weinstein, *Hate Speech, Pornography and the Radical Attack on Free Speech Doctrine* (Westview, 1999).

7. MacKinnon's publications include *Sexual Harassment of Working Women* (Yale, 1979); *Feminism Unmodified* (Harvard, 1987); (with Andrea Dworkin), *Pornography and Civil Rights* (self-published, 1988); *Towards a Feminist Theory of the State* (Harvard, 1989); and *Only Words* (Harvard, 1993).

8. See Charles Taylor, *Multiculturalism: Examining the Politics of Recognition* (Princeton, 1994); and Michael Sandal, *Democracy's Discontent* (Harvard, 1996).

9. John Dixon, "Memo," February 14, 1991.

10. Although the *Little Sister's v. Canada* (1996) case wasn't heard until 1994, and not decided until 1996 (followed by appeals to higher courts), already by late 1991 there was extensive correspondence between the Department of Justice and the Department of National Revenue, advising the latter that the prohibition of depictions of anal intercourse contained in Customs' guidelines with respect to obscene publications would not be defensible in court. See letter of deputy minister of Justice to deputy minister of National Revenue, September 24, 1991. The guideline wasn't withdrawn until a week before the Little Sister's case was heard in late 1994. For an account of the initial *Little Sister's v. Canada* case, heard in the B.C. Supreme Court, see Janine Fuller and Stuart Blackley, *Restricted Entry: Censorship on Trial* (Press Gang, 1996, second edition).

11. Among the sources for the idea of a possession offence were documents from the B.C. Civil Liberties Association, including the association's 1984 position paper on pornography written by Alister Browne, its submissions to the Fraser Commission on Pornography and Prostitution, and correspondence between the association and various provincial and federal government ministries. In a letter to B.C. attorney general Brian Smith on February 27, 1985, the BCCLA says, "One can't take a photograph of a child being used sexually . . . without it being the case that the child is really being used sexually. Canadians have agreed that the sexual use of children is so harmful as to be made unlawful, and hence we cannot countenance the making and distribution of a commodity that is produced by contriving an unlawful act."

12. John Dixon, "Memorandum re: individual rights vs. collective interests: equality rights in the Canadian federal setting," March 14, 1991.

For those with a specific interest in philosophy or philosophy of law, we should note that in our discussion of rights that follows, and in our reference in the previous chapter to the distinction between words and acts, we are not proffering a metaphysical position in the current philosophical debates between "neo-pragmatism" and forms of philosophical "realism." While we're attentive readers of Richard Rorty's *Contingency, Irony and Solidarity* (Cambridge, 1989), nothing said here, as far as we can tell, very much hangs on whether one prefers Rorty to John Searle's *The Construction of Social Reality* (Free Press, 1995). In distinguishing between words and acts, or in referring to a theory of self-governance as central to democracy, we are making no claims about whether or not such distinctions have a transcendent character. Rather, our usage is limited to the current standard usage of such terms within a theory of "political liberalism," as the philosopher John Rawls refers to such a framework. Insofar as political liberalism is assumed as the background theory for our discussion, our claims about words and acts, rights, and concepts of harm are simply meant to be coherent within that framework. See John Rawls, *Political Liberalism* (Columbia, 1996).

13. Sharon Moyer, "A Preliminary Investigation into Child Pornography in Canada," The Research Group, March 1991.

14. Kim Campbell, *Time and Chance*, p. 166.

15. *Ibid.*, p. 167.

16. *Ibid.*, p. 171.

17. *Ibid.*, p. 177.

18. *Ibid.*.

19. *Ibid.*, p. 179.

20. John Dixon, "Memo, Re: Pornography Legislation," July 16, 1991.

21. John Dixon, "Memo, Re: Child Porn/Sexual Orientation: Options," November 7, 1991.

22. The *Butler* decision has generated a considerable legal literature about the case. In what follows, in addition to our own reading of the judgment, we rely on Jodi Aileen Kleinick, "Suppressing Violent and Degrading Pornography to 'Prevent Harm' in Canada: *Butler v. Her Majesty the Queen*," *Brooklyn Journal of International Law*, 1993, v. 19, pp. 627-75, as a characteristic sound critique of the ruling. Other sources for our reading range from Ronald Dworkin's *Freedom's Law* (Harvard, 1996) to Brenda Crossman, Shannon Bell, Lise Gotell, and Becki Ross's *Bad Attitude/s on Trial: Pornography, Feminism and the Butler Decision* (University of Toronto, 1996).

23. Kleinick, *Suppressing*, p. 645.

24. *Ibid.*.

25. *R. v. Butler* (1992).

26. Kleinick, *Suppressing*, p. 646.

27. *R. v. Butler.*

28. In determining whether Section 1 requirements are met, Canadian jurisprudence has developed the *Oakes* test, so named from *R. v. Oakes* (1986), where this interpretive scheme was first established. "Under the *Oakes* test, two central criteria must be met for a limitation on a Charter right to be valid: first, the government objective for limiting the Charter right must be sufficiently important to warrant the limitation of that right; and, second, the limitation on the Charter right must be 'proportional' to the government's objective. A determination of proportionality involves three separate inquiries: (1) whether a rational connection exists between the limitation on the individual right and the government objective; (2) whether the limitation only minimally impairs the Charter right; and (3) whether the effects of the limitation so severely infringe the protected Charter right that the legislative objective is outweighed by the limitation" (Kleinick, *Suppressing*, p. 633). The *Oakes* test is not only relevant to the *Butler* case, but will be invoked by all the courts involved in *R. v. Sharpe.*

29. *R. v. Butler.*

30. Kleinick, *Suppressing*, p. 652.

31. *Ibid.*, p. 653.

32. J.S. Mill, *On Liberty.*

33. *Ibid.*

34. Ronald Dworkin, *Freedom's Law.*

35. Kleinick, *Suppressing*, pp. 666, 668.

36. Crossman, *et al., Bad Attitude/s.*

37. Jeff Sallot, "Ruling paves way for child pornography bill, minister says," *Globe and Mail*, February 28, 1992, p. 1.

38. John Dixon, "Memorandum: Child Pornography Legislation," May 26, 1992.

39. Campbell, *Time and Chance*, p. 213.

40. *Ibid.*, p. 214.

41. *Ibid.*, pp. 215-216.

42. *Ibid.*, p. 218. Accompanying Campbell's attempts in spring 1992 were a series of memos that the Department of Justice prepared for various caucus members. In addition to demonstrating that there was considerable depth to the effort to generate support for the measure, the documents discuss, in some detail, the issue of the relations between "rights" and "interests," which parallel many of the concerns in the child pornography law debate.

43. *Ibid.*, p. 228.

44. John Dixon, "Memorandum: The Appeal of Haig," August 16, 1992, and October 22, 1992. The latter memo concluded, " . . . appealing Haig would be the political 'last straw' for gay people and those Canadians sym-

pathetic to their claims. We have lost the opportunity to either steer or temper the courts with legislation. And we are without the political means (caucus would forbid it) to introduce CHRA reforms that would be consonant with the new judge-made standards. Legislatively speaking, we can neither lead nor follow."

45. Geoffrey York, "Ottawa accepts court ruling on gay rights," *Globe and Mail*, October 31, 1992, p. A10.

46. John Dixon, "Memo: Re: Senator Kinsella's Gay Rights Bill," November 2, 1992, and "Memorandum: Re: CHRA Amendments," November 17, 1992.

47. John Dixon, "Memo: Talking Points for National Caucus," December 8, 1992.

48. Campbell, *Time and Chance*, p. 231.

49. Graham Fraser, "Bill protects gay and lesbian rights; Campbell's legislation criticized for not recognizing same-sex marriage," *Globe and Mail*, December 11, 1992; Stan Persky, "Don't they know when it's time to declare victory?" *Globe and Mail*, December 21, 1992; Graham Haig, "Victory for 'lesbigays'," *Globe and Mail*, December 30, 1992.

50. Jack Aubry, "Liberals soar, Reform stumbles as gay-rights bill passes," *Ottawa Citizen*, May 10, 1996; Karen Patrick, "Canadian Human Rights Act amended," *XtraWest*, May 16, 1996.

51. "Child porn leaking through loopholes," *Vancouver Sun*, April 20, 1993.

52. Cited in Sharpe, *Personal Account*, as is much of the following material on the parliamentary committee hearings.

53. Sean Fine, "Ottawa proposes to outlaw child smut," *Globe and Mail*, May 14, 1993; Anthony Johnson, "Tougher sentencing proposed," *Vancouver Sun*, May 14, 1993.

54. Sean Fine, "Ottawa proposes."

55. Cited in Bronwyn Drainie, "How can we tell if 'pornographic' drawings are art?" *Globe and Mail*, January 8, 1994.

56. *Ibid.*

57. "Bonfire of the inanities," *Globe and Mail*, February 26, 1994.

58. Cited in *R. v. Sharpe* (1999), ruling on *voir dire*, paragraph 27.

Three: Judge Shaw Decides

1. See Mark Hume, "Man defended himself in child porn case," *National Post*, January 16, 1999, where Sharpe is quoted as remarking, "I'm used to being considered a pariah by many people. It's not an issue that can be rationally debated in public."

2. Most of what follows is taken from *R. v Sharpe*, ruling on *voir dire*, by

Justice D.W. Shaw, January 13, 1999, supplemented by our running commentary. Because there would be so much criticism of the courts in the wake of decisions on the Sharpe case, with frequent complaints that the judiciary has been wrongfully "making law" rather than properly interpreting it, it's important to say something about the justice system. Our own view of the judiciary is that it is an appropriate institution within a "checks and balances" structure of democratic government, and that the relative autonomy it enjoys through a doctrine of "judicial independence" is, on the whole, a benefit to democratic societies. The courts uphold parliamentary wisdom at least as frequently as they offer checks to legislative whims, enthusiasms, and mistakes. The court system is itself subject to checks and balances through its hierarchical structure, whereby a series of courts of increasing rank (from humble provincial courts to Canada's Supreme Court) successively apply their deliberative powers to the same case, often with varying results. Those results are dependent on the skill, insight, and intelligence that various judges and groups of judges are able to muster with respect to a given case and, of course, their decisions are criticizable in the public forum. Finally, in the Canadian system, the courts themselves are answerable to the people in the form of its representative Parliament, which retains the ultimate power to overrule even the Supreme Court of Canada through the use of what's known as the "notwithstanding clause" of the Canadian Constitution.

3. Published in *The Journal of Sex Research*, May 1988, Vol. 25, No. 2.

4. Most of the expert witnesses called by the Crown in such cases are, not surprisingly, wedded to a particular ideological view of child pornography reflective of the policies of the law enforcement or scientific institutions by whom they're employed. Sharpe's inability to call witnesses meant that significant counter-evidence, such as can be found, for example, in Berl Kutchinsky, "Pornography and its Effects in Denmark and the United States," *Comparative Social Research*, Vol. 8, pp. 301-330 (1985), was not presented to the court.

5. Jane Armstrong, "Child porn law is struck down by B.C. judge," *Globe and Mail*, January 16, 1999, p. A1; Francine Dube, "Top B.C. court strikes down child porn law," *National Post*, January 16, 1999, p. A1; Neal Hall, "B.C. judge throws out child porn law," *Vancouver Sun*, January 16, 1999, p. A1 (reprinted in the *Ottawa Citizen*, January 16, 1999, p. A1).

6. Charles Enman, "Porn ruling angers experts," *Ottawa Citizen*, January 17, 1999.

7. Neal Hall, "B.C. judge throws out child porn law," *Vancouver Sun*, January 16. 1999.

8. Neal Hall and Lori Culbert, "Surrey judge dismisses new child porn charge," *Vancouver Sun*, January 19, 1999.

9. Barbara McLintock and Holly Horwood, "B.C. moves to appeal child porn decision," *Vancouver Province*, January 19, 1999.

10. Lori Culbert, "Successful appeal of child porn ruling imminent, professor says," *National Post*, January 18, 1999. The professor predicting the decision's overturn was criminology professor Neil Boyd of Simon Fraser University in Burnaby, B.C.

11. "'Sickened' by porn ruling," *Vancouver Province*, January 19, 1999.

12. Susan Martinuk, "Justice Duncan Shaw: 'What planet is he on, anyway?'" *Vancouver Province*, January 20, 1999.

13. Shari Graydon, "There is no justifying the possession of child porn," *Globe and Mail*, January 19, 1999.

14. "Society's main concern: Safeguarding children," *Vancouver Sun*, January 19, 1999.

15. "What about the children?" *Ottawa Citizen*, January 19, 1999.

16. Ian Bailey, "Judge in B.C. child porn case receives death threat over ruling," *Globe and Mail*, January 23, 1999.

17. John Wawrow, "Sharpe 'sad' over threat to judge," *Vancouver Province*, January 24, 1999.

18. Ian Bailey, "Justice Duncan Shaw," *Vancouver Sun*, January 21, 1999.

19. Tim Naumetz, "Storm brews over B.C. porn ruling," *National Post*, January 26, 1999.

20. Tim Naumetz, "Ottawa to intervene in appeal of B.C.'s child porn ruling," *National Post*, January 27, 1999.

21. Sheldon Alberts, "McLellan rejects calls to overturn child porn ruling," *National Post*, February 2, 1999.

22. Sheldon Alberts, "4 maverick MPs ignore Liberal line over porn motion," *National Post*, February 3, 1999.

23. Mark Hume, "B.C. to fast track appeal of child porn ruling," *National Post*, February 6, 1999.

Four: An Appeal to Reason

1. The British Columbia Civil Liberties Association, "Factum of the Intervenor," April 15, 1999.

2. The BCCLA brief, mainly to highlight discrimination against homosexuals in Canada, also proposed a second issue that the court might consider. It asked if the child pornography law violated the equality provision of the Charter of Rights (Section 15) "by discriminating on the basis of sexual orientation." The kiddie porn law did so, suggested the civil liberties organization, by criminalizing the advocacy of a "consensual, non-exploitative, non-commercial sexual act, involving persons aged 14 to 17, namely, anal intercourse, a sexual act of particular significance to gay men and youth." As it turned out, the court decided not to take up the Section 15 question.

3. Janice Tibbetts, "Protecting children outweighs benefits of porn possession, Ottawa argues," *National Post*, April 15, 1999.

4. Our account of the April 26, 1999, B.C. Court of Appeal hearing is constructed from eyewitness reports and the following press accounts: Robert Matas, "Attitudes towards child porn could change, B.C. judge says," *Globe and Mail*, April 27, 1999, p. A1; Mark Hume, "Child porn will flourish without law, police warn," *National Post*, April 27, 1999, p. A1; Andy Ivens, "Child porn law goes too far," *Vancouver Province*, April 27, 1999; "Judge questions child porn law," *Ottawa Citizen*, April 27, 1999; Chad Skelton, "Appeal in porn acquittal faces judicial inquisition," *Vancouver Sun*, April 27, 1999, p. A1; John Dixon, "Balancing porn with freedom," *Vancouver Sun*, April 27, 1999.

5. Robert Matas, "Lawyers drop part of child porn challenge," *Globe and Mail*, April 28, 1999; Chad Skelton, "Porn law borders on 'thought control'," *Vancouver Sun*, April 28, 1999.

6. Chris Maclean, "Child pornography should not be a right," *Ottawa Citizen*, May 1, 1999; Luiza Chwialkowska, "Case inflames debate over judicial activism," *National Post*, April 27, 1999; Andrew Coyne, "The Charter under attack," *National Post*, May 3, 1999.

7. Chad Skelton, "Child pornography in the court," *Vancouver Sun*, May 4, 1999; Ted Byfield, "Onward, the revolution: how media and government advance the acceptance of pedophilia," *British Columbia Report*, May 31, 1999.

8. Citations that follow are from *R. v. Sharpe*, Court of Appeal of British Columbia, June 30, 1999.

9. See Chapter 1, Note 3.

10. At this point, Justice Southin briefly took up the argument of the Evangelical Fellowship of Canada, which argued that the phrase the "supremacy of God," which appears in the preamble to the Canadian Constitution, was relevant to interpreting Section 1 of the Charter. Responded Southin: "I know of no case on the Charter in which any court of this country has relied on the words [that the Evangelical Fellowship] invokes. They have become a dead letter and while I might have wished the contrary, this Court has no authority to breathe life into them for the purpose of interpreting the various provisions of the Charter." *R. v. Sharpe*, paragraph 79.

11. Paula Brook, "Unprepared and buck naked," *Vancouver Sun*, July 7, 1999; Robert Matas, "Legal to possess child porn, B.C. court rules," *Globe and Mail*, July 1, 1999.

12. Jane Armstrong, "Kiddie porn law headed to top court," *Globe and Mail*, July 1, 1999, p. A1; Robert Fife, Jennifer Prittie, and Mark Hume, "Possession of child porn legal," *National Post*, July 1, 1999, p. A1; Janice Tibbetts, "Child porn legal in B.C.," *Ottawa Citizen*, July 1, 1999, p. A1.

13. Susanne Hiller, "Madam Justice Southin not known to back down,"

National Post, July 1, 1999.

14. Mark Hume, "Judge draws on absurd examples," *National Post*, July 1, 1999, p. A1.

15. "Stick to banning material that exploits real children," *Vancouver Province*, July 1, 1999; "A clear law against child pornography is a priority," *Vancouver Sun*, July 2, 1999.

16. "Too sweeping," *Ottawa Citizen*, July 3, 1999.

17. George Jonas, "The confused embrace thought control," *Ottawa Citizen*, July 9, 1999.

18. Carmen Wittmeier, "Child porn wins again," *British Columbia Report*, July 26, 1999; Jack Keating, "Child porn law to be reviewed," *Vancouver Province*, July 9, 1999.

Five: At the Supreme Court of Canada

1. Norm Ovenden, "Justice minister under fire for inaction on child porn issue," *Ottawa Citizen*, September 23, 1999.

2. Tim Naumetz, "Liberal MPs demand action on child porn," *Ottawa Citizen*, October 15, 1999.

3. Sheldon Alberts, "Child porn petition doesn't sway McLellan," *National Post*, October 16, 1999; Tim Naumetz, "McLellan resists call for new child porn law," *Ottawa Citizen*, October 16, 1999; Peter O'Neil, "Government asked to suspend Charter rights over child porn," *Vancouver Sun*, October 16, 1999.

4. "Manitoba: Province to intervene in child porn case," *Globe and Mail*, October 23, 1999; Theresa Boyle, "Ontario joins fight to outlaw child porn," *Toronto Star*, January 12, 2000. There were also reports of town councils passing resolutions against child pornography, an indicator perhaps of the depth of feeling about the issue, but also a measure of the rhetorical attraction of the subject.

5. Ian Bailey, "SFU defends invitation to man in child porn controversy," *Vancouver Sun*, October 1, 1999; "Pedophile gets a grant," *National Post*, October 2, 1999.

6. Janice Tibbetts, "B.C. urges high court to weigh public opinion in porn case," *National Post*, October 2, 1999.

7. B.C. Civil Liberties Association, "Factum of the Intervenor," December 30, 1999

8. Janice Tibbetts, "Chief justice vows to ignore public fury," *Vancouver Sun*, January 12, 2000; Luiza Chwialkowska, "High court will be pragmatic, McLachlin says," *National Post*, January 12, 2000; Juliet O'Neill, "McLachlin credits 'justice of Canadian society' for rise to top court position," *Vancouver Sun*, January 18, 2000.

9. Christie Blatchford, "How to make the laudable proper," *National Post*, January 19, 2000.

10. Our account of the Supreme Court hearing is drawn from eyewitness accounts and the following press accounts: Janice Tibbetts, "Protesters demand court uphold ban on child porn," *Vancouver Sun*, January 19, 2000; Kirk Makin, "Child porn case spurs intense arguments," *Globe and Mail*, January 19, 2000; Janice Tibbets, "Freedom of speech not absolute in Canada, high court judges warn," *National Post*, January 20, 2000.

11. Chad Skelton, "Sharpe, lawyers at odds as porn case opens in Supreme Court," *Vancouver Sun*, January 18, 2000, and authors' interview with Robin Sharpe, February 17, 2001.

12. Chad Skelton, *ibid.*

13. Supreme Court of Canada, *Little Sister's v. Canada*, headnotes.

14. Chad Skelton and Janice Tibbetts, "A new standard for obscenity," *Vancouver Sun*, December 16, 2000; Lori Culbert, "After 15 years...", *Vancouver Sun*, December 16, 2000.

15. Cristin Schmitz, "Supreme Court 'goes too far,' oft-dissenting judge claims," *Vancouver Sun*, January 13, 2001.

16. Supreme Court of Canada, *R. v. Sharpe*, January 26, 2001.

17. *Ibid.*, paragraph 58, emphasis in the original.

18. Reactions to the Supreme Court decision have been garnered from eyewitness accounts and the following press reports: Kirk Makin, "Top court rules 9-0: child porn law stays," *Globe and Mail*, January 27, 2001; Kirk Makin, "Activist days long gone for deferential court," *Globe and Mail*, January 27, 2001; Brian Laghi, "McLellan welcomes balanced judgment," *Globe and Mail*, January 27, 2001; "Bringing proportion to the child-porn law," *Globe and Mail*, January 27, 2001; Rod Mickleburgh, "B.C. defendant unrepentant after court ruling," *Globe and Mail*, January 27, 2001; Rod Mickleburgh and Colin Freeze, "Both sides claim victory," *Globe and Mail*, January 27, 2001; Luiza Chwialkowska, "High court upholds child porn ban," *National Post*, January 27, 2001; James Cudmore and Ian Jack, "Victory for children: Liberals," *National Post*, January 27, 2001; Ian Bailey, "Children meant to have sex, accused says," *National Post*, January 27, 2001; "Sharpe Ruling," *National Post*, January 27, 2001; Janice Tibbetts, "Pornography law stands—with fixes," *Vancouver Sun*, January 27, 2001; Neal Hall, "Interview with John Robin Sharpe," *Vancouver Sun*, January 27, 2001; Lori Culbert and Harold Munro, "Walking the line between privacy, harm," *Vancouver Sun*, January 27, 2001; Douglas Todd, "Artistic merit a matter of liberal interpretation," *Vancouver Sun*, January 27, 2001; "Pornography decision a sound compromise," *Vancouver Sun*, January 27, 2001; Brenda Cossman, "A weak squeak of courage," *XtraWest*, February 8, 2001.

19. Tim Naumetz, "Law will target pedophiles who lure via Internet," *National Post*, March 15, 2001; "Child pornography, etc.," *Globe and Mail*,

March 16, 2001.

20. John Ralston Saul, *The Doubter's Companion* (Free Press, 1994).

21. Here we follow the arguments in Alexander Meiklejohn, *Political Freedom: The Constitutional Powers of the People* (Oxford, 1965).

INDEX

Abbott, Jim, 136
abortion law, 30, 32, 47-51
abuse, and individual testimony,
    19. *See also* child abuse; child
    sexual abuse; sexual assault
adolescents. *See* young people
"adults", definition of, 211
advocacy, political, 115-16, 192
"advocacy" materials, 93-94, 104,
    109, 113, 116, 148, 192, 213
advocacy rights, 115-16
age of consent, 12-13, 15, 59-60,
    137-38, 146, 210-11. *See also*
    consent, meaningful
Andre, Harvie, 84
*Andrews v. Law Society of British
    Columbia*, 79
Arbour, Louise, 176
Armed Forces, Canadian, 80
artistic merit, 97, 105, 193-94,
    214
artistic works, 92, 95-97, 193, 194
artists, 14, 96, 193
Axworthy, Chris, 88, 89

Bad Attitude/s (Crossman *et al.*),
    75
Bakan, Joel, 181
Bala, Nicholas, 118
Bastarache, Justice Michel, 183,
    200, 201, 203
Bennest, William, case of, 10, 11
Binnie, Justice Ian, 178, 182
Birch, Joshua, 82
Blais, Pierre, 86-94
Blatchford, Christie, 176-77
Bloc Québecois, 31, 95, 125
Borovoy, Allan, 92
Bouchard, Lucien, 31
Bowers, Judith, 129
B.C. Civil Liberties Association
    (BCCLA), 30, 165, 203, 206;
    intervenor's briefs, *R. v.
    Sharpe*, 129-35, 140, 146, 147,
    150, 154, 160, 163, 164, 171-75
British Columbia Report, 142
Brody, Hugh, 20-21
Butler, Donald, 68
Byfield, Ted, 142

Cadman, Chuck, 119-20
Campbell, Kim, 29-31; and abortion law, 47, 48, 49, 50; and child pornography law, 41, 58, 75, 78, 92; and CHRA amendments, 79-81, 82, 83-85; and *Haig* ruling, 83; and new rape shield law, 52-53; and political appointments, 31, 31-34, 34, 86, 95; and pornography issue, 35-36; on *R. v. Butler*, 75. *See also* Justice ministry under Kim Campbell
Campbell, Marianne, 35
Canada Customs, 2, 39-40, 46-47, 180, 181-82
Canadian Alliance Party, 180, 205
Canadian Bar Association, 95
Canadian Civil Liberties Association, 92, 171
Canadian Conference on the Arts (CCA), 14
Canadian Family Action Association, 161
Canadian Human Rights Act (CHRA), amendments to, 33-34, 51, 54, 57, 61, 79-86, 87
Canadian Judicial Council, 123
Canadian Police Association, 129, 139, 145, 177, 205
Carney, Pat, 30, 50
censorship, 40, 64-65, 72, 74, 140, 147, 182, 214, 216, 217
Charest, Jean, 86
Charlottetown referendum, 82
Charter of Rights and Freedoms, 38, 39, 65, 79, 110, 141, 155, 217; Section 2 ("fundamental freedoms"), 25, 69, 74, 100, 104, 112, 132, 135; Section 15 ("equality rights"), 43-44, 67
Charter of Rights and Freedoms, Section 1 ("reasonable limits"): and "fundamental values", 109-10; and "possession offence", 104, 112, 146, 147, 149, 151, 156, 196, 199; and *R.*

v. Butler, 68, 69, 70; and *R. v. Langer*, 105, 106;
"child", definition of, 58-59, 60, 61, 76, 77-78, 143, 190, 211-12
child abuse, as social construction, 16-18. *See also* child sexual abuse
child molesters. *See* pedophiles
child pornography: and Canada's international commitments, 136, 137; and freedom of expression, 14, 107, 152, 158; and harm to children, 26, 101, 111, 113, 118, 122, 156, 187; market for, in Canada (1991), 46, 56, 62; and payment of subjects, 136; and pedophiles, 101, 102, 108, 187; and photographs vs. other depictions, 55, 56; private member's bill to outlaw, 88, 89; real vs. imaginary, 138; and seduction of children, 101, 103, 104, 108, 187; and social discourse, 13-14; UTV special on, 8-9; various views of, 12-13; where adults dress as children, 77, 78, 88
child pornography, definition of, 55, 90; in child pornography law, 112, 132, 137, 150, 188, 189-90, 210-11; in child pornography law, and "overbreadth", 172, 173, 197
child pornography, possession of, 76, 115, 132, 187; and analogy to stolen property, 41, 55, 113-14; and harm, 187, 197, 202
child pornography, possession of, as a crime, 12, 41, 54, 89, 94, 132-33, 154; and law enforcement, 101, 202, 208; and "overbreadth" of child pornography law, 132, 135, 146; and production/distribution of pornography, 55, 109, 137, 144, 169, 187. *See also* Criminal

Code, Section 163.1 (4)
("possession offence")
child pornography law in the
making: and abusive enforcement concerns, 54, 95; and
amendments, 91, 93-94, 157;
arguments for and against, 46-
47, 53-54, 56-58, 61-62; and
bill tabled by Blais, 89-91; and
civil libertarians, 54, 92-93;
and constitutionality, 90, 93,
94; criticism of, 54, 91; and
debate over development
process, 58; and definition of
"child", 58, 60, 61, 76, 77-78;
and "depiction" issue, 77, 78;
focus of, 56, 77, 78, 90, 93-94,
96, 104; and government
control of the agenda, 57, 62,
77, 91; and Kim Campbell, 41,
58, 75, 78, 92; and lack of
demand, 46, 47, 53, 57; legislative hearings on (1993), 13-14,
20, 88-89, 92; limitations of,
78, 87-88;and Pierre Blais, 87-
94; and political context, 28,
29, 31, 36, 80, 87, 91-92;
proposal for, 41; and search for
balance, 77; and unresolved
issues (1992), 77-78; and
written materials, 76-77, 90,
93-94. *See also* Criminal Code,
Section 163.1 ("child pornography law")
children, 15, 56, 101, 178; protection of, and child pornography
law, 87, 168, 187, 188
"children's agenda", 167
child sexual abuse, 12, 17, 37, 54,
55, 56, 96-97
Chretien, Jean, 86, 95, 161, 180
civil libertarians, 12, 41, 53, 54,
55, 56, 92-93, 158. *See also* B.C.
Civil Liberties Association
(BCCLA)
Clair, Richard, 35
Clemenger, Brian, 205-6

"cognitive distortions", 101, 103,
108, 109, 113, 144-45, 157, 202,
211
collective interests, 38, 43, 45,
216
collective rights, 35, 37-39, 42-
43, 160
Collins, Peter, 26, 100, 101-3,
144-45, 147, 211
"communitarianism", 38
"community standard of tolerance" test, 65-67, 69, 70, 72,
73-74, 105-6, 182, 183, 193,
194
consent, meaningful, 114, 121,
122. *See also* age of consent
Cory, Justice Peter deCarteret,
151
Cossman, Brenda, 208-9
Coyne, Andrew, 141-42
crimes, and relativity, 12
Criminal Code of Canada, 64, 204-
5
Criminal Code, Section 163
("obscenity law"), 46, 65, 181-
83; and freedom of expression,
67, 68, 70; and *R. v. Butler*, 37,
51, 62-63, 68-75; suggestion to
redraft, 39-40, 54
Criminal Code, Section 163.1
("child pornography law"):
about, 4-6; and age of consent,
137-38; constitutional challenge of, 22-23, 25 (*See also R.
v. Sharpe*); and constitutionality, 189; and constitutional
"overbreadth", 134-35, 139,
140, 150, 160, 173, 197, 212;
criticism of, 60, 95, 97, 130-33,
134-35, 140; and definition of
"child", 190, 211-12; and definition of child pornography,
112, 132, 137, 150, 188, 189-90,
210-11; invasiveness of, 140;
media coverage of, 9, 89, 97;
passage of, 94; and *R. v.
Langer*, 96, 105; subsection

Criminal Code, Sec. 163.1 (cont.) (1)(a), 150; subsection (1)(b), 100, 115, 149. *See also* child pornography law in the making

Criminal Code, Section 163.1, subsection (4) ("possession offence"): authors' views of, 214; and constitutionality, 99-112, 121, 130, 135, 142, 153, 154, 158, 172, 174, 183, 184, 195, 199, 201, 203; and constitutional "overbreadth", 132, 135, 151, 153, 154, 156, 172, 187, 200, 201, 209; and freedom of expression, 156, 185; and market for child pornography, 156, 178; and "Oakes test", 108-11, 155, 156, 157; and personal privacy, 156, 185; and police enforcement, 101, 139, 177, 202; scope of, 187; and thought control, 160, 198; and written materials, 192, 195

Crosbie, John, 79
Cullen, Austin, 11
Customs Act, 181, 182

Dagenais v. Canadian Broadcasting Corporation, 107, 108, 112, 155
Daniels, Sergeant Keith, 118
Danson, Tim, 139, 177
Day, Stockwell, 180, 205
de Chastelain, General John, 80
democracy, 44, 54, 74, 133, 134, 148, 158, 215-17
Dickson, Chief Justice Brian, 65-66
dignity of persons, 133-34, 135, 148, 215, 216, 217
discrimination, 34, 40, 43, 51, 79
Dixon, John, 35
Dosanjh, Ujjal, 11, 119, 120-21, 122, 160, 180
Drainie, Bronwyn, 96

Dworkin, Ronald, 72, 74

elections, federal, 31, 86, 95, 180
Elley, Reed, 120
Ellison, Ross, 124
Entick v. Carrington (1765), 148
Epp, Ken, 166-67
equality rights, 35, 38, 42, 43, 45, 67, 68, 79, 134
erotica. *See* pornography, written; written materials
Evangelical Fellowship of Canada, 129, 205-6
Everitt, Marc, 6
evidence, 17, 19, 100-103, 109, 144, 197, 212
expression rights, 35, 54, 55-56, 65, 67, 106-7, 112, 198, 215, 216. *See also* freedom of expression; freedom of speech
expressive materials, 131, 181; possession of, as a crime, 132, 146, 147-48, 154, 172, 173, 174, 195, 196, 197

"Family Caucus", 33, 53, 83; and abortion law, 32, 50; and child pornography law, 31, 41, 76, 78, 92; and CHRA amendments, 34, 80-81, 84, 85; and Justice ministers, 33, 34, 36, 87
"family values", 13, 18, 36, 88, 168, 206
federalism, 37, 38
feminists, 17, 32, 35, 36, 54, 67-68
Flaherty, Jim, 169
Focus on the Family Association, 129, 168, 205
Ford v. Quebec, 109
freedom, human, 64, 72
freedom of expression, 115-16, 153, 158-59, 193, 215; and child pornography law, 134, 164; limitations on, 74, 116,

158, 179, 186; and obscenity law, in *R. v. Butler*, 69, 70; and pedophiles, 178; and personal identity, 109; and "possession offence", 104, 111, 130, 146, 154, 156, 163, 185; and privacy rights, 110; and production of child pornography, 107; range of, and appetites of deviants, 130-31, 146; and Supreme Court, 186, 214-15. *See also* expression rights; freedom of speech

freedom of the press, 93

freedoms, fundamental, 133, 134, 174, 217. *See also* Charter of Rights and Freedoms: Section 2 ("fundamental freedoms")

freedom of speech: and child pornography, 14, 54-55; criticism of Sharpe's, 170-71; and democracy, 134; illusions about, 214; and Justice McEachern, 158; and obscenity law, 67, 68; and offensiveness of ideas, 74; and pornography, 69, 72; and "possession offence", 173; and protection of children, 218; and *R. v. Sharpe*, 214; and "reasonable limits", 25; in the United States, 217; and words vs. acts, 20. *See also* freedom of expression

Friesen, Benno, 81

Gaul, Geoffrey, 165

Gay, Andrew, 129

gay constituents, 33, 57, 83

gay rights, 57, 62

Globe and Mail, 96, 97, 117, 118, 121, 122, 159, 184, 207, 208

Gonthier, Justice Charles, 177, 179, 200, 201, 203

Gordon, John, 136, 137, 138, 171

Grabb, Sergeant Russ, 118

Graydon, Shari, 118, 121

Grey, Julius, 119

"grooming" of children, 101, 104, 108, 109, 144, 145, 187, 202

group rights. *See* collective rights

Guarnieri, Albina, 124

gun control legislation, 32-33, 51

Gwyn, Richard, 164

Hacking, Ian, 16, 17, 18

Haig, Graham, 82

Haig case, 82-83

harassment, 9, 19, 20, 119

harm: caused by child pornography, 101-2, 154; to children, and "cognitive distortions", 103; and "community standard of tolerance" test, 183; concept of, in *R. v. Butler*, 69-71, 72, 73, 131, 172-73, 182, 185, 196, 201, 212; "indirect" vs. "direct", 72; morality, and youth sexuality, 212; notion of, and causality, 69, 70, 71-72; and obscenity, 67, 69-70; and scientific evidence, 185, 196-97, 212; and social science findings, 67, 68, 146-47, 153, 154

harm, anticipated, 20, 26

harm, direct, 65, 72, 173, 174

harm, measurable, 65, 67, 68, 71, 73

harm, Mill's principle of, 65, 73

harm, "reasoned apprehension of", 172, 174, 183, 185, 212

Harris, Mike, 169

"hate speech", 149, 181

Hlady, Jean, 6

homophobia, 81, 182

homosexuality, 15, 16

homosexuals, 79, 80, 85, 86, 142

Hume, Mark, 162-63

incest, 17, 19
"inclusive justice", 34-35, 42, 51,
    93
injustice, 47
Inquisition, 133
intercourse, anal, 39, 59-60, 94,
    143
Internet, 47, 101, 204
Inuit, and case of child sexual
    abuse, 20-21
irrationalism, social climate of,
    18-20

Jonas, George, 164-65
Jones, Craig, 165, 206
"judicial activism", 140-41
justice, 98, 128, 151. *See also*
    "inclusive justive"
Justice ministry under Anne
    McLellan, criticism of, 135-36
Justice ministry under Kim
    Campbell, 31-33, 34-35, 37-41,
    47-51, 52-53, 75-76; and
    pornography legislation (see
    child pornography law in the
    making)

Kaminer, Wendy, 18-20
Kay, Jonathan, 164
Kelly, Keith, 14
Ker, Katherine, 136-37
"kiddie porn law". *See* child
    pornography law in the
    making; Criminal Code, Section
    163.1 ("child pornography
    law")
Kinsella, Noel, 83
Kirkby, Gareth, 11
Kitchen, Judge William, 10
Kleinick, Jodi, 63, 71-72, 74, 75
Knopff, Rainer, 140

Lamer, Chief Justice Antonio,
    107-8

Landolt, Gwen, 165
Langer, Eli, 95, 96, 97, 105, 194
law enforcement, 54, 95, 101,
    139, 177, 202, 205, 208
Law Society of B.C., 123
LeBel, Louis, 176
Legal Education and Action Fund
    (LEAF), 37, 67
legislation. *See names of laws*
L'Heureux-Dube, Justice Claire,
    179, 200, 201, 203
liberty, 64, 72, 186
Little Sister's, 40, 180, 181, 182
Little Sister's v. Canada, 181-83,
    185, 214
Lowther, Eric, 168
Lugli, Peter, 35

McAlpine, John, 129, 150
McCausland, Mary-Louise, 6, 7
McCombs, Justice J. David, 105,
    106-7
MacDonald, Constable, 2, 24
McEachern, Chief Justice Allan,
    126, 128, 142, 156-59, 186
McKenzie, Lloyd, 123
MacKinnon, Catherine, 37, 38,
    67, 116
McKinnon, Gil, 129, 139, 178
McLachlin, Justice Beverley, 152-
    53, 175-76, 179, 181, 201, 202,
    208; majority ruling in *R. v.
    Sharpe*, 184-200
McLellan, Anne, 119, 124-25,
    126, 135, 160, 161, 166, 167,
    168, 204, 205
MacLellan, Russell, 91
McTeague, Dan, 167
Major, John, 178
Makin, Kirk, 207
Manning, Preston, 86, 125, 161
Marshall, William, 102
Martinuk, Susan, 121
Matthews, Detective Inspector
    Robert (Bob), 89, 139, 176-77,
    205

media coverage of Bennest case, 10, 11
media coverage of Langer affair, 96-97
media coverage of *R. v. Sharpe*: B.C. Court of Appeal, 128, 140-42, 159-60, 162-65; B.C. Provincial Court, 7-8, 117-18, 120-22, 123, 143; Supreme Court of Canada, 184, 203-4, 207-9
media sensationalism, 12, 117
Mill, John Stuart, 64, 72
Miller, Judge R.D., 23
"minimal impairment" test, 105, 106, 152, 154, 155, 157, 196, 197
"Montreal Massacre", 32, 33
morality, 36, 63-64, 75, 145, 182, 183, 211, 212
Morton, Ted, 140-41
Moulton, Earl, 205
Mulroney, Brian, 31, 33, 47-48, 81, 82, 84-85, 86
Myers, Suzette, 7-8

NAMBLA Bulletin, 88, 89, 101
National Action Committee on the Status of Women, 57
National Post, 117, 118, 140, 141, 142, 162, 164, 170, 171, 176
national unity, 37
Newman, Don, 207
Nicholson, Rob, 89, 94
North American Man-Boy Love Association (NAMBLA), 89, 94
"notwithstanding clause", 124, 125, 126, 141, 161, 167, 168, 205

"Oakes test", 105-11, 151-52, 153, 155, 156, 157, 195-99, 215
obscenity: and censorship by Canada Customs, 181, 182; and "community standard of toler-ance" test, 65-67;and depiction vs. description, 40; and depravity test, 64; legal defini-tion of (1957), 65; and *R. v. Butler*, 69-70, 71, 75, 182
obscenity law. *See* Criminal Code, Section 163 ("obscenity law")
Obst, Grant, 205
On Liberty (Mill), 64
Ontario Human Rights Code, 81
Ontario Provincial Police, 89, 139, 176, 205
Orris, Glen, 124
Ottawa Citizen, 117, 122, 163-64
"overbreadth", constitutional: and child pornography law, 134-35, 139, 140, 150, 160, 173, 197, 212; and "possession offence", 132, 135, 151, 153, 154, 156, 172, 187, 200, 201, 209

Peck, Richard, 129, 139-40, 150, 153, 160, 177, 178
pedophiles, 17, 88, 101, 102-3, 130, 161, 163, 170, 202
Penner, Barry, 119
"person", definition of, 189
"pervert", use of word, in media, 9, 120
photographs. *See* pornography, photographic; Sharpe, John Robin: photographs in posses-sion of
pornography: adult, and posses-sion offence, 57; and causality of harm, 71-72, 73; and changing views, 138, 139; and feminists, 35-36, 67-68; histor-ical view of as obscene, 63-64; and the religious Right, 36; and sexual assaults, 67-68. *See also* child pornography
pornography, photographic, and abuse of children, 55, 101, 102, 103, 104, 108, 112-13, 130, 147,

pornography, photographic (cont.)
172
pornography, written, 104, 109,
138, 188. *See also* Sharpe, John
Robin: writing by; written
materials
pornography legislation, 35-36,
37, 39, 63-68. *See also* child
pornography law in the
making; Criminal Code, Section
163.1 ("child pornography
law")
"porn wars", 35, 77
positive rights, 42
"possession offence". *See* Criminal Code, Section 163.1 (4)
("possession offence")
presumption of innocence, 6, 12
privacy, 113-14, 140, 187, 198;
and democracy, 177, 216; individual, and Parliament, 154,
157, 158; and "possession
offence", 132, 135, 156, 173,
185, 213
privacy rights, 110, 111, 112,
115, 122, 172, 174
Progressive Conservative Party,
28, 33, 47-48, 80, 86, 87, 91-92,
95. *See also* "Family Caucus"
Prohibition, 137
property rights, 55
"proportionality" test, 105, 106,
108-11, 146, 149, 150, 152, 153,
155, 157, 196, 198, 198-99

Quebec question, 33

R. v. Butler, 37, 51, 67, 119, 131,
149, 214; authors' criticisms of,
73-75; and child pornography,
70, 75-76; cited in *R. v. Sharpe*,
Supreme Court, 193, 194, 196,
201, 202; and "community
standard of tolerance" test, 66,
69, 70, 72, 73; and concept of

harm, 69-72, 73, 131, 172-73,
182, 185, 196, 201, 212; deci-
sion of, 62-63, 66, 68-75; and
Little Sister's v. Canada, 182-
83, 185; and obscenity, 69-70,
71, 75, 182
R. v. Heywood, 151
R. v. Hicklin, 64
R. v. Keegstra, 109, 149, 214
R. v. Langer, 97, 105, 106, 107,
194
R. v. Morgentaler, 30, 48, 49
R. v. Oakes, 105, 109. *See also*
"Oakes test"
R. v. Seaboyer, 51, 52
R. v. Sharpe, B.C. Court of
Appeal: arguments by Sharpe's
lawyers, 139-40; and BCCLA
brief, 129-35, 140, 146, 147,
150, 154, 163, 164; date set for
appeal, 126; exchanges
between Justice Southin and
the Crown, 136-39; and hypothetical examples, 140, 153-54,
155, 162; and intervenors, 124,
125, 128, 129, 135-36, 145;
judgment, and political
response, 160-61; and media
attention, 128, 140-42, 159-60,
162-65; and "Oakes test", 146,
149, 150, 152, 153, 154, 155,
157; and police brief, 139;
reasons for judgment, 142-59
R. v. Sharpe, B.C. Provincial
Court, 7-8, 23, 24-27
R. v. Sharpe, B.C. Provincial
Court, ruling on *voir dire*, 99-
112, 114-15; appeal of, 120-21,
126; authors' views of, 112-14,
115-17; and case adjournments,
120, 121, 126, 136; cited by
appeal court judges, 146, 147,
153, 155, 156, 157; and constitutionality of child
pornography law, 112, 114-15;
and examination of evidence,
100-103; and "finding of

facts", 103-4, 146-47; media coverage of, 117-18, 120-22, 123, 143; and "Oakes test", 105-11; parliamentary reaction to, 124-25; public reactions to, 118-20, 121-22, 123

R. v. Sharpe, Supreme Court of Canada, 166-69, 171-80; about, 175, 176; appeal announced, 160; arguments heard by court, 171, 177-79; date set for appeal, 165, 166; deliberations of court, 179-81; filing of appeal, 165; and hypothetical examples, 179, 197; and intervenors, 169, 171; and law enforcement convenience vs. freedom of expression, 177; political reaction to schedule for, 166-67

R. v. Sharpe, Supreme Court of Canada ruling, 183-200; and "advocacy" materials, 192; and artistic merit defence, 193-94; authors' critique of, 210-14; and constitutional "overbreadth", 187, 191; and deference to Parliament, 202, 203, 207, 209; and exceptions, 184, 197, 198, 199-200, 202-3, 204, 205, 209, 213; government response to, 204-5; and lower court rulings, 185-86; and materials caught by "possession offence", 195, 197; and meaning of terms, 188-91; media response to, 184, 203-4, 207-9; and minority opinion, 184, 200-203, 210, 212; and "Oakes test", 195-99; public response to, 205-6; and proof of harm, 196-97; and "remedies", 199-200

"rape shield law", 51-53

"rational connection" test, 105, 106, 152, 153, 157, 196, 197

REAL Women of Canada, 33, 165

"reasonable limits". *See* Charter of Rights and Freedoms, Section 1 ("reasonable limits")

Reform Party, 86, 87, 95, 180; and criticism of government, 125, 126, 136, 160-61; and *R. v. Sharpe*, 119-20, 167, 168

Reid, Darrel, 168, 169, 205

Reimer, John, 81, 85, 94

Republican Party, 33, 36

Reynolds, John, 125, 161

Rideout, George, 94

rights, 44-45, 67, 72, 106, 151. *See also* advocacy rights; collective rights; equality rights; expression rights; positive rights; privacy rights; property rights

Roberts, David, 162

Robinson, Svend, 83, 85

Rock, Allan, 86

Rogers, Rix, 37, 88

Rowles, Madam Justice Anne, 128, 142, 151-56, 159, 186

Royal Canadian Mounted Police (RCMP), 118, 205

Ryder, Bruce, 159-60, 203, 206

Sanders, Doug, 85

satanic ritual abuse (SRA), 19

Saul, John Ralston, 214

Schultes, Terry, 23, 25

search warrants, 4, 24, 101

Sekora, Lou, 167

sexism, 52, 81

sexual assault, 51-52, 67, 68. *See also* child sexual abuse

sexuality, and the law, 15

sexuality, youth, 15, 60, 145, 202-3, 212

sexual morality, 48, 64, 75, 142, 217

sexual orientation, 34, 57, 62, 79, 82, 84, 85

sexual representations, 131, 182, 189, 212, 216. *See also* child

sexual representations (cont.)
pornography; pornography
Sharpe, John Robin: about, 21-
22; activities after initial arrest,
2-3; apartment searched, 3-4;
and appeal of voir dire ruling,
126, 128-29; arrests, 1-2, 4; and
artistic merit defence, 194;
charges against, 4, 23-24, 99;
and constitional challenge to
child pornography law, 22-23,
24-25 (*See also R. v. Sharpe*);
dismisses lawyers, 22; and
freedom of speech, 170-71; and
harassment, 9, 119; media
representation of, 8, 9, 162,
176, 177; participates in panel
discussion, 169-70;
photographs in possession of,
2, 3, 6-7; poster campaign
against, 9, 119; prepares self-
defense, 22-23; public view of,
98-99; requests postponement
on outstanding charges, 142;
views of, 2, 3, 22, 123, 129,
139-40, 178, 206-7; writing by,
1, 2, 3, 6, 7, 138, 194
Shaw, Justice Duncan, 122-24,
142; public criticism of, 118-
19, 163, 185; and *R. v. Sharpe
voir dire*, 25, 26 (*See also R. v.
Sharpe*, B.C. Provincial Court,
ruling on *voir dire*); and view
of Sharpe, 98, 99
Simon Fraser University, 170
Small Press Action Network, 169-
70
social constructionists, 14-15
social science research, 67, 68, 71,
72, 146-47, 153, 154
Sopinka, Justice John, 66
Southin, Madam Justice Mary,
128, 136, 137-39, 159, 161, 162,
173-74, 186, 196; reasons for
judgment, *R. v. Sharpe*, 142-50
Stanbury, Richard, 94
Standing Committee on Justice,
88, 92, 93-94
Steckle, Paul, 167
Stock, Peter, 161
Supreme Court of Canada, 35, 37,
79, 156, 181-83; and obscenity
law, 62-63, 68-75; and rape
shield law, 51, 52; reconfiguration of, 176. *See also R. v.
Sharpe*, Supreme Court of
Canada; *names of cases*

Tait, John, 34, 35
Taylor, Charles, 38
Taylor, Kate, 96
Thomas, Jeannie, 123
thought control, 140, 160, 177,
198, 203, 213
thoughts, private, 140, 155, 157,
160, 173, 177, 213, 215, 217
Tobias, Cheryl, 178
Toronto Star, 164
totalitarianism, 133, 146, 155,
160, 173
Towne Cinema v. R., 65, 66

U.S. Customs, 1-2
U.S. Postal Service, 46, 56
utility, Mill's principle of, 64
UTV, 7-8

Vancouver Police, 3-4, 8, 10-11
Vancouver Province, 9, 88, 121,
163
Vancouver Sun, 13-14, 117, 121-
22, 142, 163, 181, 207
Vander Zalm, William, 30
Vriend v. Alberta, 151

Waddell, Ian, 93
Wappel, Tom, 88, 89, 94
Warren, Peter, 119
Waters, Detective Noreen, 3, 4, 6,
8, 10-11, 94; views of, 4, 11; as

witness, 23, 26, 88, 89, 100-101, 144
"weighing of the effects" test, 105, 106, 107-9, 157. *See also* "proportionality" test
White, Randy, 125, 170
Wilson, Justice Bertha, 66-67, 72
Wilson, Peter, 13-14
Wilson, Warren, 123
witnesses, 26, 100
Wolff, Noreen. *See* Waters, Detective Noreen
Wood, Josiah, 11
Woods, Tom, 162
world wars, and censorship, 147
written materials, 40, 104, 109, 138, 192, 195, 203, 213; and child pornography law in the making, 76-77, 90, 93-94

Xtra West, 10, 11, 209

young people, 15, 138, 202, 211; and sexual relations, under Canadian law, 59, 132, 143, 210. *See also* age of consent; sexuality, youth

Zundel, Ernst, 181